The Absence of Myth

The Absence of Myth

Writings on Surrealism

◆

GEORGES BATAILLE

Edited, translated and introduced by
Michael Richardson

VERSO
London · New York

This paperback edition first published by Verso 2024
First published by Verso 1994
© Verso 1994
Translation and Introduction © Michael Richardson 1994
From Georges Bataille, *Oeuvres completes*
© Editions Gallimard, 1976–1988

1 3 5 7 9 10 8 6 4 2

Verso
UK: 6 Meard Street, London W1F 0EG
US: 388 Atlantic Avenue, Brooklyn, NY 11217
versobooks.com

Verso is the imprint of New Left Books

ISBN-13: 978-1-80429-659-2
ISBN-13: 978-1-78960-264-7 (US EBK)
ISBN-13: 978-1-78960-265-4 (UK EBK)

British Library Cataloguing in Publication Data
A catalogue record for this book is available from the British Library

Library of Congress Cataloging-in-Publication Data
A catalog record for this book is available for the
previous edition from the Library of Congress

Printed and bound by CPI Group (UK) Ltd, Croydon CR0 4YY

Contents

Acknowledgements

Many thanks to the following for all their help: Krzysztof Fijalkowski, Malcolm Imrie, Stuart Inman, Nadia Lovell, Gerald Stack, Stuart Thompson and Peter Wood.

Thanks also to the Council of Europe and the British Centre for Literary Translation for financial help.

M.R.

Introduction

The fever pitch at which surrealism unfolded in its early years can be deceptive. Constant interrogation of motives and calling to order may lead us to perceive that the aim was the establishment of a closed circle, or allegiance to a sterile ideology. However, nothing could have been further from the truth, for one of the issues raised most forcibly by surrealism was the nature of freedom itself in a collective context. The surrealists were soon faced with a paradoxical truth: that if it is to be realized, liberty has need of a moral basis, and has no meaning except in relation to a disciplined attitude. No one recognized this more than Georges Bataille, one of the early victims of André Breton's determination to establish an authentic basis for surrealist activity. As Bataille wrote: 'It was André Breton who rightly recognized that a poet or a painter does not have the power to say what is in his heart, but that an organization or a collective body could.'[1]

Bataille's relation to surrealism is controversial, and he is often placed among its enemies, especially by those who have seen him as a precursor of 'postmodernism', who make a point of dissociating Bataille from contamination with surrealism. This goes against Bataille's affirmation of his fundamental solidarity with it, and his general agreement with the thinking of André Breton. It is therefore opportune to gather together Bataille's own writings on surrealism, especially since he had at one point intended to write a book on a subject which had intrigued him throughout his life and had a pivotal place there, even if he also displayed a certain ambivalence in relation to it. He called himself its 'old enemy from within', and defined his position as lying 'at the side of surrealism'.

In a letter written in December 1948, Bataille informed the publishers Gallimard that he was working on a book to be called *Surrealist Philosophy and Religion*. It never appeared, and he seems to have abandoned the project sometime around 1951 (it is unclear whether

'Surrealism from Day to Day', apparently written in 1951, is the first
chapter of this work or a quite separate project that equally never saw
the light of day).

Even though the book itself was not written, from 1945 until 1951
surrealism was central to Bataille's thought, and a considerable collection of material – both published and unpublished – bears witness to
the fact. This presumably constituted the research he intended to use
for the aborted book, and it is surprising that he abandoned the
project, since this material is so rich and clearly delineated that it would
not have required a great deal of further work to assemble it. It is
collected here for the first time, and gives us a rich insight into
Bataille's thinking at this key moment of his life, as well as providing
many profound reflections on surrealism. Bataille's understanding
concentrates on elements within surrealism that few critics have recognized, and thus gives us a new perspective on what surrealism may mean.

The period of these writings was the most active (from a publication
point of view) in Bataille's life. He published *L'Alleluiah, Catéchisme de
Dianus*; *Méthode de la méditation*; *Haine de la poésie*; *La part maudite*; *La
scissiparité*; and *L'Abbé C*; in addition to editing *Critique*, in which he
published a vast number of articles.

In many ways surrealism was the key to most of this work, and it is
especially significant to the themes of *La part maudite* and *Théorie de la
religion* (written during the same period, but not published until after
his death). It may seem surprising that Bataille should have been so
concerned with surrealism at this time, for the cultural context was
hardly propitious to this movement that had been so important during
the interwar period, but was then becoming intellectually marginalized. In the immediate aftermath of the war it had retained a great
prestige, but this was soon eclipsed as the French Communist Party
gained ascendancy over French cultural and social life. Equally, the
rise of existentialism tended to subsume surrealism in the intellectual
domain. For a long time the surrealists had been consistent in their
opposition to Stalinism, and could expect no favours from the Communists, while the basis of existentialism was also largely hostile to the
basis of the surrealist sensibility. By 1948 the surrealists had become
peripheral to the currents of French cultural life and, for those
conscious of trends, its moment had passed. Considered an interwar
indulgence, it was seen to be irrelevant to the needs of the time.
Bataille took the opposite view. Having often been disparaging and
sometimes hostile towards surrealism before the war, in the late 1940s
he came to view it differently and consider it to be more vital than ever.

This was doubtless due in part to Bataille's evident distaste for the mood of the time, for a postwar euphoria heavily marked by guilt and spite. Retribution for the perceived humiliation of France during the war hung heavily in the air. In this atmosphere surrealism alone seemed to have retained its prewar generosity of spirit, so that it pointed the way towards the questions Bataille wished to address, and it is perhaps primarily for this reason that he came to re-evaluate what surrealism had been and could be. Bataille had no time for the idea that surrealism was dead. On the contrary, it had barely come into being – it was almost the embryo for a potentiality that could be realized only in the future. This above all marks Bataille's own surrealism: it was a potentiality to be realized.

Before the Second World War, Bataille's relations with surrealism had been close but strained. Although he was imbued with its spirit, and numbered many of the surrealists among his close friends, he did not then appear to take surrealism itself entirely seriously. It was admirable, he appears to have felt, as the embodiment of a principle of refusal and revolt, but he seems to have been contemptuous of its pretensions in the realm of ideas. Having denounced it in 1929 as an idealism, he appears to have continued to view it as such throughout the 1930s, and did not pay much further attention to it. As Michel Surya says, he 'pre-judged [surrealism] as fraudulent'.[2]

It seems likely that Bataille was drawn closer to surrealism after the war by his friend Michel Fardoulis-Lagrange, who, although he was never a member of Breton's group, was an important figure on its margins, animating the journal *Troisième convoi*, of which five issues were published between 1945 and 1951 and in which Bataille published three articles (including 'On the Subject of Slumbers' and 'Take It or Leave It', in the present collection). The first of these texts is particularly significant, for it signals the change in Bataille's perception and the fact that he believed a reappraisal of surrealism had become necessary. Describing himself as 'surrealism's old enemy from within', he remains highly critical of surrealist practice, which he views as being too concerned with a place in the world: he considers that with its books on the shelves and its paintings on the walls, *a great surrealism* begins. This is by no means a compliment. Such 'great surrealism' suggests that surrealism has lost its vigour and surrendered to the necessities of utilitarian society.[3]

But if he perceives this negative aspect, he does not use it to dismiss surrealism. On the contrary. There is a real surrealism that remains latent, and it is surrealism alone that has any claim to addressing the crucial issues of the period: '*in terms of mankind's interrogation of itself,* there is surrealism and nothing'. It was this sense of surrealism that Bataille was to explore over the coming few years.

Before considering what this meant for Bataille, let us take a glance back at his relations with the surrealists up to this point in the story, and especially at his sometimes strained relationship with André Breton.

Unfortunately, what we know of this relationship is largely one-sided, since almost everything that has been written on it has come from Bataille's side (Bataille's own writings, and those of close friends like Leiris and Masson). Breton himself wrote hardly anything about Bataille, nor did any of those close to him during the 1930s. It is possible that some light may be shed when Breton's personal correspondence is published, but since this will not be for another two decades, we have a long wait. In the meantime, we have to rely primarily on what Bataille has written, which is generally even-handed and gives a clear insight into what was a complicated love–hate relationship.

It is in 'Surrealism from Day to Day' that Bataille sets out most fully the context of his involvement with surrealism in the 1920s. This is a revealing and extremely honest document in which Bataille does not spare himself. It is plain that from the time Bataille was drawn into the surrealist circle through his friendship with Leiris and Masson, his feelings for it, and for Breton's person, were a mixture of contempt and admiration coupled with both envy and a feeling of intimidation in the surrealist milieu. Bataille admitted as much. His initial reading – or rather, misreading, as he was later to accept – of surrealist texts also served to underline his sense of alienation. His first public comment on surrealism had come in response to a letter inviting him to participate in what was to be a notorious meeting of the Surrealist Group to discuss the implications of Leon Trotsky's expulsion from the USSR, which brought a refusal from Bataille in the most forthright and uncompromising terms: 'too many fucking idealists'. Bataille tells us that he had already made a bad impression on Breton at their first meeting, when Breton seems immediately to have concluded that he was an 'obsessive'. His response to the surrealist invitation was hardly calculated to correct first impressions, and perhaps one should not be surprised that when Bataille took on the editorship of the journal *Documents* and gathered around him most of the surrealists with whom Breton had fallen out in 1929, the latter should have regarded this as a provocation and concluded that Bataille was set upon undermining his own authority within surrealism. Breton decided on a pre-emptive strike, and the *Second Manifesto of Surrealism* included an attack on Bataille of such violence that it still shocks today. Bataille replied in kind with a text entitled 'Le lion châtré', published in 'Un cadavre', a collective pamphlet published by the surrealists who had quarrelled with Breton. Where Breton had accused Bataille of being an 'obsessive', Bataille called Breton a 'religious windbag'; where Breton ridiculed Bataille's vulgar materialism, Bataille accused Breton of hiding a sinister religious enterprise behind a phoney revolutionary phraseology that merely represented impotence: Breton was nothing but a 'castrated lion'.

Bataille always denied that, through *Documents*, he was engaged in an attempt to undermine Breton's own activity and found an alternative surrealism, but it seems clear that Bataille's attitude at the time was such as to encourage this belief. It is also apparent that Bataille's character did exercise an attraction for those surrealists who were disillusioned with Breton. In fact the personalities of Breton and Bataille appear to have been remarkably similar, and I think it is this fact above all that accounts for their immediate dislike of each other: both recognized in each other elements of themselves which they were not willing to admit at the time.

From their first meeting they both seem to have been aware of a clash between their respective personalities. At a distance from these events of over sixty years, it is plain that much of this initial hostility was due to a latent sympathy. Temperamentally the two men were very similar: both were impulsive and given to bursts of irrational anger; both were uncompromising in their personal attitudes and in what they demanded of others; both were decisive, making up their minds quickly and with a tendency to form hasty judgements. Bataille was well aware of the latter similarity, which he considered a fault, both in himself and in Breton.[4] Bataille's dislike of polemic and his deep regret about trading insults in print is a contrast with Breton, who never apologized for his impulsive anger. Even when this was unjust, Breton seems to have found apology difficult, but at the same time he did not bear grudges. His preface to the 1946 edition of the *Second Manifesto* expresses regret for the violent attacks it contains (almost all of which time had shown to be unjust), but he neither withdraws the substance of the allegations nor suggests any contrition. Breton clearly felt that the attacks, no matter how unfortunate, were nevertheless necessary in the context of the time.[5]

Certainly differences in their respective emotional responses to the world are marked – Breton was more intuitive in his judgements, while Bataille needed to back up his judgements with intellectual arguments. Equally, where Breton's writing is crystalline and lyrical, reflecting the light and transparency with whose hope he would like to imbue the world, Bataille's writing is marked by a dark humour in which any notion of hope is absent. The light which remains focused here is not transparent but dark and haunting, and emanates from a black sun.

But even these very real differences in sensibility are generally complementary – something upon which many of those who knew them both have insisted. Patrick Waldberg, for instance, wrote:

> we could take André Breton and Georges Bataille as two poles of the surrealist spirit as it has been manifested to the present. While Breton dreams of enchanted palaces constructed 'at the side of the chasm in philosopher's stone' and welcomes utopia and the 'paradise on earth' through Fourier's idea of history, Bataille, the black surrealist of catastrophe, exalts in a mysticism of unhope, in which consciousness of human absurdity is the source of an hilarious joy. Their approaches are so tied in with each other's that such a confrontation could appear intolerable to neither of them.[6]

Similarly, for Sarane Alexandrian: 'Those critics who want to oppose Breton and Bataille are very poorly informed. These two men are closely united, like day and night, like conscious and unconscious.'[7] And, as Jean Wahl testified: 'Each time I heard Bataille speak, I would see Breton come to hear him in places where he would never usually go. He came, he told me, to hear Bataille because he liked and admired him so much.'[8]

As these quotations suggest, there was a sense of complicity between the two men – something which is shown in a revealing anecdote recorded by Philippe Audoin of an occasion when Breton attended a lecture given by Bataille during the 1950s:

> When Bataille arrived, Breton rose and took a step towards him. The two men shook hands for a while and exchanged a few words which, in the general mayhem, I did not hear. Then Breton said, 'Well, my dear Master, are you going to make us suffer again?' Bataille smiled, muttered something a little wearily, and, after having politely taken his leave, climbed to the stage. A young woman who was with Breton was amazed: 'You called him Master?' 'Well,' he said with a somewhat sardonic air, 'with certain very great satyrs, it is allowed.'[9]

Perhaps it is not helpful to seek to penetrate this complicitous ambivalence. In 1947, Breton wrote that Bataille was 'one of the few men in life worth taking the trouble of getting to know'. This is a very revealing statement. Breton, an impatient man who made up his mind decisively, was rarely given to such reflection. That Breton 'took the trouble' to get to know Bataille is not simply a casual turn of phrase: it signifies that Bataille was singularly worth getting to know. Generally Breton relied on the intuition of first impressions. In the case of Bataille, his first impressions had deceived him, and he had to make an effort in order to get to know him.

Reading the polemic of the *Second Manifesto* and Bataille's response to it, one is surprised how seriously it has been treated, as though it has the quality of a debate. Breton's attack is largely devoid of content, and what little there is (i.e. that Bataille was a vulgar materialist) is provided by Bataille himself when he specifically defined materialism as 'excluding all idealism', thus defining it explicitly in the spirit of Feuerbach, even if Bataille's concept was more complex. Even so, despite taking Marx into account, Bataille never fully grasped the implications of *dialectical* materialism. But whether or not we consider that Bataille's obsessive distrust of the mind – at least in the interwar period – ties him inevitably to a 'vulgar' materialism, the fact is that this is an explicit element of Bataille's own thinking – we don't need Breton to point it out.

Bataille's response has even less to recommend it. 'The Castrated Lion' is a piece of pure polemic, rather effective so far as it goes, but showing little insight into Breton's position. Hardly better is 'The "Old Mole" and the Prefix *Sur* in the Words *Surhomme* [Superman] and *Surrealist*',[10] an attack not only on surrealism but also on Nietzsche, which is interesting in the development of Bataille's thought but virtually null and void as a critique of either surrealism or Nietzsche (as Bataille would certainly have admitted later). In this context the only value of this text is to show how much Bataille had misunderstood surrealism at the time. A further article from this period, 'The Use Value of D.A.F. de Sade',[11] has also been included in this polemic, perhaps a little arbitrarily. Bataille himself does not indicate that the article (which he thought he had destroyed) was addressed to the surrealists, and states that it was destined for an erotic review. My own view is that the tone of the article suggests that the 'Current Comrades' addressed may be his Communist friends – first because it seems unlikely that he felt close enough at that time to Breton's group to call them 'comrades'; but more importantly because it is difficult to see why Bataille would wish to convince the surrealists of the importance of Sade's 'use value', something they were very much aware of. Similarly, it seems hasty to assume that the criticisms made of the 'admirers' of Sade refer to the surrealists. He writes:

> The behaviour of Sade's admirers resembles that of primitive subjects in relation to their king, whom they adore and loathe, and whom they cover with honours and narrowly confine. In the most favourable cases, the author of *Justine* is in fact thus treated as any given *foreign body*; in other words, he is only an object of transports of exaltation to the extent that these transports facilitate his excretion . . .[12]

While the surrealists were among the admirers of Sade, they never
made a cult of his work, or considered themselves his followers. Sade
had many admirers, and Bataille's comments may well have been
aimed at the ideology of Decadence, which did respond to Sade's work
in this way. If they are aimed at surrealism, they seem singularly poorly
directed.[13] In this altercation Breton's criticisms are certainly more
penetrating (not that this is saying much), but it is clear that the focus
for both writers was polemic rather than a considered critique. It is
difficult not to feel that in Bataille's case, a blind – if understandable –
anger got the better of him.

The contretemps of 1930 was certainly violent, and after such an
exchange it seems remarkable that by 1935 the two men should be
working together side by side in the grouping *Contre-Attaque*. In fact
thereafter they never appear to have exchanged another word in
anger, at least not in print. Their violent altercation behind them, both
men seem to have been eager to assert their respect for each other, as
though they were both aware of how unfair their words had been.

Nevertheless, there is one aspect in which they did differ markedly,
and this is explored by Bataille in his article on Camus's *The Rebel* (see
'The Age of Revolt' in this collection). Bataille's criticism of Breton in
this text is somewhat surprising in that he condemns Breton for giving
way to excess and obeying only passion, while disdaining intellectual
discourse. Given Bataille's dislike of discourse, this seems odd, but in
fact Bataille, although he may have despised the objective fact of
discourse, nevertheless recognized its legitimacy as the only real arena
of intellectual inquiry. Breton, on the other hand, ignored discourse
altogether. Unlike Bataille, he did not despise it, but his intellectual
training had led him not to regard it as essential to his argument.
Breton never engages with an intellectual argument: in his writing, as
in his life, he responds in an immediate and affective way. His
response to *The Rebel* is no different in this respect from his response to
any other book, and for Bataille to criticize him on this score seems
ingenuous. But something more is involved here. Breton's article
'Sucre jaune' (which is by no means as vitriolic as Bataille makes it out
to be – one will find far worse every week in the literary pages of
today's press) attacks not so much the content of what Camus says
about Lautréamont as the perspective he adopts. Bataille mentions
Camus's response that from a literary point of view *War and Peace* is far
more important than *Les chants de Maldoror*. For Breton (as in fact for
Bataille) the merit of *Les chants de Maldoror* was to go beyond any
literary perspective, and the very fact of reducing it to literature was
offensive to him. This literary approach is essential to Camus's

method, and represents a clear distinction between him and surrealism that Bataille seems determined to ignore. In fact, in his criticism of Breton, Bataille falls prey to the very fault he discerns in Breton, since his criticism uses wide exaggerations to make its point. While Breton's treatment of Dostoyevsky in the *First Manifesto* may be completely offhand, this is the whole point: Breton was attacking not Dostoyevsky but the conventions of realism.[14] This is quite different from devoting a whole chapter to a writer. Similarly, Bataille's comparison of Camus with Lenin, saying that Lenin would only have shrugged his shoulders at *Maldoror*, is dubious. Doubtless he would have done, but he would hardly have devoted a chapter of a book to it.

None the less, there is an important point in Bataille's criticism that should be emphasized, for he raises something that few people have confronted with such clarity: the dialectic between revolt and conservatism, between excess and a need for restraint. This is preliminary, of course, to his discussion of the relation between taboo and transgression in *Eroticism*, but it also identifies the importance of what one can see as a deeply conservative strain within surrealism itself.

Following the *Second Manifesto*, the various ebbs and flows within the Surrealist Movement had been complex. For Breton the main concern in the political domain had been a fraught collaboration with the French Communist Party, which by 1935 was over, brought to a definitive end with the surrealists' tract 'On the Time the Surrealists were Right'.

Despite the unhappy outcome of the relationship between surrealism and Communism, it would be erroneous to see the conflict between them as inevitable, and any collaboration as being doomed from the start. Almost all the surrealists had seen the necessity for some form of collaboration with Communism, and they were certainly not naive in the realm of political theory. On the contrary, it was often because they understood Marxist theory better than most of those in the higher echelons of the Parti Communiste Français (PCF) that the break became inevitable, since the surrealists recognized that the abandonment of the Bolshevik watchwords 'revolutionary defeatism' and 'no national defence under capitalism' by the Comintern (and imposed on Communist Parties around the world) meant the betrayal of fundamental Marxist principles. If Breton and his friends were naive, it was in believing that the Communists were interested in a genuine collaboration rather than merely accepting them as fellow-travellers who gave the PCF a certain cultural credibility.

During the same period Bataille had been equally concerned with a collaboration with Communists, and had been closely involved in Boris

Souvarine's 'Cercle Communiste Démocratique'. Souvarine, one of the founders of the French Communist Party, was among the first to perceive the danger represented by Stalin, and had been excluded from the PCF in 1926. Thereafter he founded an oppositional 'Cercle Communiste Marx et Lénine' (the name was changed in 1930 to establish a distance from any possible 'cult of personality'). Among its members were Pierre Pascal, Pierre Kaan, Simone Weil and Karl Korsch. Bataille appears to have joined around 1930, along with many other surrealist dissidents like Jacques Baron, Michel Leiris and Raymond Queneau.

Souvarine remained on good terms with Breton and it may have been he who brought the two men together in 1935. Or it may have been Roger Caillois, whose idea *Contre-Attaque* was.[15] Whatever the case, in 1935 Breton and Bataille were working closely together in the organization of the group.

Caillois's idea was for a 'Union of Revolutionary Intellectuals', and it was this that led to the formation of *Contre-Attaque*. Caillois himself withdrew before the group was actually established, objecting to the fact that it 'had deviated too much, taking on the aspect of a political *party* with a precise programme, etc. . . . and surrendering up too much in respect of delicate ideological questions which, for my part, I wanted to see clearly discussed'.[16]

Contre-Attaque was an anti-popular front group set up 'to defend the revolutionary position betrayed by Stalin' (Breton). It lasted for eighteen months, but had only a limited impact and was dissolved after the surrealists withdrew, stating that 'the purely fascist character had become more and more flagrant'. Although this was a serious allegation, it was not accompanied by any polemic, and no individuals were cited. In a later autobiographical note, Bataille regrets this apparent pro-fascist tendency 'on the part of Bataille's friends and, to a lesser extent, of Bataille himself'.[17] The main bone of contention was Jean Dautry's suggestion that they should explore the idea of a sur-fascism, which would surpass fascism in the way that surrealism had surpassed realism. This facetious suggestion appears to have been designed as a deliberate provocation towards the surrealists, and points to the underlying disharmony within the group.[18]

After the dissolution of *Contre-Attaque*, while Breton sought an alliance with Trotsky and continued to believe in the possibility of activity by revolutionary intellectuals, Bataille engaged in a more esoteric activity around the groupings *Acéphale* and the College of Sociology. There appear to have been few direct contacts between the two men during this period, and for those of Breton's circle – judging from comments by Pierre Mabille and Nicolas Calas – there was a sense of disappointment that Bataille should become obsessed with what they perceived as irrelevancies, rather than any hostility.[19]

With the outbreak of war in 1939 and Breton's exile in the USA, those surrealists who continued to be active in Paris remained interested in Bataille, sending him their questionnaire on poetry, to which he replied in a friendly spirit. But in 1943, apparently following publication of *L'Expérience intérieure*, they issued a violent and rather childish tract, *Nom de Dieu*,[20] which recalls Bataille's own attack on Breton fourteen years earlier. This time it is Bataille who is accused of mysticism, idealism and wanting to be a priest. It shows that even under the conditions of war, the surrealists had remained provocative, but little more.

It was against this background that Bataille came to reappraise surrealism – and his own position towards it – in the immediate aftermath of the Second World War.

Breton did not return to Paris until the beginning of 1946. He immediately sought to reconstitute the Surrealist Group, and the focus around which this reconstitution was to take place was an exhibition, 'Le Surréalisme en 1947', to be held at the Galerie Maeght in Paris and then transferred to Prague.

Collaboration with *Troisième convoi* showed Bataille's new interest in surrealism, and this was stimulated by his reading of Jules Monnerot's *La poésie moderne et le sacré*, which had been published in 1945 and had a strong impact on him. At first he retains a certain contempt for current surrealist activities, which are summarily dismissed (doubtless owing in great part to annoyance over the attack in *Nom de Dieu*). This dismissal, however, seems to be wholly directed to the wartime Surrealist Group. Following Breton's return and reconstitution of a wider-based group, Bataille's attitude was transformed from dismissal to active involvement, to the extent of participating in the 1947 exhibition and contributing the important text 'The Absence of Myth' to the catalogue. This text defined one of Bataille's central preoccupations, something which linked him closely with the surrealists, and especially with Breton's own current preoccupations (the theme of the exhibition itself was 'myth'). This notion of 'The Absence of Myth' is crucial for an understanding of Bataille's thought, and it is therefore a little surprising that the issues it raised were never directly addressed in any of his published books.

His interest in myth had developed in the late 1930s through *Acéphale* and the College of Sociology, both of which were based on investigations that would try to reinvigorate myth in contemporary society. The idea was a vain one, as the Bataille of 1947 now realized. This is why he now speaks of an 'absence of myth'.

In trying to focus myth in contemporary society, one of Bataille's projects in the late 1930s had been to establish a myth around the 'Place de la Concorde' in Paris, which seemed to have all the necessary ingredients for a myth with legendary foundations, associated as it was with both the sun and sacrifice (it once contained a statue built in honour of Louis XIV, the Sun King. During the revolution this was destroyed and replaced with a Statue to Liberty, and then finally by an obelisk – an emblem of sun worship – donated by the Viceroy of Egypt; it was also the place where the guillotine was set up).

Unfortunately, such legendary elements do not a modern myth make. Bataille had wanted to organize a celebration of the death of Louis XVI each 21 January (such a celebration had in fact been enacted in the context of *Contre-Attaque* in 1936). But where Bataille wanted such a celebration to constitute a founding myth of a new society, it is immediately obvious that it could be nothing of the kind. Modern society is far too complex to be united by the notion of the death of the sovereign. Contrary to ancient society, there could be no possible consensus as to what the execution of Louis XVI represented. Few people would see it in the way Bataille did: as an act of purification by which the whole society would be renewed. If anything it was the opposite, being essentially an act that confirmed the hegemony of a particular class (the bourgeoisie). Even as such, it was subject to dispute. Few people would identify with the act of execution. For some it may have been necessary, but even so it was regrettable. For many others, even among the bourgeoisie, it was an act of barbarism that should have no place in contemporary society. To celebrate it would not be, as Bataille wished, to encourage unity, but to promote further discord. It could never become what Bataille wanted: a contagious myth by which the death of the sovereign would be celebrated as the regenerative act of the transformation of society. Unfortunately, it is probably only people who have read *The Golden Bough* who could even make such a connection, and few of them are likely to consider it appropriate to contemporary society.

Another of Bataille's apparent projects, to perform an actual human sacrifice, was still more dubious, even if it should not be dismissed out of hand. It was not conceived as scandalous – everything suggests that it would have been performed discreetly, with all legal formalities followed (it is said that Bataille had even obtained legal clearance for a sacrifice of a willing victim, although it is a little difficult to believe that French law in 1937 would have given such sanction). Bataille wanted to understand the intense motivation behind the idea of human sacrifice, and the only way of understanding it was to participate in such an act. But to do so is impossible, since we do not live in a society that recognizes the value of sacrifice as a mediating ritual. Where a sacrificer in an ancient society is performing a public – and socially necessary – function, Bataille, had he proceeded, would have been performing a surreptitious antisocial – if not illegal – act that would be regarded as being, at best, socially meaningless. Bataille soon realized this, and the realization had a profound impact on him and his thinking.

This is what impelled him, throughout the early 1940s, to ponder what myth could mean in today's society, and he came to recognize that although contemporary society was not without myth, it had denied the very basis of ancient myth, founded on a mediation between mankind and the natural world through which the cohesion (and necessity) of society would be affirmed. The myth of contemporary society, therefore, was an 'absence of myth', since that society had deluded itself into believing it was without myth by making a myth of its very denial. Furthermore, it believed that it no longer had a need for myth, that it had evolved beyond dependence upon a ritual to establish a mediation between mankind and the rest of creation, since man now had dominion over nature. The word itself had become devalued, and 'myth' now referred to something that is by definition 'false'. Both Bataille and the surrealists were convinced that this was profoundly misguided – and dangerously so: contemporary society was as much in need of mythical foundation as any other society, and by denying that fact it was simply making a fetish of its absence and denying part of itself.

Bataille believed that this was where surrealism was especially important, because it had long recognized this absence of myth, and sought to confront what it brought into play. But the surrealists, unlike Bataille, had realized very early that the reviving of ancient myths could lead to nothing. Any modern conception of myth needed, on the contrary, to begin with a concept of its absence. For Bataille, this absence of myth was merely one aspect of a more generalized 'absence'. It also meant the 'absence of sacred'. 'Sacred', for Bataille, was defined in a very straightforward way – as 'communication'. By extension, its loss also meant, therefore, an absence of communication. Quite simply, the notion of an 'absence of myth' meant a failure of communication which touched all levels of society. And a society which ceases or is unable genuinely to communicate ceases to be a society. In a very real sense it becomes an 'absence of society' or, more specifically, an 'absence of community'. At this point Bataille's analysis touches the

Marxist notion of alienation, but Bataille was more precise in defining both the symptoms and the possible 'cure'.

For Bataille, the profound sense of surrealism lay in the fact that it recognized the falsity of rationalism's ideological claims to define what is 'real'. Such a concept destroys the notion of myth, just as it becomes itself what it denies: reality is a myth. A society that denies its mythical basis therefore denies part of its essence, and is living a lie. The crucial point here is that everything about the concept of reality is mythical. Nothing solid responds to this state: the only reality we can know is defined by the use we make of myth to define our ontological principles. The thrust of Western civilization has been to deny this mythical basis, and to posit reality as an ontological given that can be located and conquered.

It is in this context that the surrealists' understanding of so-called 'primitive society' should be understood. In 'The Surrealist Religion' Bataille makes an analogy between surrealism and the Renaissance, whose break with the medieval world was framed through a 'nostalgia' for a classical past and a recovery of the riches of Rome and Greece. In the same way, Romanticism's revolt against the Renaissance looked back to the medieval values denied by the latter. In both cases, though, such an attitude was not merely nostalgia, for it served an exemplary role in providing a focus for the revitalization of society using echoes from the past. Surrealism acted in the same way, looking back to the 'primitive' – not to re-create what had been lost, but to gain an insight into it, and as a means of practical knowledge to confront the 'absence of myth' in contemporary society.

As Bataille emphasizes in this conference text (which unfortunately was never revised, and remains in a rather crude state), it is necessary first of all to re-create the notion of ritual in a society within which the value it represented (that is, the value of community) has been destroyed by the ideology of Christianity, which was the basis of capitalism. The problem for surrealism is that there is no possibility of imbuing any such ritual with meaning. No ritual could go beyond the immediate context of its performance. The absence of myth has itself been ritualized, and has in this way become absolute. Of course, this is a contradiction in terms, but capitalist society bases itself on such a contradiction, so neutralizing the contagious quality of ritual. Deprived of this contagion, which was its essential quality, any possible surrealist ritual could only be impotent, since no one outside the surrealist circle could believe in it. It was, as Jules Monnerot stated in *La poésie moderne et le sacré*, only 'prayer in a void'.

Bataille emphasizes that this is not a criticism of surrealism. It is in fact more clearly a self-criticism, since by his activity in *Acéphale* and the

College of Sociology Bataille showed himself to be far more naive than any other surrealist in believing that things could be otherwise. Indeed, it is perhaps fortunate that surrealist rituals did not have such an effect, because in the form of society in which we live, had they attained a contagious power that went beyond their immediate context, they would certainly have been swallowed up by the Culture Industry and become part of the very 'absence of myth' they sought to confront. But it remains important to establish the terrain that needs to be charted. It was not something that could be crossed by surrealism alone. The prerequisite was the establishment of a new type of society not based upon the principle of individualism and personal gain. This could be achieved only through Communism, without which surrealism was but an empty conceit. Nevertheless, the originality of surrealism was to have recognized that a society could be founded in which revolt would be accepted as a fundamental principle. The surrealists had made revolt a moral value, calling themselves 'specialists in revolt', and Bataille was later to define surrealism as a state of rage. This served to emphasize its relation to his own thought, and served especially to provide a preliminary definition for what would become one of Bataille's central precepts, the notion of 'sovereignty'.

For Bataille, sovereignty meant a state of grace in which an individual became free of given conditions without, however, transcending society. Its parallels with Breton's 'supreme point' in the *Second Manifesto* are obvious. It was a state characterized by Bataille as 'impossible'. This 'impossibility' was tied to a fundamental paradox of existence (indeed, for Bataille the condition of life itself was paradoxical) in which the highest aim – in fact ultimately the *only* aim – is the resolution of what cannot, by definition, be resolved.

It is useful to explore what Bataille meant by sovereignty by considering his relation with the thought of the Marquis de Sade, who advanced a very different idea of sovereignty which Bataille found very seductive, but ultimately rejected. The identification of Bataille's thought with that of Sade has become common, and while it is true that Bataille was fascinated by Sade, his understanding of his work was both complex and subtle. To see Bataille's thought through Sade, or vice versa, is fundamentally to misunderstand it. This is something Annie Le Brun has addressed in *Soudain un bloc d'abîme, Sade*.[21] She argues that there is by no means, as commonly believed, a close identification between Sade and Bataille, but that they were at the antipodes of each other's thought. I think she is quite right, but it seems to me that Bataille, far from being unaware of this – as Le Brun thinks – was quite conscious of the distance separating him from Sade. I think he found Sade a disturbing – even threatening – figure.

Nevertheless, Bataille did identify with Sade on several levels, most notably in his relation to writing. Like Sade he believed writing should be thrown down as a challenge to the reader; it should be a deliberate provocation, and not serve a one-to-one relation in which the reader assimilates a message from the author. Writing should have a visceral and direct relation with life, and should not be divorced from the flow of day-to-day living. And Bataille certainly identified with Sade's life, with his courage and with his intransigence. At the level of thought, however, the two men could hardly be more different.

Sade's work is a profound affirmation of life – or, at least, of *my* life, independent of that of anyone else. This affirmation is asserted to an extreme that is perhaps possible only for someone who spent much of his life in prison and who sought, with every fibre of his being, to experience to the full that free life which had been denied him by circumstances. It is an affirmation that denies death. Bataille's own statement that 'eroticism is the assenting to life even in death' would have been unthinkable to Sade. For Sade, sex served to annul death, and should be a way for us to triumph over it. Sade's sovereign man refuses death, since his life is a profusion to be experienced only for itself, and nothing exists outside of it. If we accept Bataille's terms, then, for Sade there could be no eroticism at all. This is borne out by Sade's writing, which eschews any erotic effect.

For Bataille, on the other hand, eroticism is crucial, and a comparison between Sade's novels and those of Bataille reveals this distinction clearly. What is at stake in sex for Bataille is communication between two beings, and in pushing sexuality to its limits, he wants to test to breaking point the emotional boundaries of the personality of the man and the woman. It is the relationship with the other that is important. He is not interested in sex as something that celebrates individual penchants and leads to the sovereignty of the isolated being – something that serves to strengthen the myth of the personality which Bataille wished to challenge, but which is Sade's overriding motivation.

Sex, for Bataille, is intimately associated with and necessarily includes anguish. It is the intermediary between birth and death, and in the sexual encounter we experience the chasm at the edge of existence. When two beings embrace, they momentarily experience the surpassing of life that is death. In interpenetrating, a man and a woman go to their limit, which is a state of undifferentiation in which their separate identities merge. For this reason the sexual encounter is dangerous. This sense of undifferentiation, this collapse into otherness, is what Sade both fears and denies. For him the sexual encounter should be freed of all contamination with otherness, which weakens and ultimately destroys what is unique to us. We need to assert our sovereignty as isolated beings – if necessary, in spite of the other. But, as Bataille points out in 'Happiness, Eroticism and Literature', this does not overcome anguish, since the more otherness is denied, the more sexuality is reduced to a mechanical act and, in the process, pleasure negates itself.

Bataille also affirms that life in its plenitude includes death. For him the central issue is a confrontation of the isolated being lost in his freedom. Without a social purpose in *himself* (i.e. not as a thing that serves others) man is cast adrift both from himself and from his fellow beings. This again is where myth comes in, for man is a social creature, and socialization is his determining quality. When that socialization prepares him only to serve, then he is lost in the same way as someone who is free of social sensibilities. The latter (who is, in fact, Sade's sovereign man) is, for Bataille, not a man at all. Solitude dehumanizes as surely as does servitude; therefore the central problem of existence is how to live with one's fellows.[22] Unlike Sade, whose thought is based upon an essential being that is independent of socialization, Bataille's notion of sovereignty necessarily includes engagement with social being. For Bataille, society is a social fact given in the actions of human beings but also transcending them: society has its own personality, within which each man is a part. Liberty, for Bataille, must therefore include the notion of mediation, and can be founded only in terms of a reciprocity with others. The condition of liberty is the recognition of its limits.

Sade denies any limit t﹖ human behaviour or the liberty of the individual subject, since man is a natural force not reducible to his social situation. For Sade, sovereignty must be independent of social-ization, which is merely a chain holding man down. There is no possibility of accommodation, since this would reveal a fatal weakness that would destroy sovereignty. Sade denies community as he denies death, and isolates being in a veritable orgy of sensation in which no limits must exist. Again, this is quite the opposite from Bataille, for whom existence is profoundly an experience of limits, and being itself can take form only by recognizing those limits. To deny them, or try to break completely free from them, is to deny one's own humanity.

Annie Le Brun is right, perhaps, to distinguish Sade's atheism from Bataille, whom she characterizes as religious. But only up to a point. There may be some truth in this to the extent that Sade's atheism denies all legitimacy to religion, which he sees as being imposed upon man. This creates a shackle that needs to be broken. For Bataille, on the other hand, religion is not imposed. It comes from within man's inner depths, and is realized in social reality. It is this inner necessity that must be confronted in its social context.

In the end, however, Le Brun's distinction raises a false dichotomy. As Bataille would probably reply: one can be both religious and an atheist. This is certainly what he considered himself to be. Sade, on the other hand, is certainly anti-religious, but if he is an atheist, his 'atheism' is of a different nature from Bataille's.

Essentially, the difference between Sade and Bataille is not theological but philosophical. Bataille's position is monist, while Sade's is pluralist. In Bataille's view, God *cannot* exist, because God is nothing but an idea generated by a need within man to deny his fundamental oneness. More precisely, we could say that for Bataille God *must* not exist, since God's existence is evidence of man's servitude, by which he denies his own sovereignty. As he says, 'God is merely a hypostasis of work.' The creation of God was an aberration caused by the diversion of man's socialization into satisfying only utilitarian needs. In this respect Bataille agrees with Marx that '*Man makes religion*, religion does not make man', as well as with Bakunin's 'Even if God really existed, it would be necessary to abolish him.' Or rather, more precisely, that since God did once exist within man's sensibility, we need to understand what had caused him to be born as well as examining the consequences of the fact that he had died. By denying the social, Sade cannot deny God in this way. His arguments rely on a material denial, devastatingly put forward and in a way that is probably unanswerable. But if one could answer it – if one could show that, nevertheless, God did create the world – then Sade would be forced to accept the fact. For Bataille, on the other hand, the material existence of God is an academic, meaningless question.

To this extent, too, the frequent characterization of Bataille's thinking as 'mystical' – something with which Le Brun concurs – is misconceived. The confusion arises because Bataille's primary concern is with communication. And communication, as Bataille conceives it, equals religion. But such communication cannot be with a beyond, as is the case with mysticism. For Bataille, it is conceptually impossible to know or communicate with what is beyond death, since death is an absolute limit of human experience, beyond which we cannot travel and return. The most one can experience is the vertigo of the edge of the chasm. This is the point at which the erotic and the mystical experience meet, but contrary to the aim of mysticism, Bataille believed that it was impossible to experience the fall itself without actually falling.

If Bataille was generally aware of the distance separating him from Sade, there is one point upon which he did identify with Sade's thinking in a way that appears mistaken, and this concerns materialism.

In effect, it seems accurate to say that Sade was the materialist that Bataille claimed to be, for his materialism was consistent and unyielding. His masters in this respect were d'Holbach and La Mettrie, and he took their teaching to its logical conclusion. On this point Annie Le Brun is right to insist of Sade's heroes that 'none of them really fears death, their materialism being in direct proportion to their definitive atheism'. Quite so, and here we see a sharp discordance with Bataille's proclaimed materialism, since it must follow that a consistent materialism cannot admit death. Matter does not die; it either exists or it ceases to exist. Only the mind can die, and by admitting death (and not merely admitting it, but making the consciousness of it one of the cornerstones of his thought), Bataille implicitly admits idealism. For Sade there is no death, and he certainly cannot accept its intrusion into existence, for his sovereign being can never die. Its existence may be brought to an end; it may be destroyed, but it cannot *die*. Death is otherness, undifferentiation and totality, all of which Sade's relativism denies. Only individual penchants matter: there is no order to the world, simply a permanent unfolding. This does not mean that morality does not exist, but any morality is defined as an accord with one's own natural being. Immorality for Sade begins with thought: anyone who thinks or reflects on their condition in the world, anyone who fails to act in accordance with their passions, is to be condemned. This was why he was so repelled by the guillotine, because people were being slaughtered by others acting in accordance with thought rather than passion. As such they were obeying the logic of reason, not the contrary. Like Sade, Bataille desires consecration in action, but it does not satisfy him. He knows only too well that our essential being includes thought; that to believe we can live purely in accordance with our passions is an empty nostalgia. In any event, Bataille's denial of idealism was always too vociferous for us not to suspect that we should find it lurking at the heart of his own thinking. Not that this is a criticism, of course, for if we consider Bataille a dialectical thinker, then idealism must be included in his materialism, for in a consistent dialectical materialism, the material takes form only in relation to the mental (and vice versa). And in this again Bataille's thought is remarkably close to that of Breton.

In her book, Annie Le Brun cuts a swath through much of the fanciful criticism of Sade. She does not, however, make it clear whether Sade's work squares with surrealism. In this respect it seems to me that Bataille's relationship to Sade is that of a surrealist. The surrealists can admire Sade for the same reasons as Bataille does, but I cannot see how they can have any other response to his work than that of Bataille. The very basis of surrealism is social; it assumes the very community of being in its totality that Sade was determined to deny. Of all the ancestors claimed by surrealism, Sade is perhaps the only one who, we can be sure, would have disowned such an allegiance. While he might have been drawn to the poetic quality of surrealist work, there can be no doubt that Hegelian philosophy would have repelled him in every way, especially the dialectic, which is completely alien to Sade's point of view. In the same way, there seems little doubt that he would have found the thought of both Breton and Bataille little to his taste. We have seen the distance between Bataille and Sade, but equally there is no way that Breton's 'supreme point' or his interest in magic and coincidence – quite apart from the idea of 'amour fou' – can at all be made compatible with Sadean views. Sade would have been disgusted by the thought that there could be any unity or order to the world, and he would probably have found the idea of analogical thought – the foundation of surrealism – ridiculous.

In this respect it is highly significant that in 'Happiness, Eroticism and Literature' Bataille has counterposed Sade with Malcolm de Chazal, who engaged in profound explorations of analogical thought, to suggest precisely the hidden unity of the world upon which surrealism insisted.

In Annie Le Brun's book, Sade is presented as he would have liked: as a natural force standing above social processes. This seems to be an oversimplification. In terms of Hegel's master-and-slave dialectic, Sade is perfectly comprehensible as an extreme (but what an extreme!) of a master deprived of his mastery and cast adrift in the world. His rage provides an exemplary image of revolt that will resonate as long as people deny their own inner sensibilities, but he remains closed to the experience of slavery that results in true liberation. His experience, no matter how powerful and affecting, is always limited to loss of mastery, and can never include the experience of the slave. It is this that separates him from any concept of dialectics, and ultimately from both Bataille and Breton.

The question of Bataille's supposed 'mysticism' is taken up in what remains one of the most penetrating studies of Bataille's thinking – by another surrealist, Nicolas Calas, in an article entitled 'Acephalic Mysticism'.[23] Writing in 1947, and therefore lacking access to the amplitude of Bataille's writing (the article is doubtless based primarily on *L'Expérience intérieure* and *Le coupable*), Calas is nevertheless able to go to the heart of what Bataille is addressing. Exploring Bataille's connections with mysticism, Calas writes:

If existence is informed by exchanges, and man's personality is primarily social, what are the reasons that justify him fleeing from the social nature and plunging into the wounds of ecstasy? What is the compensation for this indulgence in the state of unhappy and painful consciousness, if the answer to torment is greater ignorance of reality? If the purpose of ecstasy is not the union with God, then this heightened form of anxiety, that is obtained through feasts and yoga practices, is a sterile solution. If, nevertheless, this extremism appears preferable to the mediocrity of a compromise indulged in by the majority of mankind, then why not drive the contradiction between the ecstatic and the lower forms of the social to its extreme solution and increase the wound till it becomes one with total sacrifice? . . . Bataille, in his theory of atheistic mysticism, cannot explain the derivation of the will to oppose nature. Existentialism is the counterpoint of the old metaphysical theory of essences and, as the neoplatonists who were confronted with the task of accounting for the relation between the Divine Ones and the less perfect beings, which they succeeded in doing by developing the theory of emanation, so the existentialists must develop a theory of psychological emanation. In psychology emanation becomes will, the will by which the primary fact, existence, manifests itself. It is the will to be different from the nature of society which is the cause of anxiety. . . . If in its essence mysticism is not divine, how can Bataille avoid the psychoanalytical diagnosis that ecstasy is a pathological state?

This is a pointed critique which expresses very clearly what Bataille asked himself. But Calas is restricted in his knowledge of Bataille's thought. Bataille was quite aware of this contradiction, from which one could never escape. To divorce ecstasy from the social (in this he would completely agree with Calas) could only be a sterile solution – as is made plain by Bataille's pain at Char's phrase: 'Solitary tears are not wasted.'[24]

Nevertheless, I do not think that the will to oppose the social is what is at issue for Bataille. Mysticism is a by-product of the growth of individualism, in which God becomes substituted for social cohesion. In positing an 'absence of myth', Bataille was looking not for a new form of mysticism, but to reintegrate the notion of ecstasy into the body social, within which it would have a virulent and contagious quality. His interest was in union not with God, but with the social. The focus is integration with others, and involves tangible realization of *collective* being, which both transforms and enhances one's own individuality. It was necessary to reconstitute society. There is no individual solution, and to associate Bataille with existentialism, as Calas does, is to distort his thought. The parable of the ham-eater[25] makes this clear. The mystic who consecrates his ecstasy alone is in the same position as the ham-eater in a famine: his ecstasy is as if it had not happened.

The same thing is true, in a different way, for the surrealist, but the surrealist recognizes this as an intolerable situation, and the urge of surrealism is to overcome the isolation it implies. This is why it needs Communism, which is a stronger (or more immediate) affirmation of the demand that surrealism makes: the urge towards a society that is not based on the needs of personal interest. But Communism has the problem that even though it denies the demands of personal interest, it needs, in order to establish itself, to remain attentive to such demands even in its denial. This is the tragedy of Communism in practice, which has been trapped in an economic condition not of its own making, one that it remains unable to transcend: personal motivation remains a necessary motor for the development of technological society. By occurring in an underdeveloped country, Communism in the USSR could only succumb to the very utilitarian economic values it denied in theory. Common consecration beyond utilitarian needs could never, therefore, take shape. Nevertheless, the impulse remains, and Communism still embodies the principle more powerfully than surrealism ever could, since the demands surrealism made are left in a vacuum without the social foundation that Communism alone can provide. In other words, the reinvigoration of myth for which surrealism called could take shape only through Communism.

If eroticism and mysticism (for Bataille, two aspects of the same experience) represent the personal aspect of sovereignty, the public aspect is represented by poetry, which Bataille – in a conjunction that may initially take one aback – equates with sacrifice.

Bataille's attitude towards poetry may appear ambivalent. He declared a 'Hatred of Poetry' in the title of one of his books, and was often scathing about the emptiness of much written poetry. Yet as several of the texts in the present volume show, he also regarded poetry as one of the most important forms of the sacred.

Above all, Bataille considered poetry to be the only real residue of the communal sense of the sacred that had survived into present-day society; thus it is that he makes the equation between it and sacrifice. If this conjunction is surprising, especially when applied to such a genial poet as Jacques Prévert, it is quite consistent with Bataille's overall thinking. Indeed, Prévert is the appropriate choice for considering the sacred aspects of modern poetry since he more than any other poet has been able to consecrate a communal emotion in his work. During and immediately after the Second World War, Prévert's poetry (and not only his poetry, but also his film *Les Enfants du Paradis*) united French people in a way that excluded any facile nationalism, and gave voice to the underlying solidarity of all people. Prévert was (and remains) loved because he expressed simultaneously our most generous feelings about life and our most profound revolt.

Poetry embodies the form of revolt that surrealism sought to establish as a first principle. By definition, true poetry cannot be subsumed to utilitarian value, since it is above all determined by its affect, something that cannot be translated into a product which can be bought and sold. Bataille makes the point clearly in 'From the Stone Age to Jacques Prévert', emphasizing the difference, for instance, between a poem and an Anjou wine. No price can be placed on poetry. It is immediate, existing only as an immediacy that takes place in intimacy between writer and reader. It is an experience that cannot be recaptured beyond the immediate impact of its telling. If a poem genuinely affects, then it transforms being, doing so in a way that is beyond words; for poetry, as surrealism insisted from the start, is something that is not reducible to a poem but captures something beyond words that touches the heart. This sense of shock – of recognition and intimacy – is the essence of poetry, and it is what connects it with sacrifice, which similarly effects a common consecration beyond expression.

And again, this is where the surrealists' interest is so crucial. The need is for a new myth which establishes the communal consecration and mediation that sacrifice once effected in ancient society. Poetry is its seed, but it remains only a seed, since it is marginalized in rationalist and utilitarian society. The need, then, is to recover the primitive in a contemporary form – that is, as inflected through individualism. This is not a denial of rationalism; rather, it involves using the basis of rationalist individualism to create new collective values.

For Bataille, therefore, poetry is an affirmation of a basic humanity, and it embodies the complicity of our intimate relations with other beings. It stands against the reality principle which requires the very destruction of those same human qualities, and serves to turn us into things. Any worthwhile human activity (and this means, in effect, poetry) needs to be directed against this anonymous process by which we became alienated from ourselves; it needs to assert the singular qualities that reside within people against the uniformity imposed upon them by day-to-day responsibilities. Anything that served to affirm such uniformity was an enemy of mankind.

Present-day life is dominated by the need for subordination without reciprocity: unreasonable demands are made on us for which we are given no return except in terms of an accumulation of material goods and psychological wealth – qualities which, in the long term, really mean nothing to us. The refusal of such demands is the refusal of the weight of the world, and is necessarily the first principle for the attainment of sovereignty.

It is at this point that Bataille's debt to Hegel is most apparent, for the basis of his ideas here is explicitly drawn from Hegel's master-and-slave dialectic. It is by the refusal of given conditions that the slave (by recognizing both the condition of his slavery and its intolerability) begins the process of realization that results in sovereignty. As Bataille defined surrealism, it serves to embody this elementary state of revolt: 'It is genuinely virile opposition – nothing conciliatory, nothing divine – to all accepted limits, a rigorous will to insubordination.'[26] Towards the end of his life he was more precise: 'surrealism appears to me in its essentials to be a sort of rage . . . [A rage] against the existing state of things. A rage against life as it is . . .'[27] This revolt is a determination that has been an undercurrent of Western thought since Romanticism, but in an indistinct way. In surrealism the rage does not remain petrified in its first stage. It must lead on into restraint – something which, as we have seen, Bataille explores in 'The Age of Revolt'.[28] Surrealism was first to give it clear consciousness, so that the negation becomes positive.

If we accept Bataille's arguments about the sense of absence in respect of communal values in Western society and the necessity to confront the issues it raises, surrealism is of the utmost importance. The trend of Western thought since the Renaissance has always been focused on the great individual, the inspired genius, who determined the course of history. German Romanticism represented the first reaction against this surge, but in its later English – and especially French – forms, Romanticism served in many ways to emphasize the very individualism it had first been a reaction against. Surrealism, by establishing as a fundamental principle that 'poetry must be made by all', definitively broke the stranglehold of individualism, but in a way that was still tentative.

The failure of surrealism, according to Bataille, was to have been unable to take this very tentative step any further. But this is why it remains so important, and what distinguishes it so strikingly from the existentialism that was beginning to replace it on the intellectual scene as Bataille was writing these studies. For surrealism, freedom of choice – the essence of existentialism – is a false issue. Freedom depends not on choice, which is empty phraseology, but on the quality of life. As Bataille puts it, in surrealism 'The accent is placed not on the fact of choosing but on the content of the choice proposed'.[29] For surrealism, liberty exists independently of mankind – if we seek to dominate it, to take control over it, then liberty will dissolve. No one can enjoy freedom independently of others: the freedom of one is the freedom of all. 'Individual freedom', in this sense, is a contradiction in terms.

These writings on surrealism are clearly those of someone committed to a surrealist perspective. They do not take the standpoint of a critic, but seek to enter the surrealist sensibility. Bataille may have wished to distance himself to some extent from the Surrealist Group as such, and his critical comments serve to emphasize this distance. But such criticisms are vague, cursory and of little real substance. He accuses the surrealists of lacking intellectual inclination, but what does this mean, and to whom is he referring? Without specific examples, it hangs in the air as a vague reproach. He protests about surrealists putting themselves on show, and being content with only producing works, but again he gives no examples, and leaves the criticism as an empty allegation. Rather than being a critic of the surrealists, it seems more accurate to say that Bataille, with such assertions, was defining a paradox which was as apparent within his own work as within that of the 'surrealists'.

Bataille clarifies this paradox in these terms: surrealism cannot speak. If it speaks, it betrays itself. But on the other hand, if it does not speak, it abdicates its responsibilities. Others will then speak for it, and destroy the very intransigence it ought to maintain.

In so far as these texts pass for a critique of surrealism, therefore, the criticism is somewhat oblique. It passes, in fact, for self-criticism. Bataille is well aware that the paradox he raises applies equally to his own work, as he makes plain in 'René Char and the Force of Poetry'. Since Bataille's own books are now lined up on the shelves (rather more prominently than those of most other surrealists), the paradox he puts forward implicates himself still more forcibly.

Writing in the shadows cast by Auschwitz and Hiroshima – events which took pure utilitarianism to its logical conclusion – Bataille recognized the urgency that the 'absence of myth' served to focus. The regaining of a consciousness of collective myth was a necessity that required first of all that we refuse to allow ourselves to be treated as objects to be used. And likewise we must cease to make abstractions of others if we are not to lose our own humanity. The consciousness of this gained its preliminary recognition in the 'absolute revolt' of surrealism, and it is against this background that these writings should be read.

Notes

1. 'Surrealism and How It Differs from Existentialism': see p. 57 below.

2. Michel Surya, *Georges Bataille, la mort à l'œuvre* (1987), Paris: Garamont, p. 92.

3. This criticism is almost certainly aimed not at André Breton but at the wartime Parisian Surrealist Group, 'La Main à plume', organized by Noël Arnaud and Jean-François Chabrun.

4. See in particular 'Notes on the Publication of "Un Cadavre" ' and 'The Age of Revolt', pp. 30, 158 below.

5. Bataille writes of Breton's remorse over the allegations made in the *Second Manifesto*. Nothing in Breton's own writings, however, gives any substance to this.

6. Quoted in José Pierre (ed.), *Tracts surréalistes et déclarations collectives*, vol. 1 (1980), Paris: Le Terrain Vague, p. 80.

7. Sarane Alexandrian, *Le surréalisme et le rêve* (1974), Paris: Gallimard, p. 456.

8. Jean Wahl, in Ferdinand Alquié (ed.), *Entretiens sur le surréalisme* (1968), Paris: Mouton, pp. 167–8.

9. Philippe Audoin, *Sur Georges Bataille* (1987), Paris: Actual, p. 34.

10. This text was never published during Bataille's lifetime, and saw the light of day only in 1968, when it was published in *Tel Quel*, no. 34. It is translated in Georges Bataille, *Visions of Excess*, ed. Allan Stoekl (1985), Minneapolis: University of Minnesota Press.

11. Also in *Visions of Excess*.

12. *Visions of Excess*, p. 92.

13. If it is true that this critique may have been prompted by Breton's criticism of Bataille in relation to Sade in the *Second Manifesto*, it is difficult to see how it relates to Breton's comments.

14. In fact Dostoyevsky is mentioned only in a footnote. Breton uses a quotation from him as a deliberate provocation. It would be absurd to read this as a dismissal of Dostoyevsky's work as a whole.

15. E. Tériade had been keen to effect a reconciliation between Bataille and the surrealists during the end of 1932 and early 1933, when he was establishing his journal *Minotaure*, which in fact was named by Bataille and later effectively became the organ of the Surrealist Group. At this time, however, the surrealists were not willing to work with Bataille.

16. Letter to Jean Paulhan, quoted in Georges Bataille, *Lettres à Roger Caillois* (1987), Paris: Folle Avoine, p. 42.

17. 'Autobiographical Note' in Bataille, *Writings on Laughter, Sacrifice, Nietzsche, n-Knowing*, trans. Annette Michelson in *October*, no. 36 (1986).

18. See Robert Short, 'Surrealism and the Popular Front', in Francis Baker (ed.), *The Politics of Modernism* (1978), Colchester: University of Essex.

19. For instance, Mabille refers in a response to Jules Monnerot's inquiry on 'spiritual directors' to: 'this College of Sociology where some professors confuse the Temple with the Circus' (included in *The College of Sociology 1937–39*, ed. Denis Hollier, trans. Betsy Wing (1988), Minneapolis: University of Minnesota Press, p. 66. Patrick Waldberg and Georges Duthuit, who participated in *Acéphale* and the College of Sociology, were later highly critical of the activity of these groups in an open forum published in the surrealist review *VVV*. This forum was established at the suggestion of André Breton after Patrick Waldberg had written a long letter to his wife Isabelle about the activity of *Acéphale*, where he was scathing about his own participation, which he said now made him feel nauseous and which was particularly reprehensible for its lack of 'humour and modesty'. But the letter also contains important material about possible ways to approach myth in the contemporary context. See Patrick Waldberg, Robert Lebel and Georges Duthuit, 'Vers un nouveau mythe? Prémonitions et défiances', *VVV*, no. 4 (February 1944); also Patrick and Isabelle Waldberg, *Un amour Acéphale* (1992), Paris: Éditions de la Différence.

20. In Pierre (ed.), *Tracts surréalistes*, vol. 2, p. 9.

21. Annie Le Brun, *Soudain un bloc d'abîme, Sade* (1986), Paris: Jean-Jacques Pauvert; trans. as *Sade: A Sudden Abyss* (1990), San Francisco: City Lights.

22. In this respect, Bataille's idea of sovereignty seems to conform completely to Marx's definition of Communism as 'the *positive* supersession of *private property* as *human self-estrangement*, and hence the true *appropriation* of the *human* essence through and for man; it is the complete restoration of man to himself as a *social* i.e. human, being, a restoration which has become conscious and which takes place within the entire wealth of previous periods of development' (Economic and Philosophical Manuscripts', in *Early Writings* [1975], Harmondsworth: Penguin, p. 348).

23. Nicolas Calas, 'Acephalic Mysticism', *Hémispheres II*, no. 6 (1945).

24. 'René Char and the Force of Poetry'. Char's original phrase is difficult to translate. 'Pleurer solitaire mène à quelque chose' means literally 'To cry alone leads to something', but a literal translation fails to capture the anguish of the expression.

25. 'From the Stone Age to Jacques Prévert': see p. 137 below.

26. 'On the Subject of Slumbers': see p. 49 below.

27. Interview in Madeleine Chapsal, *Envoyez la petite musique* . . . (1984), Paris: Grasset, p. 236.

28. An attentive reader could never fail to recognize how little Bataille was an advocate of excess, since he always makes it clear that excess has meaning only in relation to restraint. In these writings he explicitly denies that he is interested only in excess (see 'The Problems of Surrealism', p. 97 below), and in 'Surrealism from Day to Day' (see p. 34 below) he writes, in a sentence that is an important key to his thought as a whole, 'I love purity to the extent of loving impurity . . .'

29. 'Surrealism and How It Differs from Existentialism': see p. 57 below.

The Castrated Lion

I have nothing much to say about the personality of André Breton, since I hardly know him. His police reports don't interest me. My only regret is that he has obstructed the pavement for so long with his degrading idiocies.

Religion should die with this old religious windbag.

Still, it would be worthwhile to retain the memory of this swollen abscess of clerical phraseology, if only to discourage young people from castrating themselves in their dreams.

Here lies the Breton ox, the old aesthete and false revolutionary with the head of Christ.

A man brimming over with respect is not a man but an ox, a priest, or even a representative of that unspeakable species, the animal with a great mop of hair and sputtering head: the castrated lion.

There remains the celebrated question of surrealism, that newly consecrated religion devoted, in spite of appearances, to hollow success.

In fact no one doubts that the surrealist religion embodies the elementary condition for religious success, replete as it is with 'mysteries' surrounding its dogmas which today extend to *occultation*, and a 'hypocrisy' with respect to people which attains, in a manifesto as grandiloquent and false as a catafalque, the level of gross indecency.

In any case, I think we need to be clear about what this involves. In speaking about the surrealist religion I do not do so merely in order to express an insurmountable disgust, but out of the desire for precision and, to some extent, for technical reasons.

I suppose it is idiotic to speak about violence while at the same time swindling an appearance of violence through darkness. It is undoubtedly possible to safeguard the most vulgar virility while at the same time opposing sloppiness and bourgeois oppression with technical trickery. The dreadful awareness that every human being has of mental castration almost inevitably translates, under normal conditions, into religious observance, since such a human being, fleeing in the face of grotesque danger yet retaining the taste for existence, transposes his activity into the mythical domain. Because by so doing he regains a false liberty and has no difficulty portraying virile men, who are only shadows, and in consequence complacently confounds his life with a shadow, even though everyone today knows that the liquidation of modern society will not turn into water as it did at the end of the Roman Empire in the face of Christianity. With the exception of a few rather unappetizing aesthetes, no one any longer wants to be buried in blind and idiotic contemplation, no one wants a mythical liberty.

Amazed to see that this liquidation happened only in the political domain, and was expressed only by revolutionary movements, surrealism has sought with subconscious obstructionism, and the deceitful politics of the corpse-like Breton, to insinuate itself as well as it could into the baggage of Communism. This manoeuvre having been frustrated, Breton is reduced to concealing his religious enterprise under a feeble revolutionary phraseology. But how could Breton's revolutionary attitude ever be anything other than a swindle?

A shifty character dying of boredom in his absurd '*lands of treasure*' is fine for religion, and fine for little castratos, little poets and little mystic-mongrels. But nothing is ever changed by a great big soft strumpet armed with a gift-wrapped library of dreams.

Notes on the Publication

of 'Un Cadavre'[1]

In autumn 1929 the *Second Manifesto* was published in *La Révolution Surréaliste*. André *Breton* implicated me, and particularly accused me of mustering the dissidents and those excluded from surrealism against him: 'Perhaps,' he wrote, 'M. Bataille is preparing to gather them together, and what happens will be interesting. Taking starters' orders for the race organized by M. Bataille are Messrs Desnos, Leiris, Limbour, Masson and Vitrac. It is difficult to understand why M. Ribemont-Dessaignes is not among them.' All in all, the *Second Manifesto* made accusations against those surrealists cited in the 'first' who, according to Breton, had lost the moral right to draw their inspiration from the movement: *Artaud, Carrive,* Francis *Gérard, Limbour, Masson, Soupault, Vitrac, Artaud,* Jacques *Baron,* Pierre *Naville, Desnos, Ribemont-Dessaignes,* Tristan *Tzara.*[2] In fact the dissolution of the group was still more serious than these initial splits would have indicated. Michel Leiris had excluded himself for quite some time, and between (round about) the writing of the *Second Manifesto* and its publication, Raymond *Queneau,* then *Breton*'s brother-in-law, Jacques *Prévert* and Max *Morise* had broken away and, as if to give meaning to *Breton*'s allegations, had entered into relations with me.

In truth there was never anything that amounted to a new heterodox group which would have locked horns with the first. Personally, my only interest at that time was eroticism and erotic subversion. I was trying to effect publication of an *Erotic Almanac,* which Pascal *Pia* (who would publish *Combat,* then become the editor of *Carrefour*) would be entrusted with publishing clandestinely (in 1927 he had published *Irene's Cunt* by Aragon, with etchings by Masson; and in 1928 *The Story of the Eye,* which I signed 'Lord Auch' – 'Auch' being the abbreviation of 'aux chiottes' [to the shithouse], which had been used by my friend *Fraenkel,* one of the first Dadaist protagonists, while 'Lord' had for me the meaning it has in English translations of the Bible – *Masson* was also

responsible for the lithographic illustrations in *Story of the Eye*). *Masson*
then gave me some admirable illustrations for *Justine*, which I still hope
to publish as beautifully as possible in a small volume; *Leiris* gave me a
text which later became *Manhood*;[3] *Limbour* produced a very charming
story which has probably gone astray. Maurice *Heine*, who did not
break with *Breton*, gave me a very beautiful unpublished text by *Sade*.[4] I
wrote my [or a] 'Use Value of D.A.F. de Sade', which I have destroyed.

The economic crisis, which soon affected the trade in luxury books,
prevented the project from coming to fruition: it was by no means an
erotic movement. In fact the signatories of the second 'Cadavre', which
appeared on 15 January 1930, were never united by anything other
than hostility. Today I am inclined to believe that *Breton*'s demands,
which ended in the generalized rupture of the years 1928–9, were
fundamentally justified; there was in *Breton* a desire for common
consecration to a single sovereign truth, a hatred of all forms of
concession regarding this truth, of which he wanted his friends to be
the expression, otherwise they would cease to be his friends – something with which I still agree. But *Breton*'s failing was to be too rigidly
attached to the outward forms of this fidelity. This resulted in an
unease all the greater for having a sort of hypnotic prestige – an
immediate and exceptional authority – which he used with insufficient
care and without real discretion. His mood is changeable, and he yields
to it more easily than to the need to respect others. It was in this way
that he could so mistreat *Aragon* (who was then – this must have been
around 1928 – at the peak of his notoriety) that the latter, returning
home with *Masson* one evening after a row at the studio in rue
Fontaine, said: 'And to think that I've broken with my family for this.'
Breton's authority had in fact something of a paternal deafness about it.
Moreover, I do not think that a more patient and more reflexive
character would have been any more able to form the community
devoted to the profound meaning of surrealism André *Breton*
dreamed about. In fact there is nothing in this principle which could
be sufficiently clear, particularly sufficiently absolute, to break modern
individualism and personal pride. There is a contradiction between
the liberty that is essential to surrealism and the rigour without which it
fades away, and any way of life replaces the sovereign course to which
it lays claim.

Whatever the case, in the narrow literary milieu which formed – not
around me, but around the review *Documents* (which, as 'secretary-
general', I really edited, in agreement with Georges-Henri *Rivière*, who
is today curator of the Folklore Museum at the Palais de Chaillot, and
against the titular editor, the German poet Carl *Einstein*). The majority
of the signatories of the second 'Cadavre' had in fact collaborated on

Documents, and this collaboration provided proof of their tenuous cohesion. It was *Desnos* who had the idea of replying to the *Second Manifesto*. Since this publication and the extreme dissolution of the group announced his death, we would prepare *Breton*'s obituary, using the form and title of the pamphlet which tarnished Anatole France's public funeral. I recall that we were sitting outside the *Deux-Magots*. I asked around: the idea seemed a good one, and my friend Georges-Henri *Rivière* immediately obtained the five hundred francs the publication would cost. When I saw *Desnos* again he said that he didn't think it was a very good idea after all, and he had really been joking; on reflection, it would not serve to discredit *Breton* but, on the contrary, to reinforce his authority. I was not sure he was not right. But I had started to put the thing into operation, and despite his reservations I managed to persuade *Desnos* to provide a text in spite of everything. Jacques-André *Boiffard* was given the task of preparing the photographic montage, taken from the page of *La Révolution Surréaliste* where all the participants of the group are represented with their eyes closed and their gaze turned inwards.

Today I am sure that *Desnos* was right. There are many other things in my life with which I do not agree, but 'Un Cadavre' is among them. I hate this pamphlet as I hate the polemical parts of the *Second Manifesto*. These immediate accusations, with no possibility of recall, came from facility and premature annoyance: how much better silence on both sides would have been. Did not *Breton* himself write in a 'preface': 'In allowing the *Second Manifesto of Surrealism* to be republished, I now see that time has served to blunt the polemical edges for me. My hope is that it may also have corrected – albeit to some extent at my expense – the sometimes hasty judgements I made . . . ' A single reservation: a certain regret for a youth when haste could be sovereign, when it did not seem that passion should ever be distrusted. I was wrong, but however painful the vanity of inexperience may seem, the need for experience is the defect of realization: if we were not so moved by the stammerings of childhood, our deepest thoughts would never have the lightness to gauge their depths.

Notes

1. As far as I can recall, 500 copies of 'Un Cadavre' were printed, but I am sure I destroyed about 200 of them when I moved house. There were copies on coloured paper. [This text, like 'Le Surréalisme au jour le jour', was written at the request of Yves Breton, a book collector. The circumstances are recounted by Jean Breton in his book *Un bruit de fête* (Paris: Cherche-Midi, 1990). I am indebted to Jean Breton for this information. – *Translator*]

[2. Bataille's memory is at fault in respect of Tzara who, far from being insulted in the *Second Manifesto*, was welcomed back into surrealism. – *Translator*]

3. This is the explanation for the dedication in the second edition of this very wonderful book (Gallimard, 1945); the first edition appeared in 1939 without a dedication.

4. The text appeared later in the insert of *Le surréalisme au service de la Révolution*.

Surrealism from

Day to Day

To Yves Breton, whose friendship inspired the idea and
possibility of writing a book that I love.

Chapter 1

1. My intention[1]

I have just finished reading the pages devoted to surrealism in *The
Rebel*. My understanding of surrealism is on a different level to that of
Albert Camus.[2] For myself, I remain connected to these minor and too
familiar details of a dispute in which my voice was unfortunately
raised. But it is necessary to bring together in a single point the
amplification of submerged life in which nothing at all can resist the
vivacity which frees us from our bonds. Minor details are important to
me, and I cannot separate my valuable moments from the humility
they give me. I am not writing this book with a view to publication. At
the present moment I am writing for myself, for those rare people who
will pass and, aided by chance, fall upon these pages (I have no wish to
intervene, except in one respect: I would prefer there to be no other
copies of these pages; I forbid their publication and I could not allow a
single passage to be quoted).

Clearly I might change my mind and pass the text to a publisher . . .
In any event, my intention is neither to harm nor to disparage. I love
those submerged, forlorn – almost shameful – antecedents, this sort of
manure in which an almost-always secret truth is nourished, perpet-
ually concealed, half embarrassing and marked by shame: this is all
that pleases me. I love purity to the extent of loving impurity, without
which purity would be counterfeit. I do not know if I compromise or
safeguard; I think I may be leading myself away or going beyond: it is
the sort of vice that has a meaning less hidden in eroticism.

Surrealism's Dadaist origins add to it an inextricable element. Something deliberate and ostentatious goes hand in hand with a vulgar childishness. The connection is so perfect, we do not know which of these failings is the more odious. But those who are unable properly to appreciate the sweet, soapy, naked quality of prostitutes do not *feel* what it is that attaches us, in a similar way, to the most dreadful failures. I may as well finally say it: it is the only chance. Otherwise men would repel me, and I would scorn their sincerity: it is connected to these foul habits, and the hateful verbal pandemonium in which everything is hideous or disfigured, bearing the promise of a mute disavowal.

I shall write by fits and starts, sorting out my memories and not hesitating to speak about myself, but this *myself* is the person I have known better than any other, and often it was only my behaviour that posed the questions that became important for me. I would especially like to introduce digressions, for the abuse of digressions seems to me the only sphere to which my argument responds. Nevertheless, my narrative could well not differ from what I might have said about my 'literary life'.

2. Michel Leiris

The first person I got to know was Michel Leiris. I met him at the end of 1924 through Jacques Lavaud, a fellow librarian at the Bibliothèque Nationale. The three of us had the vague intention of founding a literary movement, but we had only empty ideas about what form it would take. I can recall that one evening after cocktails we went to the bar of a little brothel in a street adjoining Porte Saint-Denis, which one of us had heard about. It was a good-natured, intimate brothel, and we drank a great deal, especially me, the most inebriated of the three: I drank in a disorderly and excessive way. As I recall, our discussions, in which one of the girls participated (with a lively, if misguided, interest), were certainly anodyne, and so was their extravagance. But at that time extravagance came easily to those whom it captivated, and they felt that it put an end to the common-sense world – so much so that the 'movement' seemed to us to take shape: the only thing we needed to do was publish a few of our discussions (which I noted down in my drunkenness) . . .

Beyond a tired affectation, everything else struck us, of course, as negligible. Soon afterwards Leiris got caught up with the Surrealist Group, and we didn't mention it again. I think the breadth and harshness of the developing movement gave him a shock. A couple of months passed before we saw each other again. Neither of us was accustomed to explaining ourselves, especially not Leiris. My friend spoke freely about bars and drinking. Sometimes literature was mentioned, but with no more interest than bars and drinking. (I can say that I felt dissatisfied by the fact that Leiris, who was younger than me, intimidated me: when I was with him I felt ashamed to talk about what really interested me. Not only did I live with this sense of shame, but Leiris was, of the two of us, the *initiated one*.) Finally, on my insistence, he spoke about the surrealists at greater length, and immediately it seemed to me that while the subject might be absurd, it was also solemn, even boring. I was annoyed. It had separated me from Leiris. I liked him a lot, but he gave me to understand that our relationship was secondary. Except for the desire for a dazzling life, I was interested only in the disconnected and the inconsequential . . . . I was right: the person whose life is mediocre is unable to judge anything; he thinks he is judging life, but he is really judging only his own inadequacy. Moreover, I was in torment. I sometimes felt that Leiris had been taken in, and I feared a boisterous fraud. I could respond only to a secret and provocative violence which aroused me and consigned me, I believed, to some clairvoyant fate that was worthy of being taken seriously. I immediately thought that the dense world of surrealism would paralyse and suffocate me. I could not breathe in an atmosphere of ostentation. I found myself rejected and, as if I had experienced the shock that had directly struck Leiris by contagion, I had the feeling of being overwhelmed by a strange, deceitful and hostile force which emanated from a world without secrets, from a platform on which I would never receive or accept a place, before which I would remain dumb, mediocre and powerless.

At first I sensed the change in Leiris's attitude only dimly, but very soon I had a clear sense of what it involved: a moral terror emanating from the ruthlessness and craftiness of a rabble-rouser. Personally I was *nothing* but the locus of empty agitation. I wanted nothing and could do nothing. There was nothing within me which even gave me the right to speak in a muted voice. I was suddenly faced with people who assumed an authoritative tone, found within themselves – out of weariness? or boredom? – but without acting! – who had even deliberately chosen this voice that set them apart, alien to everything.

Even before going any further, I felt the coldness that seized Leiris. Something had changed him – he was now silent, evasive, and more ill at ease than ever. He was utterly at a loss, prey to such nerves that everything slipped away from him. At the time he was elegant, but in a subtle way and without the self-consciousness that would later rob him of some of this elegance. He powdered his face completely, using something as white as talc. The nervousness which caused him to bite the ends of his fingers down to the nails gave his features a lunar relief. His words were perhaps sententious – so as to irritate himself, it seemed, so that he could more authentically be this fake, scatter-brained child caught in the act, suddenly careful to observe a fastidious discipline, a discipline which he observed with an expressionless eye, looking elsewhere . . . obliquely eager for what he dared not do: disobey or flee.

3. André Breton

Leiris introduced me to Breton only later. He made it clear that Breton was the soul of the movement. He spoke with emotion about the *Confession dédaigneuse*. When I asked what justified the sense of authority that Breton embodied, he explained it was through this text. I had read the *First Manifesto* and found it unreadable. I told Leiris so frankly. 'Perhaps,' he replied. 'But what about *Poisson soluble?*' *Poisson soluble* was the text published with the *Manifesto* which Breton offered as an example of automatic writing. My timidity, my stupidity and my distrust, all of which conditioned my judgement, were so great that I resolved to consider what it was that Leiris felt with such absolute conviction. With more honesty, I strove to admire the *Confession* (it was my dishonesty that made me like *Poisson soluble*), but I never managed to. If I admired it, it was grudgingly, or verbally, and not without remorse and misgivings. Breton declared, with that tone of exasperation by which he skilfully expanded and then relaxed his sentences: 'I never make plans' (with one exception, he said, expressing the complacency with which he pretended to accede to those of others). From the beginning I found it difficult to believe in what seemed to me to be uneasy pretension and no more than a plan. But as I had plans myself these doubts struck me as shameful!

I was inclined to be quiet and underwent a severe test, in which I hypocritically decided to outdo in contention the most contentious lawyer. The method to which Breton reduced literature,[3] automatic writing, bored me or had only a laboured amusement. I was as fond of disorientating games as the next man but, in my humble condescension and provocative timidity, only in an idle way. But what did seem to me admirable about the method was that it removed literature from the vanity of personal advantage, which I had perhaps renounced myself, but as a writer renounces it, with mixed feelings: 'automatic writing' alone stood out, it stood out against someone who had mixed feelings.

But it seemed to me that if Breton required silence from his listeners, he did not keep quiet himself. I therefore needed not only to

be quiet myself but also to hear nothing except Breton's voice, measured, pretentious and swollen with learning. He seemed to me
conventional, without the subtlety which doubts and protests, and
without the terrible panics in which everything becomes undone. What
caused me the greatest discomfort was not only the lack of rigour, but
the absence of this completely insidious, joyous and telltale cruelty
towards the self, which tries not to dominate but to go a long way. In
such circumstances I abandoned my silence and joined the horrible
game, becoming disgusted by my own pretension while refusing it in
others. I was in turn forced to raise my voice, raise it higher and more
stupidly to rave in an exaggerated way that went too far. In order to
endure a mixture of silence and childish complaints, to which I added
my share, what sum of morose energy must I not squander? I wan-
dered into successive dead-ends from which I would cunningly
emerge even more frightened or depressed by my confused speech.

4. Louis Aragon

Leiris delayed my introduction to Breton for some time. But he did
arrange for me to meet Aragon, who at that time had an incomparable
reputation. Restless and dazzling as it was, surrealism owed its gaiety
and explosive qualities to Aragon's insolence. Breton did not seduce.
Leiris had arranged to meet Aragon, with whom he was on good
terms, one evening at midnight. We met in what was perhaps the most
charming nightclub of all: Zelli's. It was easy to go in and have a drink
standing at the bar while chatting (later it changed character and
became, under the name *Les Nudistes* and finally *Le Paradis*, a strip
joint). I don't know if Leiris had been reluctant to take me. I had
doubts about the impression I made on other people. Despite a certain
extravagance of thought, I had a rather bourgeois appearance: an
umbrella with a bamboo handle . . .[4] Finally, as we had been wander-
ing around together since nine o'clock, we went there at midnight.
Aragon was there waiting for Leiris, and immediately brought him up
to date with some unsuccessful initiative he had undertaken at the
Lower House that afternoon. It was a time of sincere revolutionary will
and serious resolutions. Aragon ventured to draw this conclusion from
his failure: 'We were born too late to play at being Lassalle.' This
phrase amazed me with the extent of its absurdity.

Later I got to know Aragon by chance. I had loved *Le paysan de Paris*,
something which now demonstrates my persistent liking for an
appearance of a particularly elegant way of life which I often considered to be sovereign. . . . From the first Aragon disappointed me. He
was not a fool, but he was not intelligent either. I often wondered if my

judgement was not coloured by the fact that he immediately assumed with me the pose of the great writer being confronted with a mediocrity.[5] But I found him amusing. I thought I could grasp his liberality of spirit. He embodied both a puerile naivety and an ease of seduction that he had to resist. He very honestly craved responsibility, and tried to give himself a breadth he did not have. I felt that he was playing at being the great man in that same way as I, at the age of ten, had galloped among the Sioux in my imagination.

What we shared was a common feeling of misfortune at living in a world that we felt had become empty – of having, for want of profound virtues, a need for ourselves, or for a small number of friends, to assume the appearance of being what we did not have the means of being. The Russian revolutionaries wondered whether they were true revolutionaries: they were. The surrealists knew they could not be authentic Rimbauds, but within themselves they knew they were as far from the Revolution as from Rimbaud. Nevertheless, Aragon could give the impression of being a very accomplished and refined person, admired by everyone, but his misfortune was to know enough to be contemptuous of what he possessed, and he refused the ripe bunch of grapes dangled in front of him. He had the charm of minor luck – perhaps of the facility of luck. . . . The overly easy amusement of satisfied vanity could not deceive him, but he could never forget or deny a brilliant plumage, always at the mercy of the temptation to amaze, seduce, deceive expectations. It's true that sometimes he stopped performing and revealed what an *innocent* he really was. I recall one early morning, on the boulevard de la Madeleine, without saying a word, he showed me a very fine moth which he had caught by the wings.

One evening, as I was writing at a table in the Deux-Magots, he came over and sat down at the next table and we had a long, serious conversation. He talked about Marx and Hegel, and offered his own interpretation of the surrealist doctrine of the moment. I let him continue for some time, expressing nothing but my own ignorance, or sometimes asking for clarification of some particular point. By the end, though, I wanted to say something. 'Once again I know nothing', I told him softly, 'about all the things you have talked about so eloquently, but don't you have the feeling that you are pulling rabbits out a hat?' I was smiling, and he smiled back.

5. The 'Fatrasies'

In the meantime, I had met Breton. At the time he held court on the glazed terrace of a small café on Place Blanche, the Cyrano. (This café still exists today, but its décor has changed.[6]) Leiris, who was by then a recognized surrealist, took me there to deliver the translation of 'Fatrasies', which appeared in the next issue of *La Révolution Surréaliste*. The 'Fatrasies' are thirteenth-century poems based on the principle of a complete lack of meaning. Paul Éluard reproduced the entirety of what I translated in 1925 in his *Première anthologie vivante de la poésie du passé*.[7] I recall that Breton said of these poems: 'Nothing is more beautiful.' In support of his judgement I will quote a few verses by a celebrated thirteenth-century lawyer:

> A large red herring
> Had besieged Gisors
> On both sides
> And two dead men
> Came with great difficulty[8]
> Carrying a door
> Without an old hunchback
> Who went around crying: 'A! outside'
> The cry of a dead quail
> Would have taken them with great difficulty
> Underneath a felt hat.[9]

Around Breton were Aragon, Éluard and Gala Éluard (who would later, after being Éluard's wife, become Dali's). At that time the surrealists' appearance was striking, and one could not help but be impressed: such was their overall confidence that the silence of the world lay within them. There was about them, in their unaffected insouciance, something oppressive, vigilant and sovereign which simply made people feel ill at ease. But it was from Breton that the heaviest sense of discomfort emanated. It seemed to me that his friends of that time possessed this manner of being so insidiously out of line: it allowed an aloofness and introduced a numbness without anything further being said, and became intoxicated with a petrified attitude. I would very much have liked this allure of uncomplacent elegance, which in my eyes had the value of a sign. The majority of surrealists who came along later appeared under a contrary sign. Even today I find it difficult to have affection for people who never have this indifferent indolence, this crazy and abandoned air, this absorbed awaking that seems like sleep. But the problem precisely starts there . . .

My feelings about visiting the Cyrano were ambivalent. I was shy, and had too great a need for self-effacement to confront these distant beings who communicated to me the feeling of a majestic life which nevertheless remained caprice itself: I knew I lacked the strength *to face them as I was.* They threatened – to the extent that I loved (or admired) them – to reduce me to a powerlessness that would literally suffocate me. Breton said little to me, and in truth I could not possibly imagine having a conversation with him. He complimented me on the 'heading' I had given to the translation of the 'Fatrasies'. 'Very charming!' he said, amiably. This shocked me: I expected rigour and could imagine nothing more disappointing than to be appreciated for reasons rather different from those maintained by Breton himself, a perspective that rightly excluded the vulgarity of compliments.

It is a memory all the more comical in that I had both an unstable character and one that was clinging and impulsive, inconsequential, unconstrained and anguished. I was so tired of my empty life, with no reputation or means; so envious of the authentic life these recognized writers embodied. At the same time I was so tired of being envious, so angry at the idea of the most furtive concession. Breton said he would like to see me again, and asked me to call him. It was only some time later that I decided to do so: a female voice answered and told me to call again a few days later, without offering the least explanation for such a delay. Before hanging up, I told her, in an apologetic tone, that I had called only because Breton had asked me to. I mentioned the incident to Leiris, and he advised me to leave the matter there. I did not ask for an explanation, and only later did I learn from him that I had made a very bad impression on Breton. According to him, I was nothing but an obsessive: at least, that was the word Leiris used.

6. W.C.

Breton later wrote (in 1947) that I was 'one of the few men in life I have found worth taking the trouble of getting to know'. As I copy out this phrase, its only interest, at this point in the story, is to bring the insignificant details I report to bear on the unfolding of time – in which nothing lasts. In 1925 Breton's malevolent attitude barely interested me. For the most part I was very sure of myself, and my embarrassment was caused less by my own doubts than by an excess of certainty. It was not that I didn't find Breton's hostile attitude annoying; to judge by his influence on Leiris, his friendship seemed no less threatening. I felt the need to protect those whom I liked, or who mattered to me, from this influence. In any event, I found it difficult to live in a world in which the discomfort that Breton had extended around him burdened the best and least submissive minds, making them insensitive to anything that did not touch Breton.

In the long run, Leiris liked me. He liked to go out with me. We understood each other marvellously – that is, in spite of a tenseness which isolated him in a wretched solitude. I met him by chance during my wanderings through bars and cafés, without mentioning Aragon, Roland Tual, Desnos, Boiffard, Tzara, Malkine and others. I was soon friends with Masson, who was also Leiris's oldest friend and mentor. Two or three times I even met Jouhandeau, who was far from the surrealist influence. Soon there appeared that seductive trio of Marcel Duhamel (today the director of the 'Série noire'), the painter Tanguy and Jacques Prévert, who lived together in a small and wonderful house in rue du Château. I often saw Dr Fraenkel, whom I particularly liked and who had played his part in the good old days of the Dada movement (and who wrote the *Letter to the Directors of the Insane Asylums* that appeared in issue 3 of *La Révolution Surréaliste*). If I was able to relate so well to Fraenkel it was because he was, as I was (perhaps even more so), a very quiet night bird with a sort of nocturnal sadness, but ridiculous deep down; such was the living figure (?) to which we were both attached.

I had written a little book called *W.C.*, which I signed Tropmann. It was illustrated with some drawings, one of which depicted a guillotine with, instead of an aperture, an eye, which was also the setting sun. A road into a deserted landscape led towards this promise of death. Below I had written the title *The Eternal Return*, with this caption: 'God, how sad is the body's blood at the bottom of sound!' It was, from beginning to end, a cry of horror, a cry of horror at myself. It was a cry that had a sort of gaiety, perhaps a wild gaiety, more lugubrious than mad. I understood Breton's horror of me. Had I not encouraged it? Was it not true that I was an obsessive? What Leiris had doubtless told him about my book before he had met me must have seemed sinister to him. I also realize now that he would feel a sense of unease next to a man who was so disturbed by him, who could never breathe freely in front of him and lacked both innocence and resolution.

Whatever the case, it is vain, given that Breton is a multiple and shrewd man, to attribute simple motives to him, and the quarrel I had with him later taught me that one only lost out by following him into the domain of facile insults.

7. Antonin Artaud

I soon got to know Antonin Artaud *to some extent*. I met him in a brasserie in rue Pigalle with Fraenkel. He was handsome, dark and emaciated. He had some money, for he worked in the theatre, but he still looked half-starved. He did not laugh, was never puerile, and although he didn't say very much, there was something emotionally eloquent in his rather grave silence and terrible edginess. He was calm;

this mute eloquence was not convulsive but, on the contrary, sad, dejected, and it gnawed away inside him. He looked like a caged bird of prey with dusty plumage which had been apprehended at the very moment it was about to take flight, and had remained fixed in this posture. I have said that he was silent. It must be said that Fraenkel and I were just about the least loquacious people in the world, and perhaps it was contagious. In any event, it did not encourage conversation.

Artaud was consulting Fraenkel about his nervous complaints. He was in pain and asked for drugs, and Fraenkel was trying to make his life bearable. The two of them had a private consultation. Then no conversation followed. So Artaud and I knew each other fairly well without ever having spoken.

One evening, about ten years later, I suddenly came across him at the corner of rue Madame and rue de Vaugirard. He gripped my hand energetically. It was at the time when I was involved in trying to set up political activity. He told me point-blank: 'I know you are doing important things. Believe me: we need to create a Mexican fascism!' He went on his way without insisting.

The incident gave me a rather disagreeable feeling, but only partly: he frightened me, but not without giving me a strange feeling of sympathy.

A few years before I had attended a lecture he gave at the Sorbonne (without seeking him out afterwards). He talked about theatrical art, and in the state of half-somnolence in which I listened I became aware that he had suddenly risen: I understood what he was saying, he had resolved to personify the state of mind of Thyestes when he realized he had devoured his own children. Before an auditorium packed with the bourgeoisie (there were hardly any students), he grasped his stomach and let out the most inhuman sound that has ever come from a man's throat: it created the sort of disquiet that would have been felt if a dear friend had suddenly become delirious. It was awful (perhaps the more so for being only *acted out*).

In time I learned what happened during his trip to Ireland, which was followed by his internment. I could have said that I did not like him . . . and had the feeling that 'someone was walking over my grave'. I felt sad at heart, and preferred not to think about it.

At the beginning of October 1943 I received an enigmatic and rather crude letter. It arrived at Vézelay at a time when I was both unhappy and cheerful, and today leaves me with a memory of anguish and marvel. I saw the signature was that of Antonin Artaud, whom I barely knew, as you have seen. It had been written at Rodez, where he had read *L'Expérience intérieure*, which had been published at the beginning of the year. The letter was more than half-mad: it was about

the cane and manuscript of St Patrick (his delirium on his return from
Ireland was all about St Patrick). This manuscript, which would
change the world, had vanished. But he had written to me because his
reading of *L'Expérience intérieure* had shown him that I needed to be
converted, that I must return to God. He had to warn me . . .

I am sorry I no longer have this letter. I sent it to someone who was
working on a collection of Artaud's letters and had asked me if I had
any documents of his. I had loaned my letter despite there being little
likelihood of publication . . . I simply told him what I thought: it was
obviously the letter of a madman. But I cannot with absolute precision
recall who it was who had asked me for it – it was a long time ago – and
the only person I mentioned it to said he had never seen it. I regret it. I
was very affected when I received it. I am sorry I have to leave its
contents vague. I cannot even exactly state whether what I have
reported it as saying about St Patrick is accurate. It would be amazing if
I had really distorted it, but memory, even when it has the object at
hand, is always a little unstable and fleeting. The entreaty to become
pious, which was addressed to me in moving – even urgent – terms, has
remained clearly in my mind.

8. *Anticipation of the shipwreck*

I caught sight of Artaud on the terrace of the Deux-Magots after his
return from Rodez. He did not recognize me and I did not seek to
make myself known: he was in such a state of decay it was frightening:
he looked like one of the oldest men I had ever seen. I have been
unable to read some of the writing that was published at that time
without a feeling of poignancy. And though I think that what happened was the best that could be done in the circumstances, it was still
for me, in spite of everything, something atrocious – atrocious and
inevitable. A little earlier, Henri Parisot had shown me one day a long,
indignant and grandiloquent telegram from Dr Ferdière forbidding
the publication of the documents under the title *Letters From Rodez*.
Parisot did not have words black enough to denounce the attitude of
the director of the Rodez asylum. I found myself in agreement: it was
necessary to go ahead – the more so in that publication of the book
would yield a little money that would help the poor fellow to live. But
how could one not be worried, as a rule, about the idea of publishing
writings by a madman who might be cured, when these writings would
always bear witness to his madness? One might think that, in this case,
Artaud was beyond the categories of reason and madness. But is
anything ever so clear? Would forgetfulness not be one of the conditions for a lasting cure? In any event, the abuse generally heaped upon

Dr Ferdière seems to me unwarranted. Where Antonin Artaud himself was concerned, they are easy to understand: Ferdière had cared for him, resorting to electric shock treatment, and the patient often had reason to disagree with his doctor's decisions. But were Artaud's friends to believe him about something that happened when he was sick? I used to know Ferdière, and I can only too easily imagine him exasperating his patients in spite of himself. He is a very kind person, as secret anarchists often are, often drowning in arrogant verbalism, something of a chatterbox, and finally getting on one's nerves. He must have done his best, and if he might be criticized for applying an unsuitable treatment (but no one else will ever know; he alone would be able to say, and he would not have done what he thought inappropriate), it is certain that he greatly improved Antonin Artaud's condition. These suffocating writings, which are like the last gleams of the setting of shipwrecked surrealism (and have not ceased to bear witness to the exorbitant and stupendous aspect of the movement), would not, perhaps, have seen the light of day without Ferdière, in spite of the unreasonable telegram I have mentioned.

The unique thing about these writings is their shock, the violent shaking of ordinary boundaries, the cruel lyricism that cuts short its own effects, not tolerating even the very thing it is so clearly expressing. Maurice Blanchot has quoted him, in speaking of himself (1946): 'I began in literature by writing books in order to say that I could write nothing at all; it was when I had something to say or write that my thought most refused me. I never had ideas, and two very short books, each of seventy pages, turned on this profound (ingrained and endemic) absence of all ideas.' Commenting on these lines, Maurice Blanchot wrote: 'It is difficult to see what it would be proper to add to such words, for they have the frankness of the knife and surpass in clairvoyance anything a writer could ever write about himself, showing what a lucid mind it is which, in order to become free, undergoes the proof of the Marvellous.' For me, this last phrase by Maurice Blanchot seems to be the precise epilogue to the surrealist adventure as a whole, considered from the moment it falteringly articulated its ambitions. I think that Maurice Blanchot is right to use these last words to implicate the basic principle of a movement which has most often avoided the reef and the spectacular shipwreck that the last years of Antonin Artaud's life show us in a glimmer of disaster.

Besides, Artaud's excitement was no less significant at the dawn than it was, I believe, in the twilight of the surrealist evening. In any case, to my knowledge it was Antonin Artaud who drafted the essential part of the Declaration of 27 January 1925, which was not, perhaps, the most remarkable expression of developing surrealism, but retains a special place for me because it was the first text communicated to me (by Leiris, on his return from the South, in the circumstances I mentioned) and the occasion for an accord I conceived without reserve and which, in truth, was due to a misunderstanding.

Maurice Nadeau reproduces this Declaration in the *Surrealist Documents*, and I will quote the second paragraph:

'Surrealism is not a new or an easier means of expression, nor even a metaphysic of poetry;

'It is a means towards the total liberation of the mind and *all that resembles it.*'

The ninth paragraph adds:

'[*Surrealism*] is a cry of the mind which turns back on itself and is determined desperately to tear off its shackles.'

I read this Declaration in a café, in a greatly disordered and lethargic state of mind in which I was – just about – *surviving*. Reading it again today, I feel the same; I feel as though I misread it as 'of the mind which turns *against* itself'. Even forewarned, I fell into the trap, so strong has my hatred remained – not only of the intelligence and reason but of the 'mind'; also of the capital entity opposing its clouds to what is inextricably filthy. In the same way, I read 'liberation of the mind' as if it were a question of a 'deliverance from evil'! Besides, perhaps I was not entirely deceived, or only partly, and this is why I have spoken fairly about Artaud who, if he wrote what preceded in 1925, wrote in 1946: '. . . and the garlic mayonnaise contemplates you, mind, and you contemplate your garlic mayonnaise: And finally let's say shit to infinity! . . . ' But in the end it is as open-ended, as empty, and equal to the sound which resolutely fades away and can finally be heard no longer.

Notes

[1. This appears to be the first and only surviving chapter of the book Bataille intended to write on surrealism. The rather obscure introductory notice is Bataille's second draft, and doubtless its obscure nature would have been clarified had he completed the book. It is worth reproducing his first draft, which is considerably clearer and sheds light on what Bataille was trying to say:

I have just read the pages in *The Rebel* which Camus devotes to the *poetic* revolt of which surrealism has been the most conspicuous form. My perspective differs in part from what Camus adopts, but what I find particularly striking as I read this pertinent analysis is the gulf which separates me from seeing *after the event, from outside*. Finally, and even more so as I have distanced myself (first in time, but also in thought), surrealism has become for me especially the real actuality, very human and connected to the fortuitous circumstances as it has been. I do not at all forget the profound, universal and most immediate nature which emerges from such actuality. But I feel everything would be distorted if the minor aspects were passed over.

I do not write this book with a view to publication. For this reason I feel very free. What I will say could have no other intention than to describe for my own benefit, and for a few people, what seems to me essential to the *only* movement of the mind in our time which seems to me to matter.

Besides, even supposing that I change my opinion, I would have no desire to prejudice it, or the intention to devalue it, but to situate it clearly. I attach significance – even an exceptional significance – to the infantile antecedents of what has taken shape in a profound way. The first stammerings of childhood seem to me connected to extreme leaps of thought, even to the most obviously pathetic. They are acts of ignorance, no doubt, but it is rightly doubtful that a certain necessity to not know, to naively close one's eyes, remains at the origin of the most ambitious spiritual movements (and card-sharps, of course, do not play an insignificant, no less discreet, role than in childhood).

The greatness of surrealism is to have been, of all the possible stirrings of the mind, the most puerile. In this sense its Dadaist origins add a precise element to surrealism, something deliberate and pretentious which corresponds with a childishness which is unaware of itself. This connection is, moreover, so inextricable that my investigation could pass – doubtless with good reason – in its essence, for surrealist. Somewhat by chance, I would mingle in the disparate elements, whose interest raises several points of view, but I cannot fail to respond to my feeling of a second fidelity to the spirit of surrealism, the open attitude of which, so often 'political', has sometimes betrayed (besides, childishness is found at the foundation of these 'betrayals'). – *Translator*]

2. Written before taking cognizance of the Camus/Breton controversy published in *Arts*, October and November 1951.

3. This was the origin of what was at issue. Due to a misunderstanding? But the misunderstanding happened.

4. I mention this umbrella in *L'Expérience intérieure (Œuvres complètes*, vol. V, pp. 46–7).

5. There was nothing displeasing about this. He treated me no differently from any other newcomer. And there was no doubt he was a charming man, of unquestionable kindness and, what is more, always ready to be of service to his friends. He was greatly loved, rather more so than Breton.

[6. Today it has become a burger bar. – *Translator*]

7. Ed. Pierre Seghers (1951), vol. 1, pp. 41–4. This translation has still been published without a translator's name.

8. In 1925 I translated *with great effort*. It is this hasty translation that Éluard followed.

9. Philippe de Beaumanoir (1247–96). Known particularly as the author of some *Customs of Beauvaisis*, but his poems have been published by the *Société des anciens textes français* in two volumes which I chanced to have been given for gaining first place in an examination at Chartres School: that was when I found a few pages of the 'Fatrasies' which the collection contained and the note which introduced the poem of the same type published by Jubinal – of course, Breton often employed the same formula.

The Absence of Myth[1]

As it determines this moment in time, the mind necessarily withers away and, stretched to the limit, desires this withering. Myth and the possibility of myth become impossible: only an immense void remains, cherished yet wretched. Perhaps the absence of myth is the ground that seems so stable beneath my feet, yet gives way without warning.

The *absence of God* is no longer a closure: it is the opening up to the infinite. The absence of God is greater, and more divine, than God (in the process I am no longer myself, but an absence of self; I await the sleight of hand that renders me immeasurably joyful).

The myths which, in the white and incongruous void of absence, exist innocently and shatter are no longer myth, and their duration is such as to expose their precariousness. At least in one sense the pale transparency of possibility is perfect: myths, whether they be lasting or fugitive, vanish like rivers in the sea in the absence of myth which is their lament and their truth.

The decisive absence of faith is resolute faith. The fact that a universe without myth is the ruin of the universe – reduced to the nothingness of things – in the process of depriving us equates deprivation with the revelation of the universe. If by abolishing the mythic universe we have lost the universe, the action of a revealing loss is itself connected to the death of myth. And today, because a myth is dead or dying, we see through it more easily than if it were alive: it is the need that perfects the transparency, the suffering which makes the suffering become joyful.

'Night is also a sun', and the absence of myth is also a myth: the coldest, the purest, the only *true* myth.

---

1. Published in the catalogue of the exhibition *Le Surréalisme en 1947* (1947), Paris: Maeght.

On the Subject of

Slumbers[1]

But how have we managed to confuse the thing itself with the expression it is given by painting or poetry?

I would appear a poor choice. Whenever the occasion has arisen, I have opposed surrealism. And I would now like to affirm it from within as the demand to which I have submitted and as the dissatisfaction I exemplify. But this much is clear: surrealism is defined by the possibility that I, its old enemy *from within*, can have of defining it conclusively.

It is genuinely virile opposition – nothing conciliatory, nothing divine – to all accepted limits, a rigorous will to insubordination.

And I think that restlessness is rarely torrential, and yet . . . the desired designation could never lend itself to so free a shape. To connect it, as André Breton has done, to certain freedoms of expression, certainly had more than one advantage, and *automatic writing* was more than a petty provocation. Insubordination, if not extended to the domain of images and words, is still no more than a refusal of external forms (such as the government or the police) when ordered words and images are entrusted *to us* by a system which, one thing leading to another, causes the entirety of nature to be submitted to utility. Belief – or, rather, *servitude* to the real world – is, without the shadow of a doubt, fundamental to all servitude. I cannot consider someone free if they do not have the desire to sever the bonds of language within themselves. It does not follow, however, that it is enough to escape for a moment the empire of words to have pushed as far as possible the concern not to subordinate what we are to anything.

There was also, from the beginning, an initial weakness in the place that surrealism gave to poetry and painting: it placed the work before being. It is true that one must deliberately cease to distinguish one from the other: the work was worth so much, being so much. An admirable poem by a despicable person seemed contradictory. Possibly it is, but it does not follow that the best one must expect from a pure person is poetry.

From the perspective I have defined, action is hardly accessible (as experience indicates: if I except René Char, those connected with surrealism have hardly engaged in any action of significance which has not first involved the abandoning of their principles). And it is not a question of action.[2] I do not see the reason (other than a need to attract, to make up numbers, or the fact that many young men write poetry or paint, or the fact of falling into a rut) definitively to connect the fate of an *extreme* conflict to the practice of painting or poetry. Rather, I see that what has happened in the name of such a violent conflict has finally gone the way of its predecessors. This would leave me indifferent if extreme confusion had not, in these conditions, taken the place of extreme conflict: the latter requires a different rigour. How can we be sure that a poem or a painting accomplishes the 'sovereign operation' without which each of us serves the established order? On this score I see only a boundless opposition, and a severity of method applied without respite, as taking up the stake. The least weakness and, far from escaping the laws of the servile world, our works will serve it. It is not only seriousness and restless anxiety which constantly threaten to wipe out the odds. In point of fact, from the beginning, 'the sovereign operation' appeared rather like a dream.

What the surrealists seem most to have lacked until now is intellectual aptitude. The surrealists have even displayed a contempt for tests of the intelligence. Nevertheless, the mastery of such practice perhaps remains the key to rigorous emancipation. If individual excellence is often a sign of servility, it does not follow that we can resolve the servility of the mind by using only feeble intellectual means. Besides, if one wants to see clearly, surrealism is connected to the affirmation of its value, no less than to *automatic writing* itself, inasmuch as it reveals thought. What Breton taught was less to become aware of the value of automatism than to write under the dictation of the unconscious. But this teaching opened up two different paths: one led to the establishment of works, and soon sacrificed any principle to the necessities of works, so accentuating the attraction value of paintings and books. This was the path the surrealists took. The other was an arduous path to the heart of being: here only the slightest attention could be paid to the attraction of works; not that this was trivial, but what was then laid bare – the beauty and ugliness of which no longer mattered – was the essence of things, and it was here that the inquiry into existence in the night began. Everything was suspended in a rigorous solitude. The facilities which connect works to the 'possible', or to aesthetic pleasure, had vanished (this also extended the discussion started by Rimbaud).

But when the Surrealist Group ceased to exist, I think the failure had a greater effect on the surrealism of works. Not that works had ceased to exist with the group: the abundance of surrealist works is as great now as it ever was. But they ceased to be connected to the affirmation of a hope of breaking the solitude. Today the books are in order on the shelves and the paintings adorn the walls. This is why I can say that the *great surrealism* is beginning.

Notes

1. Published in *Troisième convoi*, no. 2 (January 1946).

2. Not that I am at all opposed to the principle of committed literature. Can one not rejoice (even insidiously?) to see it taken up again today by Jean-Paul Sartre? Nevertheless, it seems necessary to recall that twenty years ago Breton based the whole activity of surrealism on this principle. I must also recall that the second affirmation of the existentialist school (that existence precedes essence) was familiar to surrealism (in so far as it bore witness to Hegel more than to Marx). It is unfortunate, if you like, that the intellectual aptitude of the surrealists could not have been up to the same level as their undeniable power to undermine. Today the intellectual value of existentialists is certain, but it is difficult to see what energy it would support. It is equally difficult to recognize the evidence: although surrealism may seem dead, in spite of the confectionery and poverty of the work in which it has ended (if we put to one side the question of Communism), *in terms of mankind's interrogation of itself*, there is surrealism and nothing.

The Surrealist Revolution[1]

Between the two wars surrealism aroused a wide range of different reactions. No one could deny that its manifestations were greeted with a strong interest, or even a sense of fervour. But equally, they provoked a great sense of unease. It goes without saying that the more prudent were shocked by an excess taken to extremes (was not its review, *La Révolution Surréaliste*, proclaimed as 'the most scandalous in the whole world'?). The inclination towards escalation, fabrication, an affectation of bad taste and preciosity at the same time, exhausted the best (and perhaps most durable) wills.

The war seems to have put an abrupt end to a movement that was marking time. Since 1940 people have hardly thought about it.

Nevertheless, the profound and real consequences that followed from it were not so easily disposed of. Doubtless surrealism is not dead. If its forms are often discreet, if it is true that its more public activities have been abandoned (to the point where there is, at least in France, currently no manifestation of authentic surrealism as such) – in a word, if *anguish* colours it to the end, it none the less continues to dominate, and this is doubtless even more the case in the present climate than between the two wars.

And since such an equivocal situation brings the desire for resolution, it is pleasing to see a serious book[2] trying to clarify what is involved. If it were a question of a purely episodic movement (like symbolism or naturalism) it would be vain to dwell on it. But through his book Jules Monnerot at once points to quite a different significance. What he sees in surrealist endeavour is, to simplify, religious endeavour. If in his book he has brought the most genuine objectivity and the most remarkable resources of the modern science of religion to bear on the fundamentals of surrealism, this is how historical movements are generally treated when they determine the forms of human sensibility. He does not try, as a commonplace critic would, to place surrealism in the paltry sequence of literary history, but in history itself, seen in its widest application, something that correctly considers the development of our sensibility from the most distant time. How man reacts to his unexplained situation in the world, and how he can justify his presence and being, is the fundamental question raised by this book. The question examined is how these motifs end in the present day in surrealism. It is a thorough work – something appropriate in a domain which admits of only the most profound form to challenge superficial forms. If one wants to judge the external importance of the subject, we would not hesitate to say that, no matter what its defects or rigidity may have been, surrealism has given from the beginning a certain consistency to the 'morality of revolt' and that its most important contribution – important even, perhaps, in the political realm – is to have remained, in matters of morality, a revolution.

Notes

1. Published in *Combat* (1945).
2. Jules Monnerot, *La poésie moderne et le sacré* (1945), Paris: Gallimard.

Surrealism[1]

They say that only what is dead can be fully understood. This is true even if we speak of movements like the Renaissance, Neoplatonism or symbolism. And we discuss Christianity or Buddhism with rigour only to the extent (but in a contrary sense to that of Nietzsche) that they are given 'the benefit of being something dead'. Of course Christianity and Buddhism are still alive, but in a way that suggests they could endlessly be what they are. Doubtless this could be denied, but no one would dream of denying it simply in response to my position. The same thing could be said about surrealism. What it seems to be – or, more accurately, *what it is* 'for us' – has perhaps only a vague relation with *what it will be* if it is later considered to be a dead thing (like symbolism) or a living dead (like Buddhism).

For us the difficulty in speaking about surrealism has become so much the greater in that this word has now necessarily been given two meanings.

André Breton wrote:

> Surrealism is not at all interested in taking into account what passes alongside it under the guise of art or even anti-art; of philosophy or anti-philosophy; of anything, in a word, that has not for its ultimate aim the annihilation of being into a jewel, internal and unseeing, with a soul that is neither of ice nor of fire.[2]

The word surrealism signifies, in this already celebrated phrase, a spiritual authority, strictly founded on the bringing together of a certain number of people, among whom a vital bond counts no less than distinct lifestyles: this is not merely a doctrine but a church, or it is the doctrine of a church. The number of adepts hardly matters; in this respect *surrealism* has a value that is situated in the same realm as *Christianity* in an encyclical.

But Breton also wrote: 'Rabbe is surrealist in death . . . Vaché is surrealist in me . . . Saint-John-Perse is surrealist at a distance . . . ' In these expressions surrealist has the same sort of meaning as *romantic*. This use supposes the historical existence of an orientation of minds that is outside the group and independent of a recent definition.

This adds to the difficulty of grasping surrealism. In one sense it is a position taken within the sphere of literature or art. From the beginning Breton defined it as: 'Pure psychic automatism, by which it is proposed to express, verbally, in writing or by other means, the real functioning of thought. The dictation of thought in the absence of all control exercised by reason and outside all aesthetic or moral considerations.'[3] In spite of the words 'by other means' one must recognize a slippage to the moral sphere in the *Second Manifesto* as 'The simplest surrealist act consists in descending to the street with revolver in hand and shooting at random, as fast as one can, into the crowd.'

In the end surrealism cannot be considered purely as a style. It is a state of mind whose intensity and aggressive force must go to the point of modifying the course of its expression (it is not surrealism if expression is limited to the habitual platitude of language). It is also a state of mind which reaches towards unification; in which, through this union, an existence beyond the self is experienced as a *spiritual authority* in whose name it is possible to speak. But what leads to the constitution of a bond is not yet this bond, at least not in the formal sense. And the *spiritual authority* (by spiritual I merely mean: beyond the individual) that surrealism embodies is surely not limited to the few people closely connected with André Breton.

Apparently Breton strove to create a gulf between him and his friends and the rest of mankind, but he could not make the tendency and vague state of mind retain their value. The application of the principles could never assume a rigorous form (this would have been contrary to the principles themselves). Especially since it was reserved for a very restricted group of people. The Surrealist Group has tended only to unify writers and artists: this went without saying, since expression was at issue. But from this fact the *authority* of the group, in the narrow sense, is not, in the midst of a movement, of a very general aspiration; an intangible core: it could not be so without the discipline and rigour giving rise to a formal definition. In truth, the introduction of formalism is so much more discomforting here, since it assumes a use of words that is opposed to surrealism. From that moment the fundamental difficulty of surrealism falls into a dilemma. It is an impersonal state of mind, but it is constituted by denying the supreme value of categories of language: it is a horror of ways of life made explicit by discourse. It tends to substitute for discourse a means of expression that is foreign to discourse. But it is limited in these conditions to a small number of people with a rich enough means of expression at their disposal to go beyond miserable discourse. At the same time it deprives them of recourse to verbal formalism, which alone would seem to have the power to connect them. It is difficult humanly to measure the powerlessness of those who renounce discursive language. Surrealism is *mutism*: if it spoke it would cease to be what it wanted to be, but if it failed to speak it could only lend itself to misunderstanding; it was even in the impossibility of responding to the first demand that it succeeded: in forming an impersonal authority.

Obviously people will say that it speaks. But if it does speak, in the very process we predict, with each sentence it finds that the word is harmful to it, and that to the extent that it progresses, it must introduce a disorder or – to use Gracq's word – an absence into the word. Gracq himself has described surrealism as a *religious* fact taken to its furthest extent. But to assume that it really would be, it is so inasmuch as religion does not speak (the religion which speaks is already moral, in the formal sense). Fundamentally, nothing is less like defined religions, with which it merely shares a suffix. It is, once again, life itself, precarious, elusive, which cannot be defined by death (death in the event would be language) and whose infinite difficulty recalls the wretchedness – and the muteness – of giving birth.

Notes

1. Published in *Critique*, no. 22 (March 1948).
[2. In Andŕe Breton, *What is Surrealism?*, ed. Franklin Rosemont (1978), London: Pluto Press, p. 127; translation (slightly modified) by David Gascoyne. – *Translator*]
[3. ibid., p. 122. – *Translator*]

Surrealism and How It

Differs from Existentialism[1]

There can be no doubt that during the past twenty or thirty years no one has shown more concern than André Breton to imbue even the smallest action with a meaning that involves the fate of mankind. This is explained by his power to act and provoke to a degree attained by no other living writer. In the person of André Breton mankind's possibilities are taken to a logical conclusion by means of a completely novel decision and choice (a kind of re-election). Furthermore, no one has made such a deliberate step that has been so decisive for others: who today could deny the radiant power of surrealism? Not that his actions remain uncontestable, not that one does not immediately notice continual errors and misunderstandings. But the mistakes of surrealism, in so far as they affect both works and people, represent, rather, its strength. *Despite* its general ensemble – which remains deceptive – of works and men, surrealism is what remains vibrant and genuinely compels recognition.

André Breton's determination to create, maintain and develop the movement to which he has devoted his life deserves to be emphasized. Unlike other schools (Romanticism, symbolism), surrealism is not a rather poorly determined freewheeling mode of activity. For a Romantic or a symbolist it was not a question of life and death that Romanticism or symbolism should be this and not that. Established from the first as a moral imperative, surrealism thus brings everything into question. Romanticism also had a vision of totality. Its elements also reached out towards the entirety of what is possible. But it never took shape to the point of being formulated as a necessity.

Certainly surrealism must also be treated as an artistic and literary school (this is even where one must begin): as such, it is founded on *automatic writing*. It gives a decisive value to this type of thought, analogous to dream, which is not subordinated to the control of reason. In so doing it extricates the human mind from any end other than poetry. With such a point of departure there is no possibility that a poem, a painting or a film might assume, from a practical point of view, the slightest meaning. But what is crucial is less the result than the principle. Surrealist work shocks, but in the end it hardly matters if it irritates the feeble-minded; this is merely an inevitable consequence, a desirable and fortuitous *surplus*. But the moral necessity on which this activity is founded does not depend on such a feeble result. It is of a completely different order.

'All we know', wrote Breton in *Légitime défense* (1926), 'is that we are endowed with a certain degree of language by which something great and obscure tends to be expressed through us. . . . It is a mandate we have received once and for all and have never had the leisure to dispute . . .' And essentially, surrealism is maintained as much by this imperious character as by a negation of control by reason, which binds the movement's supporters together.

'This movement', writes Nadeau,

> was not an association of men of letters patting each other on the back to insure their success; nor even a school with various theoretical ideas in common, but a collective organization, a sect of initiates, a *Bund* subject to collective initiatives, whose members were linked by a common discipline. One entered it with one's eyes wide open; one left it or was excluded by it for specific reasons.[2]

Nevertheless, the Surrealist Group differed from a party – or a sect – in so far as entry was confined, as a rule, to those who express themselves in some way in art. That surrealism surpassed the artistic and literary domain goes without saying. 'It tends', as Breton said in the *Manifesto* (1924), 'definitively to bring to ruin all other psychic mechanisms, and to substitute itself for them in the resolution of the principal problems of life . . . ' But the artists have the gifts in their own right to assure them of undeniable power: they decide the aspects and occasions which attract others' attention. What intoxicates, charms and amazes is not so much the *work* of art itself as what is designated by it. The artist, as he illuminates a given point with a living light, so determines what others will see (propaganda usage underlines the importance of this power). But he does not necessarily decide freely. He obeys as he executes commands (like the artisan of cathedrals); or if he responds to the taste of the day, which is to say, the jaded public mood. When the community chooses in its original simplicity, this is not entirely a submission. But in a sick and tarnished world it is not merely servility, it can also be a betrayal. In this confused civilization, where resources are exhausted through complex activity, where every

tree hides the forest, where exhaustion endlessly substitutes the multitude of petty, fraudulent results (the luxuries others do not have) for
the possibilities of life, the artist has, in the solitude of his room, a
power of ultimate decision. He can reveal and magnify this irreducible
part that is within us, connected to our most tenacious aspirations: *he
has the power to offer life the perspective of radiance*. But just as easily he can
hide any escape, divert all attention towards the inane, and so respond
to the desire for peace of mind. The worrying thing is that humanity as
a whole ceaselessly hesitates between, on the one hand, convenience
and consciousness and, on the other hand, somnolence (counterfeit
existence, torpor) and juvenile crazes (a dangerous enthusiasm). And
the decision turns on this point. In the choice an artist makes (if it were
not so, what would be the link to art?) purity or weakness, liberty or
servitude, is determined. Thereby the necessity to choose has a privileged meaning which is imposed on him. This can be a mere caprice if
in such and such a case I choose (I am thinking of the worst scenarios
of the war), but an incomplete one. The man who acts – whether
politically or militarily; it's the same thing – is faced with the limited
possibility of whatever it is he struggles for. This possibility is limited by
the fact that political or military action is first of all a limit to the use of
liberty, and additionally that it makes liberty possible but is never, in
this domain, other than negative (fighting in order to be enslaved no
longer but to enjoy my liberty is something else). The artist alone
chooses between *positive* liberty (his own first of all, but also that of
those he influences) and everyday banality (servility, success). (This
serves to give his determination a value alien to pure morality: to
qualify it as religious would be to court misunderstanding, but it
reaches beyond morality to become an immediate consummation
openly mocking the consequences.)

I must make one point clear: my explanation here is the ballistic
study of a gunshot. The stand taken by André Breton was the shot
itself. Struck by the force of decision, he was less concerned to give his
reasons than to express the violence of his feelings. What mattered
above all in his eyes was to communicate a determined condition: it
responded to the impulse of passion rather than intellectual expediency. In the first period of surrealism his writing always connected
the pent-up agitation of fury with the expression of its object. All his
writing has engaged with the infinite destiny of mankind – something
which people in France tend to find amusing, but which also represents, at the same time, the exhilarating mark of authenticity. No
doubt this unaccustomed decisive will, bound to so much conscience
and gravity, had something disconcerting about it. In other ages, the
priest, the prophet and the saint have, with the prerogative of choice,

held the monopoly of rousing appeals. Let's pass over the politicians who have succeeded them! The first of them spoke in the name of God, the others in the name of material wrongs and poverty. But for a writer to speak in the name of the positive destiny of mankind, about which he cares with his whole heart, with a sense of rage, as the fanatic speaks of the glory of God – this is what seems so striking.

The strangest thing is that the guilty party could recognize very well under what conditions he could speak. If he had expressed himself personally, it would have made no impact. But the force of conviction animating him allowed him to bring together a number of people whose names today are known everywhere[3] – not by external ties of action, but by more intimate ties of passion. It was André Breton who rightly recognized that a poet or a painter does not have the power to say what is in his heart, but that an organization or a collective body could. This 'body' can speak in different terms from an individual. If painters and poets together took consciousness of what weighed on poetry and painting, anyone who speaks in their name must plead that it is the vehicle of impersonal necessity. The truth is that there could be no difference between submitting to the moral necessity expressed by André Breton and forming an organization, a body that gives meaning and value to this necessity. If consciousness is born from the gravity of the decision, one must express it, and this can be done only in the name of whoever, in the same way, is placed in the position of deciding. If you prefer, the consequences arising from what was imposed on André Breton guaranteed authenticity: it is not difficult today to insist on the fact that the repercussions were as great as possible, and that the verbalism or hollow excitement at the beginnings of surrealism cannot make us forget the intensity of an effervescence which was often – as it had to be – bewildering. What followed, the human consequences (the disagreements and misunderstandings which arose, the fact that the 'organization' miscarried) do not matter since the testimony offered by the most lively and penetrating people of a generation – in the ferment that seized them – cannot be withdrawn.

*

Through time and the to-and-fro movement of bedazzlement – of expectation and disillusion – it seems that at no time did André Breton cease to feel, poignantly, that the value of the *decision* he had taken would incarnate his life at every moment. Very soon this was not simply the choice of the unleashed poetry that is automatic writing, which had the significance of an upheaval for him: we have seen that in the *Manifesto* he said of this means of poetic release that it tended to 'definitively bring to ruin all other psychic mechanisms and to substitute itself for them in the resolution of the principal problems of life . . . ' This invasion of the principle of poetry in great and small determinations – which is to say in the whole of life – progressively became the object of his writings – *Nadja* (1928), *Les vases communicants* (1932), *L'amour fou* (1937) – which in one respect are formed from the testimony of his existence. His consciousness seems to have ceaselessly guided him to join his conduct with that of mankind in its entirety. Sartre assures us today that when we marry, we engage humanity in monogamy: nevertheless, we do so only by not emerging from it, and if we refuse the marriage, it remains negative. But the act by which the initiative is affirmed has a privileged value: it can engage others if it entices in a positive way. And this is what both rouses and is desirable. It then attains its full meaning only by being expressed. In truth there is no difference between acting, in the sense of seduction, with consciousness of the initiative, and giving aesthetic expression to action. To such a point, one would no longer know if one acted specifically in order to express. Fundamentally, expression is inseparable from the act. It gives a vertiginous meaning to the act, that of the determination of a common destiny.

Arcane 17, André Breton's most recent book, perhaps assumes an even more sombre tone for having been written at the time when the outcome of the war had not yet been decided. In particular, it was started at the time when the fate of Paris was still in the balance (it is dated 20 August–20 October 1944). At the time the author was in the New World, on the coast of the Gaspé Peninsula at the southern extremity of the mouth of the Saint Lawrence River.

Isolation – which, he tells us, is the condition of poetic thought – is, on this coast, 'as unhoped for and as great as can be'. The almost forgotten character of this French domain lost in English-speaking America adds to the sensation of being far away from what is happening in time: 'a very effective protective screen against the madness of the hour . . . extends as far as the eye can see'. The free succession of reflections which constitutes the book is composed on a journey in a fishing boat around a large rock populated by a bird colony. Furthermore, during the entire time the book was being written, this island, Rocher Percé, continued to cut a marvellous profile within the writer's windowframe. His imagination slowly takes pleasure in the transparent strangeness of natural forms, through which the possibility of vision is infinite. 'The great enemy of man', he tells us, 'is opacity' – thus what the city streets have to offer is narrowly limiting in comparison. Far from fixed commonplace connections, every aspect of things is entreated to deliver up a little more of the world's immense, marvellous hidden possibilities. To go to the depths of what is and to read in transparency, turning away from the work of analysis, André Breton allows the rock and the bird to speak through him as creative humanity once did in myth. At Rocher Percé, because it responds to the first desire for bedazzlement, because beauty is the prism in which all possibilities of light play, the flow of the bewildered imagination confers the power to give form to the most distant dreams:

> When the details of its structure are veiled, at dusk or on certain misty mornings, the image of an always imperiously commanded ship becomes pure in it. . . . It is the vessel, just now deprived of its rigging, which immediately seems to have been hired for the most vertiginous of long sea journeys. . . . Nevertheless this arc remains. Would that I could reveal it to everyone, for it is charged with all the fragility but also all the magnificence of the human gift. Encased in its marvellous moonstone iceberg, it is transformed by the three glass propeller blades that are love (but only when it lifts two beings to the invulnerable), art (but only to reach to its highest manifestations), and the unsparing struggle for liberty. As one observes it distractedly from the bank, the birds serve to give the Rocher Percé its *wings*.

This method has its limits (they can be laboriously revealed) which, of course, are those of chance. Nevertheless, on the supposition that one might have recourse to it without understanding what happens otherwise, decisively and cruelly (this is the case with *Arcane 17*), it assures the extent to which the whole of human potentiality is put at stake. What, then, does the arbitrary appearance of the proposed interpretations matter: by unhesitatingly putting it at stake, life is opened to the possibility of determining the *line of seduction* for itself. For 'under this charming foliage, scattered too widely and too vivaciously to suffer the disputes of man, everything spreads, must at the end of the day spread out to reorientate itself over the seductions of life'. Is it not evident that every enigma which the world poses to us is, in this world, subordinated to what is first posed to us by what *seduced us*? If it is a sense of the things we might seize, can it then lead anywhere other than to the object of our delights? And if some day we *lose* the meaning, would we not find it again as soon as, despite that, we are seduced? What does the opacity of the world matter then? The momentary rapture, which is forcibly liberated from the dusty concern with knowledge, has given us the power to say: everything is transparency! In truth it is possible to oppose it with the character of the *provisional*, which is appropriately not distinguished from *falsehood*. The objection is not insignificant: anyone who does not extend himself and has no concern with achieving the whole of human potentiality within himself is at the mercy of feeble diversions (justifying Pascal's diatribes). But he is then seduced on only one condition: first to minimize and not to accept *what seduced* as being of sovereign value. What matters for him – by his powerlessness to affirm that he loves – is seriousness, morality and work, which enfold, humiliate and overburden man. What is seductive is abandoned to spite and conceded only in its inevitable impotence. In truth, *seduction* cannot be betrayed without being rendered miserable: it wants to be loved unreservedly and desperately.

So it is that in order to reach it, one must first allow oneself to be possessed and led far away by temerity, madness and the unravelling implicit in human destiny. This would be a futile exercise if one did not begin by saying that the limits of my will are also, necessarily, the whole of human potentiality; the limits of my will are, of course, never to have limits. This is the point at which I can start – otherwise it would be mere affectation – to give seduction the image of the *child-woman* by affirming: 'Art must systematically prepare for her accession to the whole perceptible dominion . . . ' Is it depth or weariness that causes Breton to challenge 'the intelligence of the male character at the end of the nineteenth century . . . the slime of the miserly bookworm', crystallizing in a point in which, capriciously, only the feminine and the childlike offers the possibility of the transparency of being? In matters of seduction, is it not the one who seduces who has command over the limits?

What undoubtedly withdraws part of their value from such choices is that at no time are standing still and fixation indispensable. If André Breton's position demands a body in whose name to speak, if the body establishes a point of departure, it does not always follow that the agreement could go beyond the foundation (which maintains that all art that is not the liberty of poetry would be servile and betray). And if art generally, as it projects a dark light on to a point, has the power to attract attention, it is no longer able to make the connections that religions made. The only thing it can do is direct our attention towards a part of the horizon where everything is in flux. Some connections can, it is true, have a common value at certain times. And there is no doubt that Breton is not bound to the void when, on finding love in its complete form, he assumes a tone in speaking about it which we have never heard before him. The glorification of woman as value, in particular the *child-woman*, cannot so easily be the object of inevitable attachment: one can accept the surrealist demand without attaching oneself to this seductive affirmation for too long. Besides, is not the *child-woman* caprice itself? Erected as a principle, must not caprice cease to be capricious? I could, furthermore, doubt that the increasing interest André Breton has shown in magic has the same vital quality as his position in general.

This seduction to which *Arcane 17* gives an insistent expression (not without doubts about its foundation) will doubtless encounter unfavourable prejudice. For my part, I am inclined to point out that in one sense it has, like that of love as a whole, an immediate and inevitable value. What Nietzsche said about Catholicism: that it retains, despite Christian morality, a reflection of the splendours of paganism, is true – in another sense – about magic: such traditions give us a slightly uneasy image of the very ancient foundation of non-moralist religions. Breton is right to recognize necessity in the fact that modern poetry is often a tributary of esotericism (he refers to Nerval, Hugo, 'whose close links with the school of Fabre d'Olivet have recently been revealed', Baudelaire, Apollinaire and Rimbaud's revealing readings). And how is it possible not to have some nostalgia for all lost knowledge? In its time this knowledge was perhaps able to arrange *for every man* some of the most acute seductions, perhaps, that this world conceals. All the same, it is difficult to think that in still having the will to recover and *utilize* precise motifs, we do not forget what we need to do – which is not to recover what is lost without possibility of recovery.

In order to constitute itself it was necessary for rationalism to lose the profundity of modes of thought that shackled it. But if we now seek what is possible before us – all that is possible, whether or not we might have wanted to, we who no longer have any need to construct rational thought, which is effortlessly arranged for us – we are again able to recognize the profound value of these lost modes of thought. We recognize the fact only in a world where the old relations are no longer possible. Now it is rationalism that determines the domain that accrues to it, which is that of practical efficacy: in this domain those modes of thought represented by the tradition of high magic could clearly no longer have a place. They even rendered boundless development impossible. No doubt Breton, writing before 1945, already contested the consequences of this expansion, but no matter: who today wants to return technical activity to the procedures of magic? Besides, Breton is against considerations which offer a general account of ritual practices connected to myths by suggesting that they are the means of material ends. What he does not insist upon is the liberty that confers on these modes of thinking and living the fact of no longer being, as once they partly were, subordinated to such ends. But liberty implies that it is impossible to fix anything. I can no longer be connected to such an attitude, which is no longer considered materially efficacious. My caprice can just as equally be directed towards some other benefit. If André Breton now confesses that he has faith in the privileged value of a formula – which was said to have played at Eleusis – as stirring as the magical words 'Osiris is a black god' might be, one can think that having himself opened the door to the devastating eddies of free poetry, which indiscriminately bring about the return of a profound meaning for which the phrase 'Osiris . . . ' would prepare more than any other, he returns to more oppressive forms, again embarrassed by the vulgar efficacy which was once attributed to them.

All the same, this return to fixation is oppressive: it alters a distinct character of surrealism, which brings about a free poetic release without subordinating it to anything and without assigning a superior end to it. It is true that this is an attitude that is as difficult to bear as it is decisive and virilely sovereign. Yes, it really is the decisive conquest. Poetic liberty is not new. Myths and the rituals connected to them – for instance 'Hopi ceremonies of an exceptional variety, which necessitate the intervention of the greatest number of supernatural beings that could be invested with a face and distinct attributes by the imagination' – make this fact clear enough: that human 'thought' is everywhere and always ready to break loose. But it was once necessary to give a superior end to this release, a usually rather gross *pretext*. For the Hopi it is a question of 'attracting every protection over cultivation . . . the most important of which is maize'. To the extent that more refined religions maintain an element of poetic invention, the *pretext* is given in a transcendent morality, associated with salvation as a superior end. In modes of thought in which the poetic and the rational remain con-founded, the mind cannot elevate itself to the conception of poetic liberty; it subordinates the existence of each instant to some *ulterior* goal. It has no escape from this servitude.

It is the prerogative of surrealism to free the activity of the mind from such servitude. As it consigned this activity to the shadows, rationalism stressed the binding of deeds and all thought to the end pursued. In the same way, rationalism liberated poetic activity from this binding, leaving it suspended. But the difficulty which remained was to affirm the value of what was finally released within the shadow.

In this way, what has proved to be simultaneously attained and liberated is nothing other than the *instant*. This is true in that man has never before been able to give value to the instant. Man's mental machinery is made in such a way that value is always attributed to the end pursued. Or rather, we have never been able to distinguish between value and end pursued. The dissociation requires the strange, passionate and reflective approach, lucid but evading its own lucidity, which distinguishes André Breton, who has always treated the future with surprising contempt: 'I never make plans,' he writes in the *Confession dédaigneuse*. And the principle of *automatic writing* is clearly to

have done with goals. Expressed as it necessarily was in rather metho-
dical propositions, such an attitude is not without its own contradictions. Breton's language is a result of the consciousness of these
contradictions, and of the will to resolve them, if need be, by illogical
violence.

This could hardly be 'clear and distinct' straight away. If passion
rather than lucidity had made the first move, this was devoid of
meaning. The morality to which André Breton is drawn is rather
poorly defined, but it is – if such a thing is possible – a morality of the
instant. What is essential about it is the demand imposed on whoever
expresses a will to choose between the instant – the value of the present
moment and the free activity of the mind – and a concern for results
which immediately abolish the value and even, in a sense, the *existence*
of the instant. The accent is placed not on the fact of choosing but on
the content of the choice proposed. It is only the incommensurable
value of the instant that counts, not the fact that all would be in
suspension. More precisely, what is at stake (moreover, in its capacity
of being put at stake) prevails to a large extent over the fact that the
decision belongs to me and gives me authority. Liberty is no longer the
liberty to choose, but the choice renders a liberty, a free activity,
possible, requiring that once decision is fixed upon it I do not allow a
new choice to intervene, for a choice between the diverse possibilities
of the activity unleashed would be made with a view to some ulterior
result (this is the significance of automatism). The surrealist decision is
thus a decision to decide no longer (that is, the free activity of the mind
would be betrayed if I subordinated it to some result decided
beforehand).

The profound difference between surrealism and the existentialism
of Jean-Paul Sartre hangs on this character of the *existence* of liberty. If
I do not seek to dominate it, liberty will *exist*: it is poetry; words, no
longer striving to serve some useful purpose, set themselves free and
so unleash the image of *free existence*, which is never bestowed except in
the instant. This seizure of the instant – in which the will is relin-
quished at the same time – certainly has a decisive value. It is true that
the operation is not without difficulties, which surrealism has revealed
but not resolved. The possibilities brought into play go further than
they seem. If we were genuinely to break the servitude by which the
existence of the instant is submitted to useful activity, the essence
would suddenly be revealed in us with an unbearable clarity. At least,
everything leads one to believe so. The seizure of the instant cannot
differ from ecstasy (reciprocally one must define ecstasy as the seizure
of the instant – nothing else – operating *despite* the concerns of the
mystics). Far from distancing himself from these last truths, André

Breton has given a powerful account of them: 'Surrealism', he wrote in the *Second Manifesto* (1929), 'is not interested in taking into account what passes alongside it under the guise of art or even anti-art; of philosophy or anti-philosophy; of anything, in a word, that has not for its ultimate aim the annihilation of being into a jewel, internal and unseeing, with a soul that is neither of ice nor of fire.' And again in the same book:

> the idea of surrealism tends simply towards the total recuperation of our psychic strength by a means which is nothing less than a vertiginous descent into ourselves, the systematic illumination of hidden places and the progressive darkening of others, perpetual promenading across forbidden zones; and there is no danger of it coming to an end while man is still able to distinguish an animal from a flame or a stone.

It would be vain if, after reading *Arcane 17*, one adhered to the nearest landmarks. And if, purely by publication of a series of poetical texts, in a way that habitually diminishes the power of excitement – as is the case with the collection that recently appeared under the title *Surrealist Evidence* – one loses sight of the landmarks, then one falls from the heights into literature. For surrealism is not only poetry but overpowering affirmation and, in this way, negation of the meaning of poetry. To forget it even for a moment it is to efface the gleam of the countenance.

Notes

[1. A review of André Breton, *Arcane 17*, first published by Brentano's in New York (1945), and later in Paris by Éditions du Sagittaire (1947); and 'L'Évidence surréaliste', a special issue of the review *Quatre Vents*, edited by Henri Parisot (February 1946). Published in *Critique*, No. 2 (July 1946). – *Translator*]

[2. Maurice Nadeau, *The History of Surrealism*, trans. Richard Howard (1968), London: Jonathan Cape, p. 104. – *Translator*]

3. Among them Aragon, Arp, Artaud, Bellmer, Buñuel, Caillois, Char, Chirico, Crevel, Dali, Desnos, Éluard, Giacometti, Hugnet, Leiris, Limbour, Magritte, Masson, Miró, Naville, Péret, Picasso, Prévert, Queneau, Man Ray, Ribemont-Dessignes, Ristitch, Sadoul, Soupault, Tanguy, Tual, Tzara. The majority of these people have genuinely participated wholeheartedly with Breton, in this state of exasperation that is the surrealist 'state of grace'. A small number of them – Arp, Bellmer, Masson, Péret – are now gathered in the contents of 'Évidence surréaliste', but one also reads there thirty or so new names, among them those of Césaire, Fardoulis-Lagrange, Fréderique, Julien Gracq, Huidobro, Maquet.

Surrealism in 1947 [1]

Closed, commonplace minds, eager to return life to lucidity and individual choice, are undoubtedly deluded: in having brought blind poetry to life – through impersonal disorder and chance – surrealism has survived the ordeals through which it has passed. In 1942 the publication in New York of the *Prolégomènes à un nouveau manifeste* [2] suggested that André Breton himself was not yet fully convinced whether *or not* the movement he initiated would be continued after the war. But this movement responds in such a way to the expectations of a great number of minds all over the world that one does not see how it could come to an end. It is true that one external aspect of surrealism, its gaudy and even peevish sense of 'display', unfortunately under-mines part of this expectation, which requires at its limit silence, which in turn requires darkness. (It is *acceptable to wonder*, as Julien Gracq says in an otherwise very favourable article, *if the scheme (the bass drum at the temple of Eleusis) which consists in 'keeping the* (public) *frustrated before the door of a policy of defiance and provocation' was of a type to be favoured* . . . etc.) But it is difficult to see how surrealism could avoid modes of expression *it has not chosen.* Here I would limit myself to saying that certain 'surrealists', from the outside, appear to be interested in and good for only this 'display'. On the other hand, it is true that minds whose concepts are closely related to it remain at a distance from a movement which has the disadvantages of a crowd. But this last fact – discreet enough not to be easily noticed, but whose breadth, extreme meaning, or *extreme* absence of meaning, could become apparent in the long run – does not bear witness at all to the inauthenticity of surrealism: rather, it reveals its background and far-reaching conse-quences. Besides, the most elusive minds (analogous to those who, in a church, are concerned about worldly and secular attitudes), even by their refusal, realize the power that a movement, resolutely pursued in the profane world, has of informing this world what it must do to settle *accounts* with poetry.

Of course it is paradoxical to compare surrealism with a church. However, Monnerot has been the first to do so (in *La poésie moderne et le sacré*) and Gracq has followed him (in the article already cited). Why not reinforce this argument by pointing out that in a sense Romanticism, too, is a *religion* within surrealism which condenses it? Of this religion, the Surrealist Group is the Church and poetry is the God (or the Devil). (Moreover, the recent exhibition clearly manifested a professed taste for forms of ritual initiation.) No one would contest the sacred character of poetry: from the moment poetry becomes autonomous and is no longer confined to the expression of some already sacred reality, poetry is sustained by its own power, and so fully communicates the trepidation of the sacred. In truth, it is enough that poetry ceases to be subordinate, through its 'subject', to something other than itself (this is the meaning of *automatic writing*) for a poet to show himself that he is bound to give poetry God's place (something which immediately signals the power of profanation which Gracq rightly connects to surrealism – but profanation is the sacred, it is the truth of sacrifice). How can we not understand in this sense some of André Breton's comments (*Le surréalisme en 1947*, pp 115–16)?:

> *We have not ceased to repeat that a few lines of genuine automatic writing (something that is increasingly rare), an action which, even if it is very limited, succeeds in going beyond utilitarian, rational, aesthetic or moral imperatives – in the same way as the 'true dream' in the marvellous* Peter Ibbetson *– as in surrealism's early days, retain too many gleams of the philosopher's stone to cause us to dismiss the mean and miserable world that is inflicted on us. But the approach at the limit of which other horizons can be substituted for its own is not one of those which curiosity alone would have the power to reproduce. Enticed by the categorical refusal of conditions of life and thought imposed on man in the middle of the twentieth century, it can be pursued and brought to success only at the price of asceticism.*

Breton has emphasized the point. It is useful to say that he defines both the way through and the blind alley. Without asceticism, in fact, the 'display' would be kept alive on its own. But what does an *asceticism* signify when we know nothing about it that is not merely negative (namely, that it will hardly resemble those of known religions: surrealism, as a matter of fact, was the first to put forward the name of Sade)? It would be difficult to leave the question open.

There is another point on which André Breton remains ambiguous. No matter how much the world changes in the future, it cannot be entirely freed from the 'utilitarian, rational, aesthetic or moral imperatives' from which the surrealist act necessarily frees itself. Such an act can be performed only if it is accepted as a sacred act (in the *profanatory* sense of the word): *against the unacceptable world of rational utility*. The refusal this involves would gain from not being confounded with the reasoned refusal of unreasonable conditions of life. And vice versa.

Notes

1. A review of the exhibition catalogue 'Le surréalisme en 1947', edited by André Breton and Marcel Duchamp and published by Éditions Pierre à Feu (Maeght). Published in *Critique*, nos 15–16 (July 1947).
[2. Bataille is mistaken about this title – it should be *Prolégomènes à une troisième manifeste du surréalisme ou non. – Translator*]

The Surrealist Religion[1]

Ladies and gentlemen,

Surrealism has, strangely enough, been compared to the Renaissance. Moreover, this has not been to emphasize the affinities but, rather, to mark the differences. I am not at all sure that it is right to put so much emphasis on the differences, since the affinity seems to me to be of greater interest. In the first place it serves to mark out the considerable importance that apparently insignificant changes in appearances can have. In appearance, the Renaissance was limited to changes in the category of cornices and in the category of classical studies. Yet no one today would deny that the changes which took place during the fifteenth and sixteenth centuries had a decisive quality which continues to affect the present day: without the Renaissance it is difficult to see how Marxism could have been born. The Renaissance is at the base of the world of which we are a part, even though initially it was something very straightforward: an interest in a long since vanished time – the age of antiquity. Mankind in the Middle Ages, at a given moment, felt a need to return to its most distant sources, and find again in Greece and Rome a mode of existence that had been lost. Although I would not wish to overestimate the consequences that may issue from a movement in such an unforeseeable age, it is still interesting to indicate what the meaning of a movement like surrealism can become, for to a great extent it undoubtedly represents a renaissance for a society that had been lost even more completely than the age of antiquity was five centuries ago – that is, primitive society. It seems very clear and very distinct to me that the quest for primitive culture represents the principal, most decisive and vital, aspect of the meaning of surrealism, if not its precise definition. But it is immediately clear also that if we pose the question in these

terms, primitive man was a religious being – something which immediately appears difficult for us to follow, since in so far as our approach
is through the advanced movements of contemporary literature, we
are all the more separated from the religious world of mankind's
infancy. We cannot settle the question so easily: certainly a great step
has been taken towards knowledge of primitive man, and after twenty
years of the modern movement it is not even certain that we are so
much further away from the primitive than Renaissance man was from
antiquity, but we do find one fundamental difference: in essence
primitive man was unconscious in every sense of the word; he did not
have awareness of what he was, and was not generally aware of what
today we call the unconscious. On the contrary, what distinguishes
modern man – and this is perhaps especially true of the surrealist – is
that in returning to the primitive he is constrained by consciousness
even as he aims to recover within himself the mechanisms of the
unconscious, for he never ceases to have consciousness of his goal.
Consequently, he is at once both closer and yet further away.

If I now evoke conscious man, which is us, faced with the knowledge
of what the first men were, [. . .] at least under a certain form in the
sense that we cannot doubt that the first men were closer to the release
of the passions than we are, were less domesticated, were – in the
common expression – savages, savages and at the same time religious
beings. But when we direct our lucid attention to these facts, we are
obliged to recognize that when we speak of primitive man as a religious
being, we also recognize that this was a strictly materialist religion. Let
us be clear about this: it is not a question of deciding if the religious
content of primitive thought was closer to materialist or spiritualist
philosophy, but simply of placing the emphasis on this fact: it is
impossible to understand anything about primitive life if one does not
grasp the fact that all actions were embedded in material interest. The
rites studied among those who typify, in a less unsatisfactory way than
anyone else, the people who may have inhabited the world at the
beginning of humanity, the rites that animate them in the freeing of
the passions, are always at the command of the needs of material
interest. It is always a question of the good of the community, often
even the economic well-being of the community. These rites can be
studied in such a way that they are generally relegated to pastoral rites;
this could represent an exaggeration or a simplification, although no
one would deny the importance of the preoccupation with agriculture
in the data that appear to us most poetic because they relate to the life
of primitive people. The festivals that animate them, which push them
to the highest degree of trance and lead them to orgies, have as their
goal the fertilization of the earth. Within the term religion there was

from the first – since it is in these festivals that the essence of what can be called religion is gathered up – there was, in the term religion, a sort of sense of combat. When we consider primitive people, religion is not exactly what we expect when we think of moral religions like Christianity and Buddhism. Primitive religion is interested, while Christian or Buddhist religions appear to us disinterested.

In truth, it is difficult to believe that when we pass from these simple rites and orgiastic festivals to moral religions like Christianity [. . .]; but the actions in which passion continues, in spite of everything, to be unleashed under the religious yoke has lost all interest value. The doctrine of salvation has as its foundation the concern with a self-interest of being; this time it is a question of a spiritual interest, but while it is never simply a question of duration, it is never simply a question of assuring life, never simply a question of making it possible. This can serve to emphasize, this particular end can cause the antinomy contained in the term religion to stand out, to render life possible by penetrating as far as possible into the meaning of the impossible. The unleashing of the passions suppresses the possibility of life; if, for example, it is found again during primitive festivals, this is only for a short time and in order to assure the possibility of what will follow after; but in any case the impossible is never taken as such; men never anticipate this freeing of the passions (which is contained within themselves) in order to live it without any ends and with no concern for the possibility of what follows, to live it as an impossibility of living for the sole reason that they are destined for it and that the man who does not accept his destiny is condemned to the compromises and hypocrisies which continue to weigh on him, and from which the movement about which I am now speaking probably has the precise meaning of the desire to emancipate him.

Surrealism itself is certainly opposed to what could be called religion in the clear sense that the price of passion it has put forward has never been imposed by it from a concern for security, or from a concern to assure the material interests of those who take part in it. The surrealist attitude contains something thoroughly radical which has brought it into conflict from the start with what appear to be the highest forms of religion and which, in an atmosphere of compromise, preserved the equivocation between concern for an impassioned life, between concern for an affective life in incandescence, and that of personal interest, that of security. This vanishes in surrealism under the very simple form of scandal. There is a fundamental opposition between accepted religious forms in civilized countries and a movement like surrealism, and this opposition is characteristically expressed by the scandal surrealism has been and – despite appearances – remains.

Surrealism has brought to the fore and maintained, in a sometimes
discreet form, a black element which characterizes it indisputably.
Julien Gracq, in his recently published book[2] devoted to André Breton
– and, more generally, to surrealism – has brought out this accursed
side which endures through the felicitous perspectives which Breton
has given surrealism in practice. It is not simply a matter of black water
or black blood, but of a black heart; and this black element always
dominates, carries it off, and ensures some sort of tearing away from
the world which we once dominated. The formula, the last formula in
Arcane 17, 'Osiris is a black God', continues the scandalous tradition of
surrealism. And in addition to these characteristics, the ideas of
breaking with the past dominate the destiny prepared by surrealism
for the first time in the perfectly black figure of Sade. Besides, we know
that for Breton the simplest surrealist act does not consist in an
inoffensive gesture, nor does it consist of a literary act; the simplest
surrealist act, he wrote, consists in descending – would consist in
descending to the street and shooting at random into the crowd. Thus
it is not a question of some form that could be reconciled with
possibility; there is nothing possible about the act of shooting at
random into the crowd. The will to shoot at random into the crowd
decisively signals the will towards the impossible and nothing else, in
the sense that no one, after all, has ever done it, in the sense that one
cannot pass from the actual situation in which a civilized man lives to
the situation experienced by others. All the same, it is something that
signifies an orientation on which it is not possible to go back.

Some of my reservations on the question of the religious sense of
surrealism may arise from the equivocal value of another religion; the
last judgement I am going to cite relates the surrealist attitude in the
clearest way with the forms of known religions. We know that in the
islands of Malaysia there is a tradition which, from time to time,
consigns an individual to the fate Breton used to characterize the
simplest surrealist act. The custom of amok is well known: the lands in
which the custom of amok occurs recognize, as a sort of traditional
attitude, the sudden fury that overcomes an individual armed with a
dagger who rushes headlong into the crowd and kills until he is killed
himself. It is not exactly an act of madness, since it belongs to a
perpetuated tradition. Clearly, the crowd do not in any way excuse the
amok, since they kill him, but they are still complicitous with a
supposedly crazy act, since at the start it was understood that it is
natural for a man to be overcome by the folly of amok, that it is a
natural thing for a man to succumb to the obligation to confront his
brother and kill him. Let us now try to go beyond this perhaps
exaggeratedly symbolic definition to consider the religious aspects that

have generally characterized surrealism. The greatest precautions seem to have been taken to avoid drawing parallels. When I argued that it must necessarily have an intractable character, when I insisted on the scandalous characteristics that separate surrealism from Christian morality, despite the care taken to avoid a vocabulary used by Christianity, it is easy to recognize traditional forms through numerous passages in the writings of André Breton in particular. Julien Gracq has insisted on 'Degrees around the Temples of Shadows' [. . .] which has been spoken about, to the extent that without it nothing has value in his eyes; for him value is possessed only by objects or events which have caused a shiver to pass across his temple, which we can rightfully say is a sacred shiver. I do not think there can be any doubt about the fact that there was something fundamental, something that must be defined as being connected to one meaning of the word religious. Besides, the recent development of surrealism has stressed another profound aspect of religious life: the noticeable concern of contemporary surrealism for myth is one of the clearest indications in this direction. Myth is, together with the sacred, plainly one of the essential movements within religious life; with the sacred it lies at the heart of all that has been analysed by philosophy under the form of participation. And it is evident that when surrealism put forward the idea of myth, it was in response to a vibrant nostalgia in the mind of contemporary peoples, which has been alive not only since Nietzsche but even since German Romanticism. Moreover, religion is constituted by the connection to the myth of rituals. No one, then, can fail to know that the clearest certainty of surrealism is to manage to rediscover the attitudes of mind that allowed primitive man to combine in ritual and, more precisely, to find in ritual the most incisive and tangible forms of poetic life. Everything Breton has put forward – whether it concerns the quest for the sacred, the concern with myths, or rediscovering rituals similar to those of primitives – represents the exploration of the possibility we again discover, possibility in another sense; this time it is simply a question of exploring all that can be explored by man, it is a question of reconstituting all that was fundamental to man before human nature had been enslaved by the necessity for technical work. Technical work has regulated within us judgements and attitudes which are completely subordinated to an ulterior result, completely subordinated to a material result. No one would dream of contravening the legitimacy of these judgements and attitudes, but no one can fail to notice that the role given to practical activity – in particular what it has become in the modern machine age (although this is a process that started in primitive times) – is calculated to alter profoundly what, in human nature, has remained indestructibly analogous to what we notice when we are placed nakedly in front of the spectacle of nature and, more precisely, before the spectacle of the universe. The man who works is a man who separates himself from the universe, the man who works is a man already shut up in his house, who binds himself to his bosses, his tables, his workbenches and his tools. The man who works is a man who destroys the profound reality [. . .] that surrealism has over the real. And there can be no doubt that the concern of surrealism, in common with primitive rituals, has been to rediscover, outside that technical activity which weighs so heavily on today's human masses, the irreducible element by which man has no equal more perfect than a star. It is necessary to say that this could appear as an aspect of surrealism we know today, and which some people have a tendency to find, in relation to primitive surrealism, degenerate. Nevertheless, it is easy to show that the foundation of surrealism – namely, automatic writing – already bore in itself both the virtue and the necessity of these later developments. What essentially characterizes automatic writing – and this is why a man like André Breton remains attached to its principle despite a relative failure he recognizes in terms of the results of the method – is that it is an act of rupture – certainly definitive in André Breton's mind – with an enslavement which, beginning with the world of technical activity, is determined in words themselves, to the extent that these words participate in the profane world or in the prosaic world. Someone who sits comfortably, forgetting to the greatest degree what exists so as to write at random on a blank sheet the most vibrant delirium which passes through his mind, may end up with nothing of literary value. He knows that this is of no importance; he has experienced a possibility which represents an unconditional rupture with the world in which we act to feed ourselves, in which we act to cover and shelter ourselves. He has essentially undertaken an act of insubordination, in one sense he has performed a sovereign act. At the same time, he has accomplished what, within the meaning of religion itself, could appear predominant: he has achieved the destruction of the personality itself. Those who perform the surrealist act in automatic writing must first abandon the concerns of the man of letters when he writes in order to create a book with a given intent, when he writes a book in the same way as he digs his garden. At a given moment he must forget that he belongs to this humanity whose feet are attached to spades; he must forget what the man of letters expects of publication, by the necessity of doing what, in spite of everything, all the surrealists have done to a certain point – that is, carve out a literary career. At a given moment he has, in the most profound way, needed to forget himself; and Christianity itself, if I may say so, follows in the wake of surrealism, because in Christianity the self-denial is much shorter, the renunciation is so much shorter, in that what one loses in the self one gains in God. Simple as this change of general attitudes might appear, as the surrealist performs the act of automatic writing, he abandons, in a way that is easy to judge after the event as incontestably aggressive, the prerogative of a God who has never been abandoned by man, who has been upheld in just such a way by Christian man – the prerogative of God to be all-knowing, all-demanding, fully restraining and never losing self-awareness. But if we now return to the difficulties with which we have seen surrealism tussle, we notice that these operations, which I have sought to define in relation to the knowledge of primitive religious life that could be called scientific, have not been free of some extremely difficult problems. By this I mean the relation between surrealism and politics. Surrealism, if one accepts the definition I have given of it, is the most complete negation of material interest. It is impossible to go any further. Clearly limits remain within human frailty, but this frailty within surrealism is qualified by the nature of what it is – qualified with frailty. But how can modern man deny material interest? He can do so only under the form that material interest has actually taken today – in other words, under personal interest, precisely under the form of self-interest within capitalist society. The moment one has recognized the impossibility of directly attaining material interest and the necessity of passing through the form that material interest has taken in the present conditions, one notices that surrealism is a very much weaker negation of this personal interest than Communism. Communism seems, in a totally transparent way, to be infinitely more capable of denying the world of personal interest than surrealism. Everyone knows that surrealism itself has implicitly recognized this problem. After the establishment of the movement André Breton was not slow to accept an unreserved accord with Communism. It seems to me that his intention in this respect was irreproachable – indeed, the position taken by André Breton was the only one he could take; nevertheless, experience has shown that an antagonism would develop between the partisans of the struggle against the capitalist world and the surrealist view. In fact it is evident from the revolutionary experience that the Communist struggle against the material world of personal interest, far from suppressing material interest in the world, has created a historical situation in which the primacy of material interest has only been accentuated. Evidently the matter is related to fortuitous circumstances; the fact that the Revolution developed in a backward country has been a crucial factor serving to compel Communism to rely in the most oppressive way on the value of economic interest. In any case, Communism cannot deny the fact that economic interests are not interests as such; to deny that economic activity [. . .] and not man for economic interest, but in such conditions, man must first take cogniz-ance of economic activity before being able to think morally about emancipation in the way surrealism has proposed. This involves – if I am making myself understood – an equivocation both in surrealism and in Communism. Surrealism cannot escape the equivocation by its negation of material interest; equally, Communism cannot escape the equivocation, since its negation of personal interest did not entirely lead to what could be called simply common interest, but led to technical interest which is still a particular interest. I am not making a critique of Communism here, and the few expressions I am using could not, in any case, be taken in this sense. But I want to explain myself as clearly as I can about surrealism. Certainly the difficulties I have set out have established a sort of state of crisis within surrealism. At first this seems problematic. Faced with the surrealist attitude as it is manifested concretely in the life of the individuals who belong to a given group, it is, if I may say so, the idle character connected to the unreal character of values put forward. In consequence, surrealism has abandoned a certain ambiguity, which I have defined as being inherent to religion as it existed until Christianity, the poetic value which was guaranteed in the ancient rituals by the material value of the ritual, by the real value of the ritual – a value which was, perhaps, not profoundly real, but was considered as such by all those who practised the ritual; this material value has ceased to guarantee the authenticity of the ritual. Today there is no possibility of imbuing surrealist life with this guarantee which gives belief its efficacy. This results in the sort of feeling of emptiness, hopelessness, uselessness, superfluity and frivo-lousness that characterizes surrealist work. I do not mean in relation to those who want to deepen its content but, rather, in the eyes of the majority of people; and no one can actually cross this boundary in the sense that common existence alone would be of a nature to determine this character of profound reality which surrealism seeks. This surreality cannot end in genuine realities because people do not believe in it, because men as a whole do not believe in it. It seems to me that this unhappy state of affairs has been experienced not only by André Breton but by all those who are close to surrealism, whether they actually belong to the group itself or situate their activity on the margins of the group; and to this extent I have no hesitation in allying myself to this feeling of malaise and this feeling of powerlessness that seems to me, unfortunately, to characterize the result of surrealism. I must make it clear that I do not mean by this to define a failure of surrealism – in life and in history there are no results which do not imply an element of failure, and failure does not deserve to be treated as those who do not want to go any further treat it – as a sort of proof of vanity. On the contrary, the failure cannot be grasped except as something that must be sought out most attentively by those whose impatience calls for new developments. Here I will go beyond what is accepted about surrealism and set out what, in my opinion, remains possible. It is, of course, a matter of simple evocation. It is not possible to speak about what might happen without profound reservations. Prophecy is not given to people of today: we do not know, we do not see beyond the end of our noses and, what is more, that is what we want. I suppose there is nothing acceptable about transforming a simple delirium into a prophetic delirium; we would like to live within our limits, we would like to live in the present moment, and do not want to subordinate what we experience here and now to concerns that are later to be rejected. Yet this leaves us in the presence of problems which are inherent to our nature as men; faced with an impasse, we are obliged to look for an opening. In this sense I feel that I defined this opening when I suggested at the beginning of this talk that in the possible renaissance of primitive man, contemporary man could not find vanished forms except in a way entirely altered by consciousness, which is how contemporary man is distinguished. We can only be conscious, and it is through penetrating into our consciousness that we can try to transgress the difficulties of the present world. It is not up to any of us to suppress capitalist reality; I understand very clearly the meaning of what I am going to say [. . .] we can each set ourselves a clearly defined target, like the suppression of capitalism, but it does not by any means follow that we can go beyond the capitalist world in which we exist into the world which will follow on from it. It is not even possible to say that the Soviet world has effected this leap. Whether we like it or not, we are enclosed in the capitalist world; we are reduced to conscious analyses of our present position, and we cannot directly know what life would be like in a world in which personal interest would have been suppressed. The first necessity for us in this respect is the sincere comprehension of all that happens, leading to a will to transform the world. At some moments it could be painful to notice that those who have given their lives for an overthrow of social forms have been unable to achieve the results they set beforehand. There is no doubt that there is a difference between the programme Lenin expressed in *State and Revolution* and the current state of the Soviet world, no matter how one would define it. But if we purely and simply reject this effort because of the grave consequences it might have, in particular in respect of restrictions of liberty, whether they be provisional or not; if we oppose our pure and simple incomprehension to the will of people who have acted as they have in conditions they have not chosen, it seems to me that straight away we profoundly reduce our opportunities to bring our consciousness to bear on circumstances which might not be distorted by the present state of the world. I think it is only to the extent that we can sympathetically understand those who have tried to make a real world that we can begin to form conscious judgements about ourselves. To the extent that we are distorted by a milieu determined by personal interest, to the extent that we submit to this personal interest, to the extent that we are guided by it, to the extent that we live among men who are guided by it, we can make no conscious judgement about it. A profound distortion debases all the possibilities within us, especially that which I would readily call a poetic act: could it happen if two beings remain profoundly separated by their own personal interests? How can the communication of poetry be possible if the interests of the listener and the speaker are different? We know what readings of poetic works often are: each person registers a few suggestions of extreme banality on a kind of calculator and, instead of the poetic notion, substitutes a few suggestions brought forth from the existence of various interests now existing in the world. The very existence of such a trend, in particular the specific concerns of an editor or a review, profoundly distorts poetic communication in every way; everything reduces it to the need to form a judgement such as might be formed when one manufactures a product. Faced with a painting or a book, we often find ourselves almost taking the attitude of a shopkeeper. This represents a failure which must not allow us to forget so easily the concern remaining accessible but not [. . .] of a poetic access. And I do not believe I delude myself if I say that if we separate ourselves from this for a moment, if we cease to remain awake (and I use this term in the strongest sense of the word) to all poetic reality, if at a given moment we abandon this effort, however painful it might be, and pass over to protests which we know in advance are perfectly vain, then we immediately pass from the state of men who want to deny themselves and can change themselves through poetry, to that of those who live in the cycle of personal interest. I believe one cannot insist too strongly on the necessity of binding consciousness to depersonalization. It seems to me that surrealism has gone a long way in this direction, but the way remains open, and it is necessary for us to penetrate further into it. It can be valuable to dream about creating myths, about creating rituals, and I, for my part, have no objections whatsoever to tendencies of this sort. All the same, it seems to me that when I spoke about a malaise resulting from the fact that neither these myths nor these rituals would be true myths or rituals because they do not receive the assent of the community, I highlighted the necessity of going further and considering a possibility which at first could appear purely negative and which, perhaps, is fundamentally only the most complete form of the situation. If we state simply, for the sake of lucidity, that today's man defines himself by his avidity for myth, and if we add that he defines himself also by the consciousness of not having the power to gain access to the possibility of creating a true myth, we have defined a sort of myth which is the *absence of myth*. Here I am expressing an idea that is a little difficult to follow. All the same, it is easy to accept that if we define ourselves as being incapable of attaining the state of myth which remains in a state of suspension, we define the root of humanity today as an absence of myth. And this absence of myth can be found in the face of the one who lives it (who lives it, you must understand, with a passion that animates those who once wanted no longer to live in dull reality but in mythic reality), this absence of myth can be found in front of him as infinitely more exalting than in the past, when myths were bound up with everyday life. To this absence of particularity in myth – because in defining the absence of myth in this way one simply defines the suppression of particularity – is connected a bounded character which will be able to pass, which can pass for singular; it is the fact that it is impossible to contest the absence of myth. No one can say that the absence of myth does not exist as a myth; there is no one who would not be obliged to admit, even to the extent that he strives to create a particular myth, to admit the image of the absence of myth as a real myth. To this first suppression of particularity can be added – or must be added – the necessity of an *absence of community*. What in fact does a group signify, if not the opposition of a few men to the mass of other men? For example, what does a church like the Christian Church signify, if not the negation of whatever is not it? There is in the fact that all religion of the past was bound to the necessity of putting itself forward as a church, as a closed community, a sort of fundamental impediment. Any type of religious activity, to the extent that it was an unleashing of passion, tended to suppress the elements that separated people from each other. But at the same time the fusion effected by the ancient festival had for its end only the creation of a new individual who could be called the collective individual. By this I do not mean to claim that individuals are not drawn to the group together in the way they always have been, but beyond this immediate necessity, the fact that any possible community belongs to what I call – in terms which are consciously still strange for me – absence of community, must be the foundation of any possible community; that is to say, the state of passion, the state of unleashing which was unconscious in the primitive mind, can become lucid, to the extent that the limit imposed by what is contrary to the first movement in the community as it closed in on itself must be transgressed by consciousness. It is not possible to have limits between men in consciousness; moreover, consciousness, the lucidity of consciousness, necessarily re-establishes the impossibility of a limit between humanity itself and the rest of the world. What necessarily disappears as a consequence of consciousness becoming increasingly penetrating is the possibility of making a distinction between man and the rest of the world. This, it seems to me, must be pushed to the point of the *absence of poetry* – not that we cannot gain access to poetry other than through the channel of real poets, but we all know that every poetic voice contains within itself its immediate powerlessness; that each real poem dies the moment it is born, and death is even the very condition of its completion. It is in so far as poetry is taken as far as the absence of poetry that poetic communication is possible. This is the same as saying that the condition of conscious man who has recovered the simplicity of passion, who has rediscovered the sovereignty of the irreducible element which is within man, is a state of presence, a state of wakefulness pushed to extreme lucidity, the limit of which is necessarily silence.

I have sought to show possible ways of going beyond present antinomies. I would not, however, wish to insist on these antinomies. I would like to finish instead by insisting on the profound viability of the whole of this ferment which continues today. It seems to me that no matter what the difficulties, the movement of minds converges; there is on all sides – and this is something that cannot be underestimated, despite the fact that individual attitudes often give the impression of isolation – there is on all sides a ferment which promises man a return to a so much freer life, to a so much prouder life, a life which could be called wild. There is within today's man a profound intolerance for the sense of humiliation which is demanded every day of our human nature and to which we submit everywhere: we submit in the office and in the street; we submit in the country. Everywhere men feel that human nature has been profoundly humiliated, and what is left of religion finally humiliates him in the face of God who, after all, is merely a hypostasis of work. I do not think one could dream of denying this nostalgia. I imagine that if we are gathered here, whatever diverse elements could be at play in the fact of the presence of everyone in this hall, it is a dominant element which has certainly determined this presence; it is the nostalgia for a life which ceases to be humiliated; it is the nostalgia for a life which ceases to be separated from what lies behind the world. It is not a question of finding behind the world something which dominates it; there is nothing behind the world which dominates man, there is nothing that can humiliate him;

behind the world, behind the poverty in which we live, behind the precise limits where we live, there is only a universe whose bursting open is incomparable, and behind the universe there is nothing.

G.-A. ASTRE Ladies and gentlemen, it is a tradition of 'Club Maintenant' to encourage discussion after a talk. Georges Bataille's has been so rich that I feel that if we wanted to deal with all the problems he has raised, we would be here until tomorrow evening. But I would very much like the debate to be centred around the crucial issue raised, which is the destiny of surrealism. Is there anyone who would like to ask questions about, for example, the definitions which could have been given as the objectives of surrealism? I know that in the hall there are a considerable number of writers who have either a distant or a more intimate interest in these questions, and I would very much like one of them to take the floor. Before M. Jean Wahl went to America, he was in the habit of raising a number of tricky questions. I don't know if there is someone here this evening who will take on a similar role. Patri, are you completely in agreement with what Georges Bataille has said?

AIMÉ PATRI Certainly not, but I'll wait.

ASTRE Klossowski, are you in agreement?

PIERRE KLOSSOWSKI Completely in agreement, but in different terms.

ASTRE Has M. Guibert anything to add? No? I would have thought that considering the issues raised by surrealism concerning the problem of politics and temporality, there must be plenty of questions. Patri, let's hear from you . . .

BATAILLE I am rather amazed by Klossowski's affirmation, since Klossowski is a Catholic. I don't completely follow him.

KLOSSOWSKI You are a Catholic.

BATAILLE I'm a Catholic? I won't protest, because I have nothing to say. I can also be anything you like.

ASTRE These are precise questions.

KLOSSOWSKI I want to ask M. Bataille why the resources of writing must be connected to a literary career. It seems that this is an idea, this is direct movement towards a form of prostitution. In order for these resources to be connected with a literary career, is prostitution acceptable to you?

BATAILLE I don't think you have understood me very well. Everything I said was directed against the fact that writing ended in a literary career.

KLOSSOWSKI But you said that it must end there. I want to ask

something else: you said that we are in a capitalist world; I claim that
we are no longer in a capitalist world. This is to deny all resistance
which is encountered, and the strength of poetry goes further than the
personal interest you spoke about, and poetry must be made for all.

B A T A I L L E   I am mainly in agreement with you, but it seems to me
that poetry is less effective than it seems. It can be efficacious, but to a
degree which seems to me very limited.

K L O S S O W S K I   This is not, in my opinion, connected to capitalism
or non-capitalism; it is a question of classes – there are privileged
classes who customarily welcome it.

B A T A I L L E   It seems to me that you are speaking very well, perhaps
more clearly [. . .]

K L O S S O W S K I   I have found you Catholic at certain moments.

B A T A I L L E   I don't feel in the mood to protest against being called
a Catholic. If you say something completely without foundation, I will
not reply.

P A T R I   I don't consider you a Catholic but, rather, a Buddhist.
Because finally it seems to me that the Catholics have often been
criticized for placing too much emphasis on personal interest, they are
too mindful of salvation; but Buddhists consider the person as an
illusion, and for them true deliverance consists in establishing a
distance from such interest. But on this point surrealism and
Communism would also converge, in the sense that in both cases it is a
question of aiming at the destruction of the myth of the personality.
Am I right about this?

B A T A I L L E   That is roughly what I was trying to say, in a rather
vague way.

P A T R I   Then you consider yourself a Buddhist?

B A T A I L L E   I don't consider myself a Buddhist, because Buddhism
recognizes transcendence. It does not matter how little this transcendence is connected in Buddhism to the maintenance of personal well-
being under a rather well-known form. It is certain that the cycle of
metempsychosis and the concerns of this cycle, which plays an eminent
role in Buddhism, cannot be considered neglectful of personal interest. I feel closer to Buddhism than to Catholicism. In so far as the
convergence of Communism and surrealism is concerned, it is not very
clear, for the very good reason that it is situated completely in the
future; but one could not deny that in Communism there is a will to
deny the person, at least in the sense of personal interest.

P A T R I   It seems to me that on this point there is a confusion
between Marxist Communism and that of monastic Orders, because
it's not the same thing: if one refers to Marx's text, he never says
anything of the kind; on the other hand, if one refers to monastic

Communism one finds in fact all sorts of things against personal interest, but there is nothing like that in Marx. There are formulas which come from the humanism of the Renaissance: I am still referring to intentions rather than bothering with realizations.

B A T A I L L E   Even so, material interest in the present form of society predominantly means personal interest, which it would not be in Communist form. In fact there is a sort of confusion – more exactly, of fusion – in Marx between common interest and personal interest, but there is negation.

P A T R I   There is no fusion; he very clearly upholds a society in which the liberty of all will become the condition of each; the liberty of each is not suppressed, it remains the stated aim [. . .] the end remains individualist.

B A T A I L L E   Yes, of course.

P A T R I   These are realizations.

B A T A I L L E   One must say that in such questions it is realizations rather than projects that count.

X   [. . .] I think that due to the separation between the world before the Revolution and the world after the Revolution, due to the fact that the Revolution has been delayed, we see that there is a question, that of a problem which can appear only after the Revolution [and which] already appears, of more profound questions and these social forms [. . .] I am trying to speak about the essence of existence in the absurdity of existence. There is something profound, there is a deeper malaise which will not be resolved by the Revolution. Where does Bataille stand on this question?

B A T A I L L E   In these questions surrealism is defined through the person of André Breton, who said something like this: that the artificial condition, the artificial precariousness of present social conditions, hid the real precariousness of the human condition from us, and on this point I could only – I have had some difficulty in following you, but I could emphasize only my own personal position in the sense you have spoken of, and it seems to me that a felicitous model would be to say that a man like Rimbaud would have had as much reason to flee from a post-revolutionary world as from the present world. Very simply, it seems to me that this means that the possibilities which emerge in today's world could be multiplied in a future world and, in truth, this does not come into my mind as an unalloyed blessing. I did not want to say very much about fulfilment in a post-revolutionary world. I do not want to say that I consider that this world will not be separated from its situation. Man will be separated from his profound situation, which is more like an abyss than a footpath. Clearly the world as it could be after a revolution – the world in which, quite simply, there would no longer be anything to do except observe the world of the abyss, because all problems would be resolved – is perhaps, for me, something rather theoretical; such a world would even be very frightening. In truth, it seems to me that man is bound by this fear, and to be separated from it is also the gauge of his affliction.

A S T R E   Are there questions dealing more specifically with surrealism? Especially concerning 'indistinct' consciousness in relation to the world. Do you think the role of consciousness is to achieve a fusion with the universe, as you stated at the end?

B A T A I L L E   Clearly it is one of the themes of all religions, and in particular of mysticism. For my part, I am inclined give a greater importance to this principle.

A S T R E   Do you believe that the ideal of surrealism is lucid consciousness?

B A T A I L L E   The route of consciousness could not be avoided, it seems to me. If one envisages, beyond a narrowly defined surrealism, a larger surrealism, one immediately sees the precise possibilities of this lucidity appear. It seems to me that the time is ripe to speak about Maurice Blanchot's effort towards this lucidity, which is made concrete in an analysis of the position of Sade, who could be considered exemplary, who cannot be regarded as alien to surrealism, just as surrealism cannot be considered external to him.

x   It is difficult to consider Georges Bataille a poet, because he has denied himself the right of the necessity to predict the future. The opacity which forbids us from predicting the future makes plain what you have tried to express by the absence of poetry, and this defines you as an absent poet. I believe that there is a surrealist poetry to the extent to which there is prophecy and vision in the future. I believe that poetry must present the true life which is absent today.

B A T A I L L E   I don't see what I could say against this. I have indicated that I was of a contrary opinion, that's all. I do not see why poetry should be condemned to speak the future. That is a general judgement about the future, not a judgement about poetry. You can see the future in Rimbaud, but you could equally well not see it and still be stimulated by poetic communication.

x   There is communication between a poet and a reader who reads poetry to the extent that the reader participates in a life which is not present, and this present life is situated in the future.

B A T A I L L E   This is exactly what I have always spoken out against. I have tried to be precise, I have continually placed the present moment against a concern for the future, and for me poetry is defined by concern for the present moment. For all that, this does not mean that I claim to be a poet.

x How does this relate to painting?

B A T A I L L E   For Breton, painting is the same thing as poetry, and painting exists only in so far as it is poetry. I am more or less in agreement with him.

D U R A N D [?³]   There are several points on which there could be reflections to offer. Will you allow me to point out that what you have said about the Christian position involves a certain interpretation which a Christian would not share? You said that Christianity seeks salvation as if salvation were the desire, as if salvation were inspired by a quest for personal interest, but the salvation the Christian seeks – perhaps not the common-or-garden Christian, but the Christian who has reached a certain depth of understanding – is a collective salvation, and this notion becomes concrete in the idea of the mystical body. It is so true that sanctity is always accompanied by an expiatory will: the subject, the saint himself, chooses an expiation of sins. I believe that if interest there is, it is an interest which crosses the frontiers of individuality, and besides (I would not dream of saying that you are a Catholic), I believe that this is, on the contrary, very much a pivot of the most thoroughgoing sentiment. But it is on another point that I would like to ask a question. This is a problem considered by surrealism, that of reason. I know that I will expose myself to extremely sharp criticism if I utter this word, which I do not give the limited meaning of logic but consider symbolic of a whole order of relations such as language, such as living in society, such as ethics – such as, in a general way, the consideration of secondary values in relation to the values of the instant. Let's suppose that we say there are two sorts of values: those of the moment, which I would call primary values; and those in which the individual seeks with no concern for the future, with no concern to integrate simple immediate satisfaction to new experience. It seems to me that it would not be too inaccurate to define surrealism as a sort of religion of primary values, but what is to be done in the world in which we are constrained to live whether we like it or not, what is to be done about all the problems with which we are faced because we are not sure that we have an interest [. . .] and it is here that reason constitutes a problem for surrealism which it eludes or declares non-existent, but cannot refuse to consider if it really wants to justify the meaning of its activity. What would a world in which everyone was a surrealist be like? And what sort of activity would this world produce, and would life, language, ethical categories still be possible? That is the question I would like to ask you.

B A T A I L L E   So far as Christianity is concerned, you are perfectly right to insist on these elements, which are, however, minor elements. The most general element is that of man's personal salvation; this element presents itself; it has value in general definitions of a church and in the custom of piety; it is soon perceived as intolerable, and it seems to me that in so far as Christian piety leads towards sanctity, in particular towards mystical sanctity, it could not avoid being divided along the lines I have indicated, and one would find between the surrealists and the most astute mystics, for example Bossuet [. . .] in so far as reason is concerned there is no doubt that reason is continually menaced by the unleashing of the passions, and in fact, if I had fully and properly expressed this analysis, it would have been centred on the fact that everything continually stands still between the impossibility due to the release of the passions and the possibilities reintroduced by the existence of reason. It is through this release of the passions that we enter into the instant, it is by the use of reason that we dominate the future, and human life is defined by a certain capacity to dominate the future; what we dominate is in fact never in the present but in the future. Industrial domination is always carried towards the future; plainly it ends in gratification, but it leaves a small residue and is determined in its general activity as a constitution of the future. There remains the question of knowing how conciliation between the two is possible. It seems to me that the history of religions consists precisely in this, and as for defining exactly what surrealism represents in this respect, it seems to me that for this reason it is quite simply impossible, in that surrealism today is represented only by rather restricted groups and has no influence over the fate of the world. It seems to me that when surrealism – if it ever does – has an influence over industry and over the whole of human activities, these human activities will have been profoundly changed – that surrealism also, for its part, will have developed in ways we could not have predicted.

D U R A N D [?]   If surrealism and reason were two different positions, I believe the future would, in effect, allow some synthesis and possible conciliation, but if the question is posed in terms of an absolute antinomy between surrealism and reason, I do not see how surrealism could be reconciled with reason without losing its essence, for that is where its essence is located. Each person, in surrealism, will seek the sort of rapture Breton has spoken about, and he will find it in acts which could be social, but which we can easily predict – if we refer to some of the declarations in your lecture – will rather more certainly become antisocial. This is the position I do not grasp. On the other hand, you say that the thought of the future [. . .]. One can conceive of a constitution of life which would not necessarily be capitalist, a perspective under which the capitalist or non-capitalist problem would be posed, and a slightly different perspective which has no relation to the real issue. In this surrealist society what will become of poetry or, more generally, art, understood as an assembly of techniques, the fruit of a collaboration of past generations and the present will to creation? Here again I have the impression that surrealism will proceed into the sense of pure instantaneity, into the sense of the negation of all modes of transpersonal communication. I have no clear insight into surrealism's potential to give birth to an inhabitable society.

BATAILLE To the extent that it is possible to judge a future surrealism by current surrealism, one sees possibilities of survival. I would like to add my personal response. As far as I am concerned, I do not see the meaning that [. . .] potential beyond a certain point, silence. It is apparent that silence resolves – singularly perhaps, I will not say oppressively – the problem you posed.

DURAND [?] This is mystical practice, not action.

BATAILLE Of course, action is perhaps left to others, and experience shows clearly enough [. . .] to suppose that surrealism will one day lead towards a form of new mystic experience, but it is not clear if at that point the incandescence reached at certain moments will leave man intact to respond to all the problems posed for him. These are unsatisfied passions rather than passions that have reached the limits of consummation which create a considerable disorder in the world. One must take this into account: I was talking with some friends about the animal state, especially about their sexual activity, and we were completely in agreement in considering that this was literally a hell; an animal's sexual passion ends in something practically torturous, something we see every day in the activity of dogs, in which we have a spectacle which is literally terrifying, to the extent that one cannot imagine a more frightful, more comical or more powerless martyrdom. And I believe that the more we find ourselves in animality, and the more powerless passions are, then consequently one's means of satisfying them will increasingly lead to a more or less frightful devastation. However, this difficulty is encountered again at the other extreme. Blanchot's article under a different form, but simply under a form of pure meditation – this article by Blanchot is fundamentally centred on the fact that sadism is comprehensible from the moment one perceives that what is at stake in Sade's conception is really complete destruction, not simply of the object of sadism but of the subject. Sadism is conceivable only on condition that for him the tortures he inflicts on others, which give others the most unbearable distress, are transformed for him if he experiences them, in his turn, only as delights. What, then, is the life of the mystic if not a moral transposition of the character of Sade as Blanchot defined him? The mystic is fundamentally a man for whom tortures become delights.

x   In Dante, souls in Purgatory repudiate themselves in their torments, not by pure disinterested transformation of their torments into delights, because they see an end in them.

D U R A N D [?]   And particularly because they take their delights to a logical conclusion.

x   But I believe that here the question of pleasure is secondary.

B A T A I L L E   I don't know Dante's *Inferno* particularly well, and I don't follow you too well. My impression is that you are putting forward a fundamental problem about mysticism, because mystical experience is the act of a man, and at root man is necessarily concerned with projects. Mystical experience is pursued to the extent that it becomes impossible, and it is always limited by the fact that the more it is realized, the more impossible it becomes.

x   And in this sense I understand that you connect the mystical position to the surrealist position.

D U R A N D [?]   On the contrary, I am saying that if the mystic accepts and solicits torment for himself it is in a spirit of charity, not at all in an egoistic way or in a spirit of personal gratification.

B A T A I L L E   It is true in the history of mysticism to the present day.

D U R A N D [?]   The basis of mysticism lies in the idea, in the observation, that the presence of evil in the world can be overcome only if one voluntarily agrees to offer oneself as a victim. But without playing on words, there could be no greater difference – how do we identify these two experiences?

B A T A I L L E   I have the impression that what is at issue every time is the suppression of both subject and object. The difference consists in the fact that in sadism we begin by suppressing the object, while in mysticism it is necessary to suppress the subject.

Notes

1. A conference at Club Maintenant, Tuesday 24 February 1948. There appears to be no written text for this important conference: this is a shorthand transcription taken at the time, and it contains some lacunae marked by [. . .].

[2. Julien Gracq, *André Breton, quelques aspects de l'écrivain* (1948), Paris: José Corti. – *Translator*]

3. Corrected by hand to 'Duron' or 'Durou'.

Initial Postulate[1]

I can, as a truth of experience, crudely put forward this proposition: *If, at a given moment, I elude my concern for the next moment* (and equally all those that follow after):

– in the realm of aesthetics I reach the purest form of ecstasy (which justifies well-known descriptions of it: conflagrations, excessive joy[2]);

– I place in the realm of aesthetics the only value which is subordinated to nothing else (even in the idea of God, omnipotence induces an action extended into time, and to this extent I am asked to approve the *creator* – something which implies the whole hierarchy of moral values brought back to works: if Christianity stands out from it, it is a paradox);

– in the realm of knowledge (by definition) I interrupt the development of the possibilities of knowing by clear distinctions (it is a powerlessness and an external consideration if I say *after the event* 'I place', 'I attain', 'I interrupt': if I *placed* whatever this was in *the instant*, I would reduce it to its own status, just as the worker puts the final touches to the finished object).[3]

This perspective allows me to recognize the possibilities of a discipline that is different from those which traditionally limit the domain of the human mind. This discipline to which a number of isolated approaches separately respond has not, like philosophy, theology, aesthetics or morality, been given a distinct constitution, but it could receive one. Such perceptions, which are external to philosophy and are not allowed to be reduced either to aesthetics or to ethics – for instance, the idea of 'time recovered' in *À la recherche du temps perdu*, of automatic writing or the aims[4] of surrealist activity as set out in André Breton's *Manifestos*, or others, and (always inseparable from such disjointed teachings) the approaches which preceded them, accompany them or are proposed as their ends – indicate the possibilities of a whole which is external to frameworks that have already been constructed. This perception is aimed at neither goodness nor beauty, neither truth nor God, but an immediate, which has no need of processes that are connected to moral, aesthetic, scientific or religious research. Thus no one could say that Proust or Breton is a philosopher, and if they advance in their privileged direction, equally no one could limit their approaches to those of art. To define them as religious would also introduce confusion: the object of religious desire is always associated with some supporting end (salvation is the least onerous).

These given approaches are the first steps of discoveries which allow entry on an equal footing into the domain to be defined – in which we live without ever recognizing it. Considered methodically, this domain seems accessible on several levels simultaneously. We do not possess a single mode of perception – at least, vague perception – of the instant. We must endlessly choose between immediate interests and concern for the future: the instant is at stake in the slightest desire. But normally it is represented by the shifty lawyer, who expects everything from the judge's exhaustion and timidly pleads for the rights of minors. The significance of the present moment lies in its puerility: I am a man to the extent that I know that I prefer the future. And no matter how great erotic and comical moments of life may be, they have the place for us that playtime has for children. Reason subordinates the heroic moment to services rendered. The poetic and the tragic are highly regarded, but as adornments for minds consecrated to higher ends. Like the hero, the religious man is justified by a set of duties (to the extent that the confused term indicates something that can be isolated) and ecstasy, its purest form, which is less afflicted with subordination, is brought back to the boundless negation of the fugitive moment. All in all, this hardly changes: whether one speaks of the Eternal or of the Void, one concedes the common incapacity to place value in what is fleeting.

If I now do so – not without groping, continuing in the steps of those who started – I establish a new order of thought and behaviour. The perception of the instant, without making an indulgent concession and without justification, presupposes a new discipline. I must:

– acquire knowledge, as clear and distinct as possible, of the domain defined by the words *erotic, comic, poetic, tragic, ecstatic* . . .

– determine how they respond to the desire for the instant, how they leave the door open to provision for the future; how they imply, in contradiction with the value of the immediate, miserable calculations;

– without the shadow of duty and without any *reason* (except this: what is postponed until later will in the end either be reduced to the fleeting instant or will be only a lure ensuring my 'servitude') *live* erotically, comically, poetically, tragically, ecstatically;

– subordinate all thought that touches on the erotic to eroticism, all thought on drunkenness to drunkenness, etc., as theologians subordinate theology to God. The discipline thus depicted in fact differs from philosophy or science in the same way as theology. But God is still a compromise. He is transferred on to an object – conceived on the model of objects from the sphere of activity – of the divine attributes of the immediate. God is the reduction of the immediate to the necessity of dominion. And so theology – itself subordinated to the experience of God – never had more than rights of arbitrary supremacy over philosophy, founded, rather, on a distorted but accessible experience (on the experience granted a few times for all and actually having become inaccessible) of the revelation (the experience of the revelation involves the distortion of all subsequent experience, which is reduced beforehand by faith simultaneously to be both desire and fear of the immediate). It is only in reducing the instant to the instant, the ecstatic to the ecstatic and, at least during the instant, *sine glossa*, that without revelation I advance a discipline (logic and a-logic, morality and immorality, aesthetics and the negation of aesthetics) which has the immediate as its object, as the heir of theology. It was not a folly of the Middle Ages to make philosophy the *ancilla theologiae: the philosophy of a constitutive means is an ancillary activity*. From the moment one ceases to make use of it, and constrains it, it becomes only a floating mass, separating and coming together again, responding to the silence of the sky with a drifting discordance of abstruse discourse. In fact it can resolve nothing. It cannot even attain the absence of a solution. It is only on condition of defining objects of thought on which thought cannot grasp – such as the immediate or the perceptible object is, or such as God was – that it avoids reducing the world to thought (which arranges an endless succession of subordinations). The most perfect – that of Hegel – still results in a system that is so perfect in its servitude, with such a burden of equality in the connection with what is to come (in which nothing ever means anything except in relation to something else), that when all is said and done, totality is reached and the circle is closed, it would no longer differ from the immediate. On the contrary, I assume that it is to the extent that this servile totality is shocking and completely *impossible*[5] (perfect revolt is what one imagines to be most calm) that it *slips* into an *impossible* liberty, into a free madness of the immediate.[6]

Moreover, there is another aspect to this ancillary nature of philosophy. If a man considers himself a philosopher, if he accepts being considered as such (this involves more than being a pastrycook or a

singer), he abandons being a 'complete person'. A pastrycook or a
singer cannot claim to be a 'complete person' as a pastrycook or singer.
To the extent that the philosopher wants to be a 'complete person', he
wants to be so as a philosopher. But in advancing such a claim it
immediately becomes apparent that philosophy is merely a specialized
activity, and that the 'complete person' justifies his character only when
lost in the immediate, and loses it every time he limits himself to a
definite action with a view to an ulterior end. It is the philosopher's
contradiction to be led to confuse a miserable *instrument* with the
totality of being. It is his contradiction, and also his poverty – so much
so that he is profoundly drawn to this ridiculous activity. He had some
difficulty in giving way in the face of the dangerous shadows evoked by
theology: but this is nothing compared with the puerile caprice of the
instant! For the entire being, the immediate, which has no other end
than itself and cannot surpass the instant, departs from the limit of the
puerile only by going beyond that of the possible. If power is sought, it
is absolute authority which opens up to it, but the absolute authority of
the instant is the *amok*, it is the utmost degree of powerlessness.

The relation of the *amok* to totality is expressed in a very beautiful
but disarming way by André Breton in the *Second Manifesto*:

> The simplest surrealist act consists in descending to the street with revolver
> in hand and shooting at random, as fast as one can, into the crowd.
> Whoever has not, at least once in their lives, had such a desire to make an
> end of the trivial system of debasement and cretinization in place had his
> own place marked out in the crowd, belly in line with the barrel . . .

*The discipline I dream about would finally be to philosophy what a complete man
is to a philosopher – or rather, if you prefer, what a theologian would be if he were
God himself!* This proposition certainly relies on a joke: the best thing is
silent, angelic, a sentiment of divine mockery. The inaccessible nature
of the totality of the instant motivates humour (at once angelic and
dark) rather than remorse. Thus: intellectual superiority, as it reduces
the adversary to silence, implies an unbearable task and betrays the
principle it allowed to triumph: I pull the rug from under myself. And
no matter: I am free, powerless, and I will die: *in every sense of the word* I
do not know the limits of duty.

Notes

1. Published in *Deucalion*, no. 2 (June 1947).
2. The common feelings of beauty, pleasure, ugliness, pain, tragedy, comedy, anguish
. . . also respond to moments of greater importance within the given instant, but concern
with the future retains first place there.

3. It is interesting to see a writer as removed from reflective thought as Henry Miller giving this proposition a form that is at once decisive and concise: 'I am a man without a past and without a future. I *am* – that is all' (*Black Spring* [1963], New York: Grove Press, p. 24.); an aesthetic form: 'One must act *as if* the next step were the last: which it is' (p. 26); a lyrical form: 'murder is in the air, chance rules' (*Tropic of Capricorn* [1961], New York: Grove Press, p. 210). This last phrase deliberately comes back to the sentiment of the present moment. We know that Miller considers ecstasy a principle of value.

4. No doubt one could propose the immediate as an end that is without contradictions, but the fact of introducing the instant into the categories of language always creates difficulties. It is not that, in speaking of the instant, one would be wrong to oppose it to ends that had hitherto been sought; it is that in speaking about it in any way one sets in motion a system that is completely in contradiction to its nature.

5. In the sense of 'more than intolerable'.

6. It is true that the immediacy I am talking about is the same thing as Kierkegaard's 'religious' feelings, and it is reached only by means of the negation of ethics. But although the negation and affirmations of K. can be inserted into the closed circle of Hegel's system (which is a dialectic of action and of history), because they are bogged down in history and in action, the negation I introduce takes place only once the circle is closed, beyond the domain of history and action. In fact the instant cannot be 'most important' except to the extent that man no longer has anything to *do*, when he has found Hegelian gratification in which his own dissatisfaction is no longer connected to the active negation of such and such determined form, but to the negation, which no activity can absorb, of the human situation. Thus one sees that this doctrine has a character of anticipation – so much so that social relations would be what they are according to André Breton: 'the artificial precariousness of man's social conditions . . . would veil the real precariousness of the human condition from him'.

Take It or Leave It[1]

To René Char

I have the unshakeable conviction that, come what may, *what deprives man of value – that is, his dishonour and indignity* – carries him away, and must carry him above everything else, has earned the right for everything else to be subordinated to it and, if need be, sacrificed.

In any case, what is *sovereign* is indefensible: in wishing to defend it, one betrays it. It becomes nourishment for the dogs: it is that *which gives man worth, honour and dignity*, as André Gide put it.

Within me there is only the ruin of *sovereignty*. And my visible absence of superiority – my state of collapse – is the mark of an insubordination which equals that of the starry sky.

He who knows only the sovereignty of one of us, itself also analogous with the starry sky, finds no expression other than a powerless silence (a voluntary and unviolated silence simply serves verbosity).

The most idiotic vanity: this silence which conceals anything other than shame.

A sovereign silence: '*Let's dance the capucin . . .*' A *guilty* child: there is no longer an obstacle between my mirror – the immensity of the deep night – and myself (who . . .).

Friends: the laugh up one's sleeve, the hole in the backside, the ecstasy, the night that is completely black.

Perfect *derangement* (abandon to the absence of limits) is the rule of an *absence* of community.

Poetry, written or illustrated, is the only sovereign cry: that's why it leads to those servilities that are worthy of helots made drunk with poetry.

It is not desirable for anyone not to belong to my *absence of community*. In the same way, the *absence of myth* is the only inevitable myth: it fills up the depths like a wind that empties it.

The Problems of

Surrealism[2]

To the extent that my indifference to evil increases, the equanimity founded on harmony and the *yes* given to the universe *as it is*, the imperceptible light-hearted hatred for the revolutionary idea (based on the conviction that the good of the world depends on change), I am conscious of becoming alien, in spite of my own determination but at the same time in an assured way, to the thought of those who read me. Like a stone or a glass of water, like the paucity of a madman's existence.

The sense of escaping from the clockwork regulation of thought (of existing in the beyond as the stone does) is founded on humility: it implies a retreat from the world, and to speak about it is to break the silence only in a superficial way. Today I write to affirm that I am devoted to my absence, again to link up what I say to some less fragile affirmation.

In truth there is nothing daring about my position. There is nothing that calls for a change in those who read me, except in this: they could learn from me that they resemble me, in so far as they do not already realize the fact.

That would be like a death for them!
To exist in the instant is to die, but my death is my imposture; my anguish is disguised delight, and in general unhappiness and death represent only a luxurious setting for life.

Writing is powerless. I do not possess the face and the nakedness of a prostitute and am unable to accuse human life enough for turning itself into an empty façade of which only debauchery gives a faithful presentation.

Like debauchery, truth is silent. It lies as soon as it affirms, it slips away, and it is because language cannot slip away with it that it disguises human life, making of it the things that are a judge, a poet or a political activist.

There is only one man, only one being, only a *liquid* incandescence of eternal instants. Every *thing* slips inevitably towards crime, death or the excess of joy which destroys it, like lumps of coal in the incandescence of a fire.

The incessant and light play of hesitation, the dull allure of language and the laughter of morning, or the excessive opacity of a hearse, does not change the transparency of the universe: from the blind man to someone whom the light floods with joy the distance is nil; knowledge cannot be separated from ecstasy, nor can ecstasy be separated from the horror of non-knowledge. In the same way joy is bound up with unhappiness, modesty with obscenity. What I am saying has simultaneously distinct clarity and obscurity, meaning and absence of meaning, complete ecstasy and complete horror. The intensified horror of Thyestes, experiencing his own cries of horror as an overwhelming delight, were bestowed in the meaning and absence of meaning of each instant. Thyestes, it is true, limited himself: he needed revenge and in the same way, having shabby motives, we escape Thyestes' truth. But the modesty tied to my cheerful obscenity that seeks results is what the pedestal is to the statue, or the altar to the sacrificial murder.

If each person did not consider himself distinct from all others, and separated from others by death (which is, within him, at the same time, ridiculously, nothing less than the end of the whole universe), the sense I have of being a stranger to myself, in the contempt, hatred or powerlessness of passion, would slip away from me: the sense of slipping away from myself in a cruel and voluptuous way would itself slip away from me, and I would not be this obscenity that modesty engenders, this cry of rage prolonged into laughter, this church spasm, this actor's tears.

This is so tortuous that I am sure people will consider my evidence stupid. To consider oneself an ordinary person, but guilty of all crimes, speaking the language of all, with the memory of everything cowardly, false and stupid that language has always translated (and the whole sublime concealed within the multitude) – in a word, to be aware of the *gutter*, not without the light-heartedness and thoughtlessness of the newcomer, being insignificant to the point of horror, without the benefit of horror, finally knowing oneself as eternal – in the eternity of each instant – without hope, pondering pain and the night of all the dead, becoming the monster to whom monstrosity is familiar, for sweetness and purity fuse with spite – spite with sweetness – this is the fate of a silent being, who adds only his tomb to infinite life, only the immense oblivion of what he already is.

> This is tortuous beyond, well beyond, what is acceptable, and yet:
> This summit of waking sleeps.
> The summit of waking is sleep, and through it absolute silence.

II

There is nothing less innocent (such a trivial reason at the origin of determination!) than the writer's starting point. Nevertheless, he writes as if the phrases were already displayed outside time, as in a book:

'There can be *nothing* sacred. The sacred cannot be a *thing*. The instant alone is sacred, which is *nothing* (is not a *thing*).

'A group, a party, a doctrine, a principle put forward as sacred, signifies what is sacred put in the service of a group, a party, a principle which cannot itself be sacred.

'What is sacred is ungraspable.

'In order to grasp it, I place it at the service of *that* which I determine, which I turn into a thing. I confound it with *that*. From this moment I can subordinate myself to. . . . It is not enough.

'Does something sacred direct all my actions? But if it is true that an action must necessarily be subordinated to some sacred end, must finally have only the meaning of a useless consummation, prepared by it, action is first what cries out within me the possible consummation, which is its exact opposite: it is an effort made with an end in view.

'But how to express the unease of the person who perceives this impasse, who perceives it at the summit of the possible and cries out: "The summit is the impossible"? He awakens for a moment at this response, which has the simplicity of death. But if he writes, he has already fallen asleep again.

'Apart from Communism, there is only a verbose and pitiful agitation connected to individual errors. Communism itself depends on problematic affirmations, but it has the merit of not being bound to them. Its universal and silent strength neither expresses nor affirms, but offers itself in the precision of acts.

'To my mind the immense value of Communism is to create silence – wildly, grossly – through a language deprived of meaning, which has truth only for one class, itself deprived of truth (and forced to act). Only the silence would be absolute, but the language whose banishment established absolutism has the advantage over what cannot be an equation of silence, but wants to be. What is sacred for a worker is always the illusion that the *thing* is: it is the *life of the worker*, but Communism has the crazy strictness to deny in action the *very thing* which it established as the sacred reason to act. It thereby – precisely because of that – goes beyond the naive machinery by which the sacred *thing* needs to maintain itself as both *thing* and sacred. The greatness of Communism is founded on the falsehood imposed at the same time on the world and its own followers; in this it maintains precisely that for Communism *nothing is sacred*.

'Hatred of Communism, which does not connect its affirmations, reduces to a complacent affirmation, to a mournful paralysis, to the powerlessness that duplicates the vain hope – or the necessity – of affirming sacred *things*. The lie of the enemy of Communism is greater than that of Communism itself: in no way can it surpass it; it limits itself to verbal respect for an idol which it knows is false, since it no longer has any doubt about the fact that *nothing* is sacred.

'Poetry is sacred in so far as it is *nothing*. The truth of modern poetry is to have deprived poetry of *substance*.

'Just as a *thing* cannot be sacred, so liberty cannot be contained within laws. As the sacred consumes and destroys things, so liberty is opposed to laws.

'*How* to write, except as a usually chaste woman getting undressed for an orgy?

'The existence of Communism and its rigorousness, its undeniable power to deprive those who attack it of truth, the impossibility of finding anything outside it other than passivity, inanity or servitude, is the test to which we are put. It requires of us displacement and incessant vigilance. Who can sleep in the face of the Communist resolution condemned to substitute prison walls for our verbiage? Who does not see that he will either come out of himself *awakened*, or go to the dregs? How can we not admire the excessive tension in which we are held? But how do we resist the test?

'People wrongly think that I am a nihilist interested only in Diony-sian excess. *The awakening to the impossible* is not a misfortune (any more than it is good fortune). Beyond the liberation is the *calm* of waking in which, following the necessary displacement, begins man's *friendship* with himself.[3] It would betray him at the first moment of relaxation.

'Communism is the contrary of this *peace* of man with himself. But *peace* demanded the tension that Communism has created. This *peace* would be servile to the least release of tension. Sovereignty has no right to the least servitude.'

Notes

1. Published in *Troisième convoi*, no. 3 (November 1946).

2. But why connect these problems specifically to surrealism? Are they not, more generally, those of mankind itself? But in general man is *silence*. There is no problem for him, everything has been brought into play, everything finished. While the surrealist, just like those who, in their turn, advanced liberatory possibilities – like the little girl playing hopscotch – leaps ahead on one foot. By declining the possibility of *taking rest*, he remains alone in the world.

3. Of course, one could be mistaken. I am not surprised that, according to Claudine Chonez, Albert Camus said (*Portrait d'Albert Camus* by Claudine Chonez, in *Paru*, October 1948): 'Bataille's Nietzscheanism doesn't seem very orthodox to me . . . [Nietzsche's] critique of European nihilism is still relevant, and can still be used against Bataille himself.' Camus adds (again according to Claudine Chonez) that nothing remains positive in Nietzsche except 'pride and its philosophical justifications'. 'We have paid,' he says again, 'and we are still paying a high price for some of them.' I don't doubt that I have left a false trail, and I do not protest, but to the end I have sought the implications and significance of Nietzsche's experience. I have discovered there *only* the most open experience beginning from a collapse, in which I speak, as far as I am concerned, of repetition. I could well have given these pages the title 'Nietzschean Problems', and I would have done so if I did not feel so alone in my 'repetition'. Some of Camus's words about Nietzsche are perhaps not correctly reported, but they seem to me to imply the usual judgement of Nietzsche; his experience is considered from outside. The remainder of the conversation about me between Claudine Chonez and Camus seems to turn entirely on a misunderstanding, because finally for me, as for Nietzsche – and *as for Camus* – there could be no world beyond. I gladly take these words – this time very Nietzschean – of Albert Camus for my own part: 'Europe's secret is that it does not like life, and so it has chosen to love what is beyond present-day life' (p. 13). But Europe here is *Communism*, the grandeur and poverty of which in fact arise from the negation of the present moment. It is true that death does not seem to me to be the contrary but, rather, the profusion of life, and the affirmation of the present moment (certitude that primacy of the future brings war, while that of the present moment is the only measure of peace) brings me closer to Camus than he thinks. I opposed him at first: I had the

hope that *my opposition* would show him not the diversity but the *unity* of mind in collapse. Then, that the collapse, or the absurd, releases rather than destroys the truth of awakened man. But this is a difficult truth (for a mind formed by logic). I mean that it called for happiness *now or never*, and that this requires a rigour of principles of economy, politics and morality in proportion to the tension of the present world. I put forward nothing by chance.

The Moral Meaning of

Sociology[1]

The generation that reached maturity between the two wars approached the problem of society under conditions that deserve to be recognized. In the humanist culture of its elders, which it inherited, all value was placed in the individual. Through the implicit judgements it made, this culture reduced society to an evil – a necessary one, perhaps, but even its necessity was brought into question. Juvenile ardour, but little more, followed an instinctive negation that expressed a revolutionary will. Or at least, its trace was there. In those days I do not recall that anyone before me had defended the rights of society against those of the individual: founded on the exploitation of man by man, it was the edifice itself that had to be destroyed, and one could have no other ambition than to precipitate the collapse. Such a clear principle was a cause for celebration, and was not subject to discussion. All the same, difficulties were encountered in practice.

If it was necessary to fight to bring down the social edifice, then one also needed to sacrifice an individual's desires to the necessities of a revolution. And the revolution soon reveals its true nature: it is a collective movement, having as its end the instigation of a new society, which expects nothing less than the previous society had of the individuals who comprise it (and may even require more).

This recognition led the intellectuals of this generation to see in collective reality and its meaning for the individual an experience that was unexpected and even oppressive. That of which they had been, in a constitutional fashion, the negation (they denied with every fibre of their beings the constraints of collective values), by a reversal suddenly became their affirmation, but this affirmation no longer related to the old system of hypocrisy and deception with which it was possible to come to an accommodation. It then became necessary for them to affirm what, in the revolutionary order, was of a sudden nature and, if they affirmed it, it could only reduce the individual they had been to silence.

The temptations of compromise became unacceptable, and even those who could not or would not give way no longer existed merely in an empty and false world: there was a reality that was superior to them, which called into question for themselves life and death. No doubt they could still curse it, but they were condemned to live within the terms it imposed.

On the other hand, the extinction of the possibilities of individualist culture coincided with a reminder of the brutal truths of a historical world. By its ambition, poetry – and, more generally, literature and art – as it unfolded, finally exceeded the limits imposed by the cultivated individual, the distinguished (rich or poor) bourgeois, constrained to isolation and to distinction. Between the two wars poetry ceased to be seen as the supreme honour of an isolated individual. From this perspective surrealism was decisive; it caused the poetic text to become the expression of common elements in a way similar to what was revealed by dreams. It was seen that features inaccessible to the majority, and the disregard for a reality that was independent of personal fortune, reduced the meaning of a written text to social distinction – in other words, to the void. On the other hand, liberated in principle from individual anxiety and generally from all inherited rules, modern art assumed elements in common with so-called primitive art. And the artists themselves were tempted to assimilate their work to the collective creation of exotic peoples. In particular, myths, analogous in certain respects to dreams, cannot be entirely separated from recent poetic findings. It is true that a modern poem has none of the meaning of a myth, but a myth sometimes has the same attraction as a modern poem. Without providing a solution to such questions, psychoanalysis, to the extent that surrealist invention derives from it, was itself a connecting feature between these different domains.

From the beginning, the desire for a revolutionary action had been drawn towards an interest in Marxist sociology, as well as to the revolutionary society of the USSR. Interest in myths and the various religious activities of exotic peoples drew attention to the superiority of collective over individual creation, and thereby to sociology and ethnography, in particular to the Durkheimian theory defining religious activities and myths as a manifestation of a collective being superior to the individual and named society.

*

Until about 1930, the influence of Durkheim's sociological doctrine had barely gone beyond the university domain. It had no influence in the arena of intellectual fever. Durkheim had been dead for a long time when young writers emerging from surrealism (Caillois, Leiris, Monnerot) began following the lectures of Marcel Mauss, whose remarkable teaching was fully in accord with the founder of the school. It is difficult to define exactly what they sought; this differed somewhat between individuals. There was only a vague orientation, independent of the personal interests which explain it. Detachment from a society that was disintegrating because of individualism and the malaise resulting from the limited possibilities of the individual domain was combined here. Although we cannot assume the same value for every one of them, there was possibly a great attraction to realities which, as they establish social bonds, are considered sacred. These young writers felt more or less clearly that society had lost the secret of its cohesion, and this was precisely what the obscure, uneasy and sterile efforts of poetic fever sought to address. Occasionally they ceased to despair, and no longer considered the possibility of rediscovering it absurd. This sort of research alone seemed to be vital and worthy of one's energy against the effeminate magic and tricks of art.

Besides, they were less interested in a new experience, which would have continued surrealism, than in scientific research. They felt a certain aversion to a past connected to literary ferment, and what they refused most adamantly was any possibility of a compromise, in a superficial science that would be used for the ends of a doubtful enterprise. No doubt they considered whether the sterility of pure knowledge did not follow on in this way from the powerlessness of art, but the demand for rigour and intellectual honesty was opposed in them to the need, which was stronger for others, that thought should engender action. The need for society to create the rarest values and the impulse towards sociological studies did not, in fact, lead to action, and if it is possible to speak about it today, it is rather in order to determine the sense of lack and a nostalgia related to the present condition of social life. In fact it is doubtful whether, in the limited sphere of scientific knowledge, great consequences could result from it.[2] But this new area of interest undoubtedly bore witness to a considerable sense of unease. A work like *Les faits sociaux ne sont pas des choses*, the most recent of the publications related to these 'sociological' tendencies,[3] owes part of its importance to a rather remarkable coincidence: the categories Monnerot puts forward as being the basis of a science of society respond to the needs I mentioned, and bear witness to their necessity.

I even feel that it is difficult to appreciate the significance of this book without being aware of its moral origins. This does not mean that Jules Monnerot's argument would be deprived of scientific value in

having a subjective character: his development justifies these corres-
pondences, and the method he has used is for the most part as rigorous
as anyone could require. But the general description of social forms,
which is the result of it, does not make any less explicit the content of
tendencies that were given birth in the conditions that existed during
the period between the wars.

Monnerot judiciously sets sociological research in motion with
modest statements, and limits himself to defining a small number of
categories, simple 'points of departure which the development of
research will later bring into question or serve to place in a completely
different perspective'.

The most important of these categories are those of the sacred and
the profane (which Monnerot generalizes into *heterogeneous* and *homogeneous*), societies of affect and of contract, of 'Bund' and secret society.

Monnerot underlines the significance of the category of the sacred,
and does not limit it to a vague definition founded on the traditional
use of the word. Since the end of the nineteenth century, sociological
research had in fact shown that the domain represented by this
category had been double in the primitive sense, designating, as it does
today, both the purest elements and their contraries, those that are
absolutely impure (in the Middle Ages we can still find the expression
Morbus sacer being used to define a venereal disease). In order to
displace accepted limits (if one is talking about a domain defined by its
distinct character) and anticipate difficulties, one consequently had to
admit the necessity of basing definition on characteristics that are not
made explicit. It cannot be denied that the Hindu category of *Untouch-
ables* has a 'sacred' character. But if the way Europeans treat unfortu-
nates does not have the same excessive and ostentatious quality, its
source is exactly the same, and has the same meaning. There is a sort of
'horrible majesty', an unassimilable quality, about the man of the lower
depths in our towns, which is not foreign to the character of the sacred.
One must at least determine a more general characteristic founded on
the equivalence of a beggar in London and an *outcaste* in Bengal.

The interest of this comparison – which brings into question important aspects of the description of society – could at first appear to be
external to the subjective preoccupations implied by 'sociological
trends'. But this category of heterogeneity – within which species the
sacred should be considered as a genus – is not like the sacred
primarily determined externally (that is, by an ethnologist's observation comparable to that of the biologist observing an insect), but more
generally from both inside and outside, since it is conditional upon
reactions which we experience ourselves. And it is Monnerot's merit –
as well as his overriding aim – to show us that social facts cannot be

considered as things. Besides, if the representatives of 'sociological trends' had seen in social facts only things, in their eyes they would have taken no other meaning than the constraint which had first opposed them to society. But by starting with Durkheim's thesis identifying the sacred with the social, a preliminary extension of the envisaged domain to lived experience established a perceptible bond, which is independent of constraint by the social. And the 'man of the lower depths' is not the only one who offers a possibility of living an experience of this type: the poet, above all the accursed poet ('accursed' being a variant of *sacer* in the inauspicious sense) is no longer anything more than a ragamuffin reducible to the standards of present-day life; he is no more *useful* than a ragamuffin. 'The heterogeneous', writes Monnerot,

> can be shown to be anything irreducible to assimilation: the madman, the 'accursed poet' like Lautréamont or Rimbaud before he fled to Harrar, the unyielding insubordinate, the 'intractable criminal on whom the prison door always closes', but also the outsider with no profession (since a profession is a mark of homogeneity) like Marx or Comte, who lived off the subsidies of their friends; Kierkegaard and Nietzsche, who both in their own way refused to comply with the general; Blanqui, who was almost always in prison and, as soon as he was released, always exhorted the people to rise up against the established order; all those who are 'in breach of convention': not merely the kind-hearted prostitute but the prostitute *per se*, the pimp, and everyone who would be part of what the old jurists would have called the 'dangerous classes'.

In this way, though, through an inevitable slippage, the category of the sacred extends to the realm of our own lives.

What is remarkable is that considered within the limits of the present time, it rarely seems any longer to have anything to do with social cohesion, and even seems most often to be antisocial in character. Where it had once been the sacred – or heterogeneous – elements that established cohesion, instead of constituting society and social bonds, it could well now represent nothing but its subversion.

This possible reversal can usefully be compared with the other distinctions Monnerot considers fundamental. Following Tönnies he introduces the categories of 'belonging' (in German *Gemeinschaft*, usually translated as community) and 'contractual society' (in German *Gesellschaft*, in general the equivalent of society). It seems to me that Monnerot, in opposing *Gesellschaft* to *heterogeneity*, could have translated it, in a way that would have retained Tönnies's meaning, as 'homogeneous society'. In fact what it involves is a mode of association in which exchange is fundamental, 'in which the principle of exchange has been taken to its logical conclusion so that everything becomes exchange.' This describes industrial society, which is founded on personal interest and in which every thing and every being has its proper place. It even seems to me possible to argue that it is in just such a society (or any society with a tendency to reduce itself to homogeneity) that the sacred (or heterogeneous) elements generally acquire a subversive value. While social bonding, or the community, as a rule excluding both selfish motives and conscience, is, on the contrary, founded, in conformity with Durkheim's schema, on elements of the same order which are no less irreducible to homogeneity than rebels are, but no less differing from the latter than saints. In such circumstances the reversal of values would be determined by social evolution. If you like, it could crudely be said that what is of a sacred nature founds the social bond in an authentic society, but within an aggregate that is no longer founded on social bonding but on personal interest it tends, on the contrary, towards its destruction.

The category of 'Bund' – of a secondary community – introduces a final distinction into this list of possibilities of collective life. What Monnerot defines under the name of belonging is, on the whole, the basis of society: it is the community of blood and vicinity. Every society defines its bonds of belonging, but such bonds do not always extinguish the desire people have to combine together with those like them in a social bond. Mere belonging is doubtless a significant response to the desire to bind, and the necessity for common action assures its continuance. But occasionally the knot that founds it – whether subjectively, through the acts of the individual, or objectively, in the act of perceptible dissolution – can eventually have only the force of an attenuated attraction. From that point the individual is available, and new aggregates become possible. In the majority of cases the new bond does not involve the renunciation of the first bond: the belonging of fact remains fundamental. I can join the Communist Party, the Freemasons, or some international religious Order, without for a moment ceasing to belong to the French community. If need be, the new bond follows on from a choice taken (as the belonging issues from contiguity); anyway, it is not reducible to simple proximity: another element intervenes. Since this element is not given in fact, the secondary community needs a commitment and must have recourse to some form of 'creative effervescence' if it is to endure. Like the community of fact, every secondary community tends to decline, but the form this decline takes is often no more than a reduction to the state of a community of fact (Islam has taken this reduction to its logical conclusion; the Christian Church stops halfway, but one is still born Christian as one is born French; to belong to a church differs little from a community of fact).

The importance of the last category should be emphasized. If it is true that the social bond brings our most distant aspirations into play (brought into the light under the name of religion) and that we can respond to such aspirations only through the formation of the social bond (which would testify to the fact that the separated being is not complete, that an individual is complete only in so far as he ceases to distinguish himself from others, from his fellow beings), the possibility of secondary communities becomes necessarily, for each of us, the decisive question. The belonging of fact cannot satisfy us, since it does not allow our relation with others to be founded on what is, according to the choice we make, most important for us. We are complete only outside ourselves, in the human plenitude of an assembly, but we become complete only if, as we gather together, we do so in a way that responds to our intimate demands. Thus to the extent that we no longer want to be disfigured and ridiculous in our own eyes, we are in search of a secondary community whose aims are in complete accord with our being. The consciousness of these truths was fundamental in the renewed interest of which sociology was the object. But the 'sociological tendencies' served only to give a character of precise research to commonly shared anxieties.

I will cite only the most singular of examples. From his adolescence to his death, Nietzsche had hoped to found an *order* (what we know of his life and his writings testifies to it). Usually his philosophy is considered to exist at the summit of individualism, but this had meaning in his own eyes only in so far as it was connected with the idea of a community. It was a preoccupation that was also transferred to the intellectual field: Nietzsche submitted to the organicism of Espinas. He tended to consider the entirety of individuals comprising the social being as analogous to the unity of cells forming the individual being: the 'great individuals' (I am using a term used by Monnerot) meant something only in so far as they constituted a mother-cell of a new whole, of a secondary community, of a recast and rejuvenated society. 'Your nobility', he said, 'shall not gaze backward, but *outward*! You shall be fugitives from all fatherlands and forefatherlands! You shall love your *children's land*. . . . You shall *make amends* to your children for being the children of your fathers.'[4] One could not more clearly oppose the secondary community to the belonging of fact.

A preoccupation of the same order animates surrealism. In his first book (*La poésie moderne et le sacré*) Monnerot underlines the 'Bund' character of the surrealist group in the interwar period. But the desire to establish a cohesion on a myth, to give the group a form that would recall that of initiatory societies, still seems uppermost today in André Breton's mind. Among other passages, the *Prolégomènes pour un troisième manifeste du surréalisme ou non* (1944), as well as the series of articles in *VVV* devoted to an aborted attempt (otherwise external to surrealism), bear witness to this.

*

Here it is necessary to register a regret. . . . Monnerot's book reveals these problems but it does not, as I have just done, give the details. On the whole, he approaches them in an ephemeral way. This bias seems legitimate, given that this is a scientific work concerned precisely with methodology. But as the title indicates, the author's aim is to show that social facts cannot be taken for things, and their actual *meaning* ought to matter, especially to the sociologist. It is regrettable, therefore, that Monnerot, as a sociologist, has not made explicit the *meaning* that is conjectured in the midst of the categories he examines.

Had he done so, I do not believe that his distaste for talking about himself would have been called into question, but he would not have taken his judicious critique of Durkheimianism to the point of neglecting essential elements of the doctrine. These parts seem to me also to be the most solid. But most especially, as it is passed over in silence, the *meaning* sociology took is not made explicit. I believe that Monnerot's avowed aim has not really been to make this meaning explicit. But his book would have gained in clarity had he done so. And as this would have meant that he would have done justice to Durkheim, the criticisms made about him would not have seemed excessive.

The essential and solid part of Durkheim's doctrine seems to me to be based on two propositions:

- that society is completely different from the sum of its parts;

- that religion – or, more precisely, the sacred – is the bond, the constitutive element, of everything that is society.

No doubt the extremely inflexible conclusions Durkheim drew from these principles, without waiting for – even denying in advance – any opposition encountered through experience, themselves have an excessive quality which Monnerot's critique is far from sharing. But it is dangerous to criticize only excessive propositions, for finally they leave the principle intact. To make a distinction between the whole and the parts by no means implies, as Durkheim wanted it to imply, that the determinism of society would be exclusively sociological, in defiance of any psychological cause. But to admit a psychological – or economic –

factor does not, in its turn, signify that the whole would be the sum of its parts. Monnerot does not say anything about this, so he deprives his sociological principles of a fundamental element, both in the realm of scientific research and on the plane of the inevitable *meaning* of the research. It even seems to me that in neglecting this point he is induced to put forward some confused propositions. Speaking of animal societies, he accepts Raboud's theories, in which physiological factors of inter-attraction become the basis of social fact. Hymenopterans and halictidae are sometimes attracted by each other, or others, and thus form undetermined groups. But a society, particularly an animal one, is not an open and indefinite aggregate: it is a defined whole which is no less founded on inter-attractions between its members than on the inter-repulsion of individuals of the same nature but belonging to different unities. Raboud's error even has an advantage: it serves to define the essence of social fact. This distinguishes a molecule: it is not a *mélange* of atoms but a hermetic whole that is different from a juxtaposition of atoms. And what distinguishes society is the fact that – radically differentiating it from a crowd, which is formed by the inter-attraction of similar individuals – it is a whole limited by individuals forming a whole that is different from a crowd.

*

It may even be that the consciousness of this radical difference, to which we are brought by more and more rapid subversions in the forms of social life, may introduce a new possibility into history: possibly people will finally realize clearly that there is no internal debate so profound that the historical movement of human societies alone cannot give it a *meaning*, and recognize at the same time that the *meaning* of this movement is not exhausted unless it is taken to the source of its intimate echoes.

Notes

1. Review of *Les faits sociaux ne sont pas des choses*, by Jules Monnerot (1946), Paris: Gallimard; published in *Critique*, no. 1 (June 1946).
2. In this respect the work that Jules Monnerot brings to bear today on the foundations of sociology is certainly not negligible (it could reveal the point of departure for future research), but he is isolated and a long way off the beaten track of orthodox science.
3. Jules Monnerot's first book, *La poésie moderne et le sacré* (Paris: Gallimard, 1945), already bore witness to this orientation. All Roger Caillois's books have a relation with the tendency even if Caillois disavows his earlier position today – at least in certain

respects. Michel Leiris's sociological work has generally remained on the purely scientific terrain, and has made little notable impression on his literary works (with the
exception of *L'Afrique fantôme*).

[4. *Thus Spake Zarathustra*, trans. R.J. Hollingdale [1961], Harmondsworth: Penguin,
p. 221. – *Translator*]

War and the Philosophy

of the Sacred[1]

The realm we call the *sacred* cannot be left to sociologists, even if, in our civilized world, the use of this word has become questionable if we do not frame it with reference to sociology. It is sociology alone that has given it a meaning without which it would apparently mean something rather different. Doubtless theology will refuse to withdraw from the field completely, but as a rule theology rejects a considerable part of the sociological domain. In particular, it does not take into account the religions of primitive and ancient peoples . . . When it does emerge from its ignorance, its knowledge is taken from sociology. In this way the use of the word is strictly controlled by science.

This is neither insignificant nor untenable, but it cannot be entirely justified. Science always *abstracts* the object it studies from the *totality* of the world. It detaches, it separates the atom or the cell and studies them in a detached way, and if it reintegrates these objects into greater wholes, it must still maintain their isolation: they are objects of science only to the extent that they can be considered separately. It might in turn be pointed out that the *sacred* can just as easily be envisaged on its own. Possibly it can, and the results obtained may support such a proposition. The writings of sociologists have a power not only over those who read them but also – and perhaps even stronger – over those who write them. But a question remains: suppose that the *sacred*, far from being, like the other objects of science, subject to separation, is defined as the exact opposite of abstract objects (things, tools, and clearly definable elements), precisely as the concrete totality itself is resistant to it.

Certainly, at first sight, this seems false. The *sacred* cannot be identified with concrete totality, at least to the extent that the *profane* itself must comprise part of the totality we must propose if we are to define the *sacred*.

But when one looks closer, what is the profane if not the sum of objects abstracted from the totality? The sacred world is a world of communication or contagion, where nothing is separated and a special effort is required to remain outside the undetermined fusion. It could even be said that the profane state is the necessary prerequisite for abstraction of the object from the totality of being. Take the example of the corpse: it can be dissected and treated as an object of science only to the extent that it passes – even if this scandalizes the devout or superstitious – from the domain of the sacred to that of the profane.

I can think of no better way to measure the difference between *profane* and *sacred* than to consider this distressing situation. From my own perspective – that is, as the author of a review – this is not without difficulty. The subject engages me at a distance. On the other hand, as I speak of the *sacred*, I need to recognize that I am still in the arena of the *profane*. It is true that I would like to escape from it, that I contest one's right to speak of the *sacred* in the way sociologists do – that is exclusively, as if it were the first thing to hand in respect of objects of science. It is none the less necessary to emerge from the ambiguity to which I am condemned. It is then that I realize how difficult this is. In fact, if I speak of the *sacred* as such – especially, as far as possible, avoiding disguising it and first transforming it into the *profane* – I fall subject to an even graver prohibition. I cannot ignore it, but I come from it at the moment of rupture.

To return to the example of the dead body, something which as a rule is considered to be sacred everywhere, but which ceases to be so on a dissecting table, where it has the status of a profane object, an abstract object, an object of science. From the first, therefore, it appears that the same object can be both sacred and profane, depending on the situation in which it is located. Let us now consider this dead body of a child upon which the scientist works and for whom it is an anatomical object presented to scholarly observation in its concrete totality. If I wish to extend the whole range of possibilities I cannot leave things there, but must move on from the scientist's reactions to those of the mother, if we can imagine her in the same room.

For the mother, what is at stake at that moment is the totality of being . . . . And without any doubt, her grief will accuse the scientist of placing her child's totality of being at risk. She would, nevertheless, be wrong: the scientist has before him nothing but an abstract object. Only the philosopher has, if not the opportunity, then the obligation to experience what the child represents for the mother through her grief (even dearer and more sacred because of the death which has for ever separated him from the banal and futile objects by which, when he was alive, he escaped the empty horror – which is totality, which is time – in the gulf into which everything is thrown in advance and confounded).

I have not wanted to express in a few words *everything* that the *totality* of what exists represents for the philosopher. By this example I merely wish to show a correspondence of relations. What concrete reality is in relation to objects considered in isolation, the *sacred* can be to the *profane*. The totality is itself defined in opposition to objects. And the profane object is not essentially something different from the *sacred*. In both cases there is simply a change of perspective.

In every respect it seems that my reflections illuminate the difficulty that surrounds study of the object of religion, the *sacred*, if it is considered merely within the perspective of the profane.

The *sacred* cannot simply be what it expresses as an object to which I would remain as remote and indifferent as I am to the banal parquet floor. On the contrary, the *sacred* is offered as an object which always matters intimately to the subject: the object and the subject, if I speak of the *sacred*, always interpenetrate, or exclude each other (in resistance to the strong danger of interpenetration), but always, whether in association or in opposition, complete each other. And there can be no doubt at all that I cannot escape from the consequences. The *sacred* cannot be limited to the distant experience of ancients and primitives, any more than it can be limited, in so far as we are concerned with it here, to the experience of 'revealed' religions. For us it is not a question of religion: the world we live in remains, in its depths, permeated with the *sacred*. In particular, our behaviour in relation to death and the dead does not differ less from that of animals than from that of people who have remained very religious: it differs from it precisely in that death and the dead deeply upset us, although if we reacted rationally, we would have to consider them in the same way as the scientist does. What is more, our irrational reactions are already in existence. When we see one of our fellow men alive, if death cannot congeal his features without rending my heart, in a sense his face is already sacred for me.

This does not by any means go against the data of objective science. In *Elementary Forms of Religious Life*, Durkheim himself, as he objectively envisages the behaviour of Australian Aborigines, generally considers the individual, the human being, to be one form of the *sacred*. But the question is not so much to know whether we can, from outside, gain access to the distinct knowledge that the forms of religion embody as to know if this type of disinterested knowledge does not itself serve to alter the meaning of what it reveals, even if we claim to be able to separate it from the heart-rending that affects us in the face of death. Besides, this debasement cannot be considered inevitable, but if, having defined the *sacred* objectively, we can consequently no longer transform this external knowledge into intimate and subjective experience, has this not served to sacrifice the substance for the shadow?

*

The issue is in fact presented in a complex way. I suspect that in addition to Durkheim's rules of objectivity, a sort of modesty has often prevented French sociologists from indicating the line from subjective to objective knowledge. But this scholarly modesty finally engenders considerable disquiet. If the archaic world is compared with ours, the domain that sociologists describe cannot fail to look impoverished. Even if science had the desire to explore both its archaic forms (which, in the way of things, seem accessible only externally) and its current forms, the latter, from the first, would have been treated only as evidence, as vague survivals of a marvellous past. As a rule the consciousness of the *sacred* risked, from the beginning, assuming a character of nostalgia rather than experience. Only within narrow limits can we speak today of what we take to be sacred: if we dream of vanished civilizations, or of those which are in the process of disappearing before our very eyes, what is at issue is *the quest for a lost paradise*. In current society, in which rapid changes are often deceptive in so far as they distance us from a world whose ruins and irreplaceable beauty give us only the sense of a decline, it seems to us that we indeed lack an essential factor of life. But the science of sociologists, which reveals this lack, not only does not guide the quest which follows – its fundamental principles serve to prevent us from even undertaking it.

These considerations are necessary if we want to understand the significance of Roger Caillois's book. It is above all the work of a sociologist, and is essentially limited to objectivity. Caillois seeks to speak of the sacred in a *general* sense (this much is apparent from the title he has chosen), but this generality is restricted by the commitment to objectivity. The first edition, which was published on the eve of the war in 1939 (and for this reason did not receive the attention it deserved), is a masterly exploration of what science has learned about archaic societies. Our first impression is that this involves little that affects our own lives.

But such an impression is deceptive. I do not simply refer to the fact that at the end of the book the author devotes a few pages to the evolution of the *sacred* in the modern world. This adds nothing of great significance to what precedes it. Caillois discusses the practice whereby not only is nothing examined in depth, but nothing can be. Moreover, he rightly insists on one point: the modern world tends 'to consider everything as profane and to treat it accordingly'. He is more precise:

The sacred becomes internalized and now is of interest only to the soul. . . . All external criteria appear insufficient from the moment the sacred is abstracted from collective manifestation towards a pure attitude of consciousness . . . It is with good reason that, in such conditions, we use the word '*sacred*' outside the properly religious domain to designate what each of us considers embodies what is most precious, what we each possess as a supreme value, what is venerated, and for which we would, if necessary, sacrifice our life.

And so what is sacred is conditioned, even determined, only by freedom of adherence.

Everything takes place, as though the mere attachment to a supreme end and the consecration of one's life to it (which means devoting one's time and energy, interests and ambition, and if necessary sacrificing one's existence to it) is enough to render a particular object, cause or being sacred.

To my mind, this is hardly more than a banal extension of the meaning of the word. Likewise, in an even more offhand way, a merchant who sells off stock cheaply says that he *sacrifices* it. Caillois even believes that gold has become sacred for the miser (and this is by no means his most profane example). The *sacred* seems to me to be opposed both to utility and to the passions whose object conforms with reason. Passion, of course, can be so great that the value of its object might become *comparable* to that of the *sacred*. Nevertheless, a taboo is still to be found at the base of the *sacred*, one established against convulsive behaviour which, detached from calculation, was originally animal. Omophagia, that form of sacrifice in which the victim is devoured alive by the unrestrained participants, is doubtless the most complete image of the *sacred*, implying as it always does an element of horror and criminality. Even for a Protestant theologian like Otto, the *sacred* is not only *fascinans*, it is also *tremendum* and terrifying. The *sacred* demands the violation of what is normally the object of terrified respect. Its domain is that of destruction and death. Caillois understands this, for he concludes the main part of his book with these words: 'The truth of the sacred resides simultaneously in the fascination of the flame and the horror of putrefaction . . . '[2] Moreover, this truth is connected to a more precise statement, founded in a well-known experience, that of Saint Teresa of Avila:

contact with the sacred inaugurated a sorrowful conflict between the intoxicating hope of definitively falling into a deep abyss and the kind of sluggishness with which the profane weighs down every movement towards the sacred. Saint Teresa herself attributes this to the instinct for self-preservation. Returning this being that dies to life, so that it should not die, this sluggishness seems like the exact counterpart of the ascendency exercised by the sacred upon the profane. It always tries, for its part, to renounce time in favour of a leap in the ephemeral and extravagant glory.[3]

*

I have drawn these two insights from the final pages, in which Caillois has sought to make an incursion – for which he apologizes – into the domain of 'metaphysics'. I conclude from the fact that he indicates – albeit implicitly – that *for us* the consciousness of a value of the *sacred* goes beyond what it is possible to gain from scholarly knowledge. Finally, it is necessary for him to allow a glimpse of the fundamental truth that man has always chosen between two options. On the one hand there is the need to protect the future, something which demands a 'constant search for a balanced or just equilibrium that permits living in fear and moderation without exceeding the limits of the allowable. One is content with a gilded mediocrity'[4] . . . 'the departure from this tranquillity . . . is equivalent to the entrance of the sacred into the world'.[5] This is an oversimplification, since we can leave security behind and sometimes risk everything without ever rising above a sordid calculation of advantages and disadvantages, dominated by profane interest. It is necessary to point out that even in those religious rituals in which the *sacred* is most readily apparent – in sacrifice, in festival, in orgies – the profane perspective remains, in a sense, an immutable backcloth: such rituals have, for example, agrarian aims, but the extent to which they are subordinated to these ends seems uncertain. In the course of the festival, such goals have less meaning than the festival itself. Of course it is possible to conceive that the festival possesses a value independent of the advantages expected from it: its emphasis is placed on the present time. In the usual transition from security to risk, the emphasis remains on the expected result. What remains *essential* is something which is closer to us and can be formulated in this way: whatever form it is given, no matter how awkwardly, we cannot evoke the world we must name as *sacred* with impunity: the examination of the *sacred*, of moments of consumption that are so intense that they are frightening (because death soon seems to be its limit), leads us without duplicity to confront the dilemmas Caillois has clearly posed, to which a more immediate examination is nevertheless pertinent. It is a matter of properly defining what in our behaviour is gained by immediate interest (this is also the question raised by Kant), which is opposed to interested behaviour which, in the last analysis, gains to the extent to which we await later possibilities of disinterested behaviour. In a word, it is a question of defining what *pleases*. Alerted by a rigorous consideration of the *sacred*, we would not be amazed to recognize that *pleasure* is always an intense consummation of energy and resources. That is to say, this intensity is something dangerous, not to say frightening. The role fear plays is clearly definable: without fear it would be an insignificant consummation. A worthwhile consummation is always the most frightening that can be faced without fainting – without fleeing or turning away. Of course, if he were strong enough, the only complete consummation a man might make of himself would be death, which always remains the privileged sign of the *sacred* (of the *sacred*, that is to say, of *life* at its most intense and audacious): 'death, that leap of momentary and squandered splendour'. Death, at least, has the advantage of putting an end to this burden that causes us to seek for ourselves a greater power of generosity, instead of directly beneficent conditions. Even more unsatisfactory, perhaps, is the power of being avaricious, something which causes our being to become burdened with values that close off all thought, and our character to assume the form of wretches greedy for that vanity whose unity is called 'philosophy'. Death alone leads thought towards the fear that dissolves it, and causes it to believe that silence alone terminates it.

At this point it is necessary to be precise about what this essential dilemma supposes: the *sacred* places being itself in question inasmuch as it is fragment rather than totality, yet is itself attached to the fragments. That is to say, *in so far as it has the fault of not being dead*. Thus the study of the *sacred* is itself extremely perilous, since it either leads the mind away from the object which it has perhaps thoughtlessly selected (then, by externalizing it, reduces the sacred to the form of the object analogous to other sociological objects); or casts us adrift with a temptation of a 'burst of ephemeral splendour'. . . . In this respect I cannot fail to recall the essential features of the public life of Roger Caillois, who was not primarily a sociologist. Above all, it seems to me, it would be a mistake to regard his passage through the Surrealist Group as insignificant. Of course this did not imply any real affinity: Caillois was soon disappointed. But in my opinion this meant that first, against the usual limits of scholarly activity, which is always necessarily specialized, Caillois above all retained the element of totality, and intended to place being itself in question in his life (rather than as a fragment, as the object of science is). And this originating resolution survives in *L'Homme et le sacré*, so contradicting the sociologist's usual resolution. It is remarkable that the writing of such a book requires the act of a man who wanted totality, but then disowns it, having first seen only the deficient elements. He disowned it but in choosing a limited object of study he has chosen the object whose nature is to annihilate its own limits; he has chosen the object which is not an object, since it is above all the destruction of any object.

The result is, perhaps, the best that could have been hoped for. If the author had chosen to immolate himself, his impatience would have deprived him of the power to reveal clearly the basic data uncovered by the detached mind of a scholar. He could have added nothing to the scattered results of the latter if he did not share a nostalgia for fleeting splendour. We sense that at every moment he is restive, perhaps even tormented, by the thought of going further than scientific objectivity allows and perhaps, within himself, is scornful of the nostalgia which eventually served to bend his will but he cannot help but be betrayed by the direction of his book.

It is also worth noting that *L'Homme et le sacré* is, after all, the only work Roger Caillois the sociologist has taken to a conclusion. Later, the concerns that determine it engaged him in a course in which he never ceases to make a febrile tension about his position apparent. He aims at the best assured conviction, in the service of an unassailable order, and he obviously cannot establish that such an order might not have the ambition to enclose the totality of being, in its affirmation and organic negation. But it seems to me that the key to the books he has written as a *moralist* (like *Le rocher de Sisyphe*, *Circonstantielles*, *Babel*) lies in *L'Homme et le sacré*. With this book he concedes the misfortune of the mind: the mind 'dreads giving of itself, sacrificing itself, and is aware of this wasting its very being'.[6] 'But,' he adds immediately, 'to retain its gifts, energies, and resources, to use them prudently for all practical and selfish goals – as a consequence profane – saves no one in the final analysis from decrepitude and the tomb. Everything that is not consumed rots away.'[7] What in the study of the *sacred* maintained the author in time was observation of the cautious precepts of science. And his more recent position, put forward in his work as a moralist, ceaselessly alternates in its turn, between acceleration and putting on the brake: he has never found the straight and wide road in front of him which would have allowed him to yield to the temptation to speed. If this has any value as a critique, it is perhaps only in a general sense. It is time to confess that the nostalgia for the *sacred* necessarily can end in nothing, that it leads astray: what the contemporary world lacks is the offer of temptations.

*

Or those it does offer are such odious examples that they serve only to deceive those whom they tempt.

Nietzsche had already seen that the rigours of asceticism and holiness have ceased to be attractive for our age, and that only revolution and war offer the mind comparably exhilarating experiences.

In the same way Roger Caillois, who was left unsatisfied at the interrupted character of his book (in the state in which it was first published in 1939) by the feeling of the void in which sacrifice and caution are equally impossible, replied (and his reply concludes the second edition in 1950) to the crucial question posed by the retreat from the *sacred* in the contemporary age. At first he considered that the archaic festival (whose decadence is apparent) had been replaced by the holiday. But this superficial hypothesis did not satisfy him: now he has no hesitation in regarding *war* as the counterpart in modern societies of the paroxysm of festival: war, the time of 'excess', 'violence', 'outrage'. War is the 'unique moment of concentration and intense absorption in the group of everything that ordinarily tends to maintain a certain area of independence'.[8] Like the festival, war gives rise to 'monstrous and formless explosions that serve to break up the monotony of normal existence'.[9]

Both allow actions which are otherwise considered to be the clearest violations and the most inexcusable crimes: in the one incest is suddenly prescribed; in the other murder is recommended.[10]

. . . when the hour for combat or the dance arrives, new forms emerge. Acts hitherto prohibited and deemed abominable now carry glory and prestige.[11]

Like incest in the festival, murder in war is an act with religious repercussions. It is connected, one might say, to sacrifice, and has no immediate utility . . .[12]

There is an end to bowing before the dead and honouring them, while concealing their horrible reality to the eye as well as to the mind . . . It is the hour in which one can pillage and soil this greatly revered object, the mortal remains of man. Who would deprive himself of such a revenge and profanation? In the end, everything deemed sacred is reclaimed by death. At the same time that it causes trembling, it wants to be defiled and spat at . . .[13]

The festival is the occasion for immense waste . . . Just as all disposable foods are amassed for the festival, so loans, levies, and requisitions drain the varied riches of a country and throw them into the abyss of war, which absorbs them without ever being amassed. Here the food consumed in one day by the multitude would be sufficient for a whole season's festival, for even the figures make one dizzy. The cost of several hours' hostilities represents such a considerable sum that one could believe it possible to put an end to the misery of the world with it.[14]

This interpretation is shocking, but it would not do to close our eyes. To do so would be to fail to understand the *sacred*, as it would be to fail to understand war. And finally, it would be to fail to grasp a fundamental knowledge of real people. Roger Caillois poses the question: 'is it the fault . . . of the gradual disappearance of the domain of the sacred, under the pressure of profane mentality, harsh and greedy?'[15] To a question with such serious consequences there are insufficient elements for a reply, which Caillois would be the last to give. But let us insist: the study of the *sacred* gives the feeling of an insoluble difficulty and a malediction of mankind. Without the *sacred*, the totality of the plenitude of being escapes man; he would no longer be anything but incomplete. But the *sacred*, if it takes the form of war, threatens him with complete extinction. In the paragraph devoted to the effects of atomic energy, Caillois concludes: 'The festival . . . was the creation of the imagination. It was facsimile, dance, and play. It pantomimed the destruction of the universe . . . It would no longer be the same. The day in which energy was liberated in a sinister paroxysm . . . would definitely break the equilibrium in favour of destruction.'[16]

Notes

1. Review of Roger Caillois, *L'Homme et le sacré* (1950), Paris: Gallimard. Published in *Critique*, no. 45 (1951). [This book has been translated into English as *Man and the Sacred* by Meyer Barash (1959), Illinois: The Free Press of Glencoe. The references which follow are to the English-language version. – *Translator*]
    2. p. 138.
    3. ibid.
    4. p. 137.
    5. pp. 137–8.
    6. p. 138.
    7. ibid.
    8. Appendix III, 2nd edn, *Guerre et sacré*, p.167. Of the two other appendices in this edition, the first, *Sex and the Sacred*, does not appear to me to have the necessary breadth its subject requires. The second, *Games and the Sacred*, is of rather greater interest but nevertheless touches on only one aspect of theoretical interpretation.
    9. p. 169.
    10. p. 167.
    11. ibid.
    12. p. 238.
    13. p. 169.
    14. p. 170.
    15. p. 179.
    16. p. 180.

Poetry and the Temptation

of the End of the World[1]

Of all those who scan the horizon or the skies to decipher the signs of what is to come, there can be few who have subjected them to a more persistent interrogation and with a greater avidity for discovery than André Breton. But perhaps no one has recognized as clearly as he the significance of this sign that has recently appeared: the threat of an annihilation of the world and of a definitive night that would turn the universe into a 'non-universe', *a theatre where the performance has just ended.*

'If civilizations had only considered themselves to be mortal,' he writes, assuming Valéry's sonorous tone,

> they would have taken consolation and learned from the fact. A ray of light subsisted. . . . But suppose reality in its entirety enters into night in a flash of lightning; suppose the earth, at the mercy of a failure in the administration of explosives, shattered in a way that apparently happens at times in the depths of the sky when a world fragments, leaving in its wake only a long and immense flash that will never come to our attention?

As a matter of fact, 'science' cannot, without a new order of things, take this possibility into account – or at least, it considers the possibility so remote that it can practically be ignored. After all, the fact is that it exists, and if it is no more alarming today than the risk of a more general catastrophe, not provoked by man's hand, it has become possible to talk about it. Otherwise, a future that one imagines near at hand risks opening wide the door that today is only half-open. The scientists do not yet tremble, for fear that they may themselves cause the globe to explode, but the problem is presented, and could be resolved. From that moment it is unlikely that the earth would survive.

Whether such an end would exactly be universal night is another matter. In one respect, would not a world in which there was no form of consciousness have that value which consciousness tends to destroy,

that of poetry? One must also say that science today recognizes
through experience what the theory yesterday tended to deny: the
possibility of numerous systems in the universe and, in consequence,
other humanities and other consciousnesses. Be that as it may, the
antagonism between poetry and consciousness (the latter connected to
reason) is at the heart of our lives. And faced with the possibility of this
night descending over us, Breton is led to take into account a *poetic*
tradition whose authenticity is not in doubt:

> Do not numerous studies in course of publication, establish that for a
> century they [poets] – and consequently the most acute modern spirit –
> have drifted towards the temptation of the *end of the world*? In fact there can
> be no doubt whatsoever that the state of mind of men like Nerval, Borel,
> Baudelaire, Cros, Rimbaud, Lautréamont, Mallarmé, whose sensibility, for
> the most part, has conditioned ours, was governed by the old Manichaean-
> ism and Sade.

Breton cites Baudelaire: 'To amuse myself I calculate to myself . . .
whether a prodigious mass of stone, marble, statues, and walls crash-
ing down together would be stained by the multitude of brains, human
flesh and broken bones . . . ' One should also point out that poets do
not seem to be the only people to experience this poetic temptation of
the *end of the world*: it is something that equally concerns scholars. One
of them, who works on atomic research, told me that although he
personally might find himself beyond temptation, he took it for
granted that one day or another a physicist would succumb. To have
such a monstrous possibility available would go to the head and would
finally, he said, be too much to resist.

I am less certain than he is . . . . André Breton always resolutely
separates himself from such an intoxicating proposition. About this
'end of the world' he no longer feels, in conclusion, 'the least embarrassment in saying that today *we no longer want it*'. 'We no longer want it,'
he continues,

> since we see the features under which it takes shape and which, against all
> expectation, strike us as having become absurd. We feel only repugnance in
> relation to this universal swoon, to the extent that only the alienation of
> man could have yielded a *reason* for it. Such an end of the world, arising
> from an inexcusable false step of mankind, more decisive and therefore
> more inexcusable than its precedents, is devoid of all *value for us*, and is
> deplorably grotesque.

This sentiment is founded on an almost general sensitivity which
makes us hostile to everything that used to be seductive about war, and
we should not be surprised to see André Breton express it so clearly.

He is determined to continue from that point to the 'total reversal' which has become indispensable for him. He insists on a 'reversal of the sign' whose possibility, he says, with great *exactitude*, is governed by 'a *pure perceptible fact* thanks to which the principle of contradiction can be surmounted'. 'The examples', he insists, 'are not lacking, precisely in Baudelaire, Rimbaud and Lautréamont.' He concludes: 'I am drawn into the great poetical mystery, the one that was determined during the Terror when, at the price of his freedom, Sade . . . argued against the death penalty.'

The movement of André Breton's thought, despite its cloudy appearance, often has this character of necessity and coherence: the situation of the *end of the world* must be considered from this perspective. André Breton's 'second thoughts' mark the difficulty – in one sense the falsehood – of facile vertigo, which attributes to itself simultaneously the mortal effect of the fall and the preservation of consciousness. Consciousness experiences what really slips away from consciousness, what really annihilates it, as a sorrow and an exaltation: the play of the imagination gives a (misleading) meaning to an impossible reconciliation; in point of fact the end of the world gains consciousness only on condition that it does not happen. If it did, then consciousness would no longer exist. But the falsehood – or the *black* Romanticism – does not resist an impulse. *Contradiction* alone is its truth, and the impulse immediately reduces the *black* to the condition of the *pink*, the pink to the truth of the *black*. Everything is reconciled in the *instant*, which is the *instant* only on a *black* foundation – on the foundation where nothing exists any more, but which is pink only by a negation of this *black* which will be, that the *instant*, if it is appropriate for it, can maintain as indifferent, indeed not envisage. In this way the *pure, palpable fact* – or the instant – surmounts (and alone surmounts) the principle of contradiction. *Sexual pleasure*, and with it *calm* and *luxury*, is given to man only in the night, but the truth of the night is finally merely the possibility of the day, to which night alone can give birth.

This cannot go against the fact that there is never, in our intimate returns to the *pink* depths of life, a time of pause. This ignores the *calm* (which Baudelaire made the positive image of *sexual pleasure*) which takes it for rest. *Calm* is *energy* conferred in immensity. It is not the sleep of the just.

This – genuinely Hegelian – negation of black Romanticism very felicitously introduces the pages devoted to Malcolm de Chazal. Chazal's fate is singular: having come unobtrusively from distant shores, his book at first had the welcome it deserved (even in the press), but today doubt seems to have succeeded devotion. The hesitant mind could pause attentively at the praise which revealed Chazal as the first writer to achieve *the equivalence of sexual pleasure and language.* If we reflect that the human is the same thing as language, that language is characterized by a powerlessness not to betray (if it wants to express it) the extreme moment of sexual pleasure, it will seem less strange to give Chazal's message the significance it demands of us. But Chazal, they will say, speaks about God. Here an agreement of minds could form: the word *God* is always a mask. I stand by the passage in which Breton, commenting on Chazal, through the acknowledged intimate relation between sexual pleasure and death, discovers an astonishing truth – and announces a 'recourse to everything that can constitute the *sacredness* of life'.

In truth, my description minimizes a conspicuous aspect of the book: its indignation at the horrors of the present day. In fact one could not know if one would first suffocate with indignation upon awakening to such overwhelming truths. It sometimes seems to me that *in the end* such an *awakening* represents the care denied to such afflictions, but with this clear reservation: I have no intention of resolving a major difficulty.

Henri Pastoureau:

La blessure de l'homme[2]

A young surrealist writer, a former prisoner of war in Germany, could not be a more appropriate choice to portray 'the irremediable pain of the human condition'.

To this end he considers it important not to impose himself. Rather, it is Pascal and Baudelaire he allows to speak, while 'wishing neither to comment on their words nor to set them against each other'. He simply puts the propositions and quotations forward, and comments no further. We know nothing about his intentions except the little he discloses in the two pages of the preface. He adheres to a conception that excludes 'all perfectibility of man or of the world'. According to him, 'our sins suppose no remission. Our misfortunes suppose no pity. Our wound supposes no cure. Our captivity supposes no escape. Our revolt supposes no revolution.'

It would seem that he is turning his back on the principles of surrealism. Still, in the publicity note, the author has let slip this passage: 'This work raises a question which Henri Pastoureau has been careful not to answer. But the response to it tomorrow will revolve around the point at which contrary solutions would cease to be perceived contradictorily!' This is an allusion to the crucial passage in the *Second Manifesto* in which André Breton declared:

> Everything leads us to believe that there exists a certain point of the mind at which life and death, real and imaginary, past and future, communicable and incommunicable, cease to be perceived contradictorily. It would be vain to seek in surrealist activity any other motivation than the hope of determining this point . . .

Could one not be more precise and say: *To determine this point it is crucial that I grasp as an inescapable truth: 'Our wound supposes no cure' (in fact I am already dying . . .); and that, as I recognize this fact, I will experience no less pleasure than restlessness. In other words: how, if I fail to recognize that there can be no cure for my wound, could I perceive the truth expressed so bluntly by this phrase of Char's: 'Though we inhabit a flash of lightning, it is the heart of the eternal'*?

With this principle set out, the outstanding thing about Pastoureau's restrained book is that such an *extremist* surrealism, which breaks with one tradition of the movement, does not hesitate to invoke the experience of a believer (while it is true that Breton sometimes cited Christians like Raymond Lulle in his thinking, it was for reasons external to Christianity). In fact it could be said to be dangerous for surrealism to situate experience exclusively on the evidence from writers and poets, and neglect the extreme rigour and passion of those who wanted to take the human adventure to its limit through Christianity. In one respect the free violence of poets alone responds to current enthusiasms, but it lacks a resolution that exhausts what is possible. The first *enemy* of Christianity, Nietzsche, seems to me to be much better informed when he writes: 'We want to be the inheritors of meditation and of Christian insight – to go completely beyond Christianity by means of a *hyperchristianity* rather than be content with breaking away from it.' I recall that a long time ago Breton read me a letter from Dali – whose innate buffoonery gave him such latitude – which began something like: 'It is high time we surrealists thought about becoming priests . . . ' And it sometimes seems to me that poets would gain by becoming, if not priests, then theologians or, even better, *a-theologians*, familiars of an illusionist abyss. It is remarkable how man devotes so little consideration to adding up the sum of his most remote *knowledge* (or does so poorly) . . . . No doubt it is not inspiring to note the effects of a few stray impulses, but one cannot be surprised finally to see, and perhaps seriously, a man who does not challenge the surrealist tradition proclaim: ' . . . After the experience of the past twenty years, it would today be a radical-socialist stupidity to refuse to save a place for a Pascal or a Rimbaud, and the same thing goes for a Kierkegaard, Baudelaire, Nietzsche, Dostoyevsky or Chestov . . . ' (Jean Maquet, in *Troisième convoi*, no. 1).

Notes

1. Review of André Breton, *La lampe dans l'horloge* (1948), Paris: Robert Marin. Published in *Critique*, no. 33 (1949).

2. Review of Henri Pastoureau; *La blessure de l'homme*, (1946), Paris: Robert Laffont. Published in *Critique*, nos 8–9 (1947).

René Char and the Force

of Poetry [1]

If I want to raise myself and attain the heights, I tell myself that the opposite – degradation, debasement – is no longer without its charms. In truth this comes from my fear of limiting myself to a defined possibility – which does not only lead me away from another, equally narrow one – which separates me from the *totality* of being, or from the universe which I cannot renounce. But two fields of action open to my thought: the first is that of confined existence, distinct from the rest of the world, and whose well-understood interests are sordid; the second is that of sovereign existence, where I stand, which is not in the service of any enterprise, not even of its own egoistic interest. No one can, by any displacement, enslave the truly and fully sovereign being: the only thing that concerns him is to exist in that instant, without expecting its plenitude to depend on anything and without undertaking anything whose result counts for more than the present moment, without any will or intention except the empty space. But this intangible sovereignty presupposes that I *raise* myself out of the commonplace to which action is devoted, which calculates and demands that the endeavour should respond to necessity. In fact I cannot, without *raising* myself, offer the immense horizon to my gaze where it is freed from those arduous enterprises which demand of it exact care and submission. Thus I overcome doubts for a moment and convince myself about such heights which I attain, in this elevation which intoxicates me; they do not limit me at all: it is only servile inclination which would limit me and connect me to the irksome tasks of a work.

*

Besides, I would provoke laughter in the reader who notices that I discuss, write and make erasures without knowing how to emerge from such a manifest contradiction: how, if I write, can I attain these

heights, when what I write commits me to write no longer!? If I talk of
the heights, or would attain them, I would immediately cease to talk;
otherwise I would betray the heights I talk about. The difficulty seems
explicit, but if, as I let go of my train of thought, I copy these words (I
feel that, as he wrote them, René Char's discomfort was no less than
mine):

Solitary tears are not wasted,

I notice that writing, beyond being an enterprise which is organized
and, as such, is commonplace and deprived of wings, can suddenly and
discreetly break open and be nothing other than the cry of emotion. In
order to understand me properly it is necessary to stand firm by the
fact, on the one hand, that reflection is cold and must even exclude
warmth or exaltation of the spirit; and that a genuine elevation, on the
other hand, takes me beyond the concern to make of a flow of thought
a confined object that accommodates the principle of utility. But from
that moment, I must sadly measure the distance which separates action
and intelligence (to which I still devote myself, and whose object is in
any event *limited*, had I defined it as being *unlimited*) – once the spirit
gains some elevation, everything slips away as *far* as the eye can see.

*

But perhaps to *feel* this – far, very far, away from the interminable
obligation to write – is both a sorrow and a state of grace. In this most
recent book, in which the movements of an overhasty thought are
shaken free, and which refuses to allow the reader to remain
unmoved, René Char writes: 'Every association of words encourages
its contradiction and runs the suspicion of imposture. The task of
poetry, through its eye and on the tongue of its palate, is to cause this
alienation to vanish by revealing how ridiculous it is.'[2] In fact nothing is
more ridiculous than the difficulty of thought which is obliged to
embrace what would exceed, in so far as the totality of it would be
palpable, any status as a limited object. But a dazzling energy – or a
grace – is necessary . . . . The same energy – the same grace – is
demanded of me if I want to make apparent the imposture of a life to
which death would not add the trap of anguish: this would be not a
totality but a fragment. Waking lacks sleep in the same way as the
lucidity of the philosopher lacks the monstrous insignificance of the
fly. Finally, the knowledge of totality would lack the oblivion into
which the minds most avid to know *everything* have abandoned
totality.[3]

*

At first, as one reads Char, the provocative insight he brings is not obvious. Poetry is apparent as we read *À une sérénité crispée*, but it can escape the reader that the book which dazzles him also questions him. This is not a sermon but an insomnia, prompted at the heart of a sleep which prevails. I cannot think of a more perfect moral *lesson*. Not that it offers rules of conduct, but it draws us towards the heights I have spoken about, where we cease to see those objects of narrow interest which orientate the 'commandments' in isolation. This book calls for the negation of our limits, it brings back those it disturbs to the totality they have denied. 'But', he says, 'who will re-establish this immensity around us, this density which really was made for us and which, on all sides, not divinely, bathed us?'[4] Here the flame and the sputter of sparks appear in the air, fully announcing the waking and impercept-ible anger of happiness. The sentences rollick with ease and bristle up like fire: 'How is it that we are attacked from all sides, smashed, devoured, hated and beaten into submission, and yet somehow we still manage to rise up up up, exploding with our execrations as much as with our loins?'[5] There is not a twig the blaze doesn't crackle: 'This instant when Beauty, having been made to wait a long time, rises from common things, passes over our radiant field, connects everything that can be connected, and inflames all that must be inflamed with our cluster of shadows.' How could the pressure fill the expanse any longer, or in a warmer way? But nothing tempers this plenitude: 'Where do you fall, birds we stone at the pure moment of your vehemence?'[6] In excess, the very disorder of language requests the pleasure of the consciousness of wisdom! The insipidity of the *possible* ceaselessly reminds us that we exist, that *existence* is the guarantee within us of the impossible: 'The poet prefers the experience that life contradicts.'[7] If we limited ourselves to what is possible, we would never go beyond our limits, we would remain enclosed, moribund – or rather, we would not *exist*. If we aspired to fathomless totality, how could we limit it? What would the *existence* within us be if it accepted banishment from the totality of being? What is totality if not existence exceeding the limits of the possible and going to the point of death? Our whims, and this taste for the impossible which we have in our grasp, alone signify that we never concede the separation of the individual fixed in the feeble limits of the possible.

*

The impossible always appeared in relation to a position defined as the contrary position. The leap beyond what is possible destroys what became clear: thus the impossible is the distressing contrary of what we are, which is always connected to the possible. But this is also what we lack, that alone by which we restore ourselves to totality and that alone by which totality restores itself: so death delivers us to a totality which requires our absence no less than our presence, which not only composes the world so naively expected of this presence, but suppresses first its necessity and then the memory and traces of it. (In the same way obscenity is the *impossible* which the woman who retches at the very thought lacks.) Totality is always what causes us to tremble,[8] what, in this small fragment detached from the world (where we feel secure), is *completely other*, what is horrifying and gives us a sacred shiver, but for want of which we could claim the 'pure happiness' the poet speaks about, this happiness 'screened from the eyes and its own nature'.

In this way I also indicate poetry's essence, and, in this sense, I quote Char's aphorism in its entirety: 'The fear, irony, and anguish you experience in the presence of the poet who bears the poem in the whole of his being is not mistaken, it is pure happiness, happiness screened from the eyes and its own nature.'[9]

*

But today humanity sees its right to exceed the possible in a sovereign way denied: everywhere, it is called up to limit itself and deny its sovereign immensity. The time will come when we will be asked rigidly to immobilize ourselves and, in a word, no longer *exist*. 'Is this hitherto always ransomed world going to be condemned to death before our very eyes and against us? Criminals are those who stop time within man in order to hypnotize and perforate his soul.'[10] But this Anticyclops – who, by way of enigma, is invoked by Char for the decisive battle – cannot yet be submitted to a penetrating clarity which would betray him. The entire meaning of *À une sérénité crispée* is contained in this epigraph: 'Today we are closer to the catastrophe than the alarm itself, which means that it is high time for us to compose a well-being of misfortune, even if it had the appearance of the arrogance of miracle.' In these lines there is a vital quality which urges struggle. 'We are strong,' he adds. 'Every force is banded against us. We are vulnerable. So much less so than our aggressors who, if they have crime, do not have *second* wind.'[11] In all senses, *virtue* reigns in these passionate aphorisms, in which a word never conceals the heart. Char's morality is not an abdication: it is calm exuberance: 'To fight against the absolute of hiding away and holding one's tongue.'[12] It reminds sovereign man that nothing can prevail against him.

*

I do not know if the light emanating from these charged pages will soon reach the eyes it will have the gift of dazzling. But between the furtive glimmers which animate us there is nothing more strange, more beautiful, more worthy of being loved. I can imagine that there are those who could not go for long without reading and rereading this book, and being imbued with its virtue.

Max Ernst, Philosopher![13]

I can imagine the present universe being succeeded by the ridiculous absurdity that would be *undifferentiated being*!

In this perspective, I consider in thought what opposes one thing to another. Nothing remains, and if I still speak, it is of the immensity of whatever is nothing . . .

As I collapse, my whole being evidently collapses into this thought which is suddenly the death of all thought, the death of all being and of all thought.

In this universal vanishing, in this failure of all possibilities, there is nothing which doesn't slowly collapse. For ever . . .

But nevertheless . . . . A *chink* could remain . . .

From this disappearance, which could not have been perfect, the universe of Max Ernst would remain (as I playfully imagine it) . . . a fragile, useless and last caprice in the instant which will follow, ready to squander itself.

As a young man Max Ernst would have liked to become a philosopher, to study philosophy. As I situate myself at the limit of this universal collapse I have mentioned, I allow an absurd question to open up inside me: from a dissolution which develops within him, from all things, creating the universe from his fascinating work, did Ernst turn away from this vocation that he once thought he had perceived in himself? Did he turn away from it? Not at all – has he not responded to it in a *playful* and *violent* way?

Philosophy is faced with two paths.

The first is that of work: the philosopher is at leisure successively to elaborate, in a detailed way, the particular issues which are presented to him, then the mass of issues, in their cohesion.

The other path is death.

Usually only the first path is considered, in ignorance of what a possibility of glimpsing ourselves and the world for a moment represents – something which dissolves within us the question (the questions) we consider.

However, philosophy will never be able to declare itself alien to the possibility of such a moment. Life cannot escape the perspective of death; likewise, philosophy cannot escape the perspective of the instant when the ground will slip away, of this instant in which nothing more will remain which does not slip away. The possibility of such a moment always *mocks* the philosopher, suggesting to him the *stake* which could intoxicate him.

It's true: this moment is nothing other than death.

Nevertheless, it is play. Being disappearance, it is play *par excellence*.

As he mocks philosophy, or talks about the death of philosophy, the philosopher sheds no tears; such a death is the play within him that announces the triumph of the game, the powerlessness of work. Both play and death throw the possibility of work into disorder.

What is the foundation of the turbulent and violent world of Max Ernst if not the catastrophic substitution of a game, of an end in itself, for laborious work, with a view to a desired result? The serious philosopher conceives philosophy as a laborious activity and in so doing he imitates carpenters and locksmiths. . . . He constructs his philosophical furniture, a well-oiled philosophy responding as a lock does to the key made for it. The person who recognizes the powerlessness of work, on the contrary, is dazzled and fascinated by the *play* which serves no purpose.

If he announces, if he calls for, the death of philosophy, the philosopher *who plays* sees in the locksmith a brother, but one to whom he is connected through distress. . . . But before the *inspired hill*, which dazzles him, he is the brother of Max Ernst. What he would like to portray, what disturbs and astounds him, the painter, his friend, portrays in his paintings. Next to this friend he accepts being swallowed up in this collapse of the real, in which death, half-glimpsed, compellingly represents the decisive move, in which the world, as it ceases to exist, falls apart; where thought is only the measureless applause given to the death of thought.

Max Ernst, philosopher! If one day philosophy acquired the imprudence of hilarity, could we still say that Max Ernst, creating the universe from his canvases, would turn his back on it?

Notes

1. Review of René Char, *À une sérénité crispée* (1951), Paris: Gallimard. Published in *Critique*, no. 53 (1951).

2. *À une sérénité crispée*, p. 15.

3. If we speak of totality, we could not separate man becoming knowledge from totality; or rather, totality implies the knowledge man has of it.

4. *À une sérénité crispée*, p. 40.

5. ibid., p. 31.
6. ibid., p. 35.
7. ibid., p. 33.
8. It is the *mysterium tremendum* of Rudolf Otto (*Le sacré*).
9. *À une sérénité crispée*, p. 35.
10. ibid., p. 45.
11. ibid., p. 21.
12. ibid., p. 28.
13. Published as *avant-propos* to *Bataille* (1960), Paris: Gonthier-Seghers.

From the Stone Age to
Jacques Prévert[1]

Poetry once adhered to rules: at the same time it took from these rules both the origin and the consciousness of what it was generally understood to be. It was language expressed in verse. But what now comes to mind when we use the word 'poetic' (which is still opposed to 'prosaic') cannot be independent of what our grandmothers perceived. Is this not the same thing? Without doubt. . . . But our grandmothers' thought is intelligible to us. For the naive respect given to rhymed words and the rhythm that holds the sequence of effective action in suspension has been substituted the inverse vagaries of a world in which licence, doubt or rapture, rather than constraint, rule . . . this is what limited, yesterday as today, the powers of boredom connected to rational behaviour. The processes, rhymes, long and short syllables, the number of feet and the fact that poetry depended on them, disconcerts: but if it is necessary to 'bestow sight'[2] (at a time when the necessities of rational life – morose, suspicious, tied up with business affairs – prevent *sight*), it is necessary to give words the power to *open eyes*. Then the word becomes imbued with possibilities that are independent of the meaning of the terms, a rhythm which can be raucous or pleasant at will, and a voluptuousness of sounds, due to their recurrence and their surge. And this rhythm of words – which can even be musical – awakens the sensibility, and carries us directly to intensity. Reciprocally, emotion leads us to use words (which no longer serve the ends of *knowledge* but of *sight*, and which respond not to reason but to the senses) as if they were no longer intelligible signs but cries, which one could modulate at length and in diverse ways.

Powerful emotion has always been expressed poetically. It could not be expressed absolutely – that is, translated into words – except by means of poetry. More precisely, every emotion *was sung out* (for purely literary poetry is a sort of mutilated song). Interest in hermetic poetry, the desire to affect in the rarest poetry, cannot cause us to forget the truth: that we must consider people rather than poets. It was the people of every age who defined the domain of poetry as they sang. What cannot be sung is outside the domain of poetry. (Its antipodes, *business affairs*, exactly determine its nature.)

It is true that this rudimentary definition – with which no one would disagree – would introduce tedious problems if its meaning were not immediately made explicit; and, strange as it might seem, if the extent of its lyrical possibilities were not brought back to it. It is necessary and worthwhile to glimpse what poetry is *from outside* (whether or not we accept it, we are side by side with the unreflective mass of men, and the movements of the mass determine our possibilities *from outside*), but the meaning of poetry is no less intimate. From this perspective, poetry is *also*, for us, *literature which is no longer literary*, which escapes from the rut in which literature is generally entrapped. For us, 'poetic' cannot have a set value in the same way as an Anjou wine, or English cloth. 'Poetic' undercuts the desire in us to reduce things to the dimensions of reason. The businessman may esteem a wine or a fabric, but such evaluations cannot modify the order of values on which his self-confidence is based. With poetic emotion it is otherwise, since by definition it withholds that confidence for a moment. I know that such an emotion, which in the back of my mind does not cease to disturb me, prevents me from satisfying the demands which govern business affairs. It even deprives me of savouring literary pleasure as one should. I cannot be both a *lover* of literature and also *surrender* to the overwhelming power of poetry. A woman may expect to be loved *sovereignly*: in the same way, someone who is not touched with a *sovereign* emotion cannot experience poetry, in which nothing is withheld. At least, not at that particular moment, and this signifies nothing oppressive or pompous. But poetry cannot be a pastime; even less can it be something to be acquired: it is the actuality of men *outside the self*, when its power is to communicate the condition of the poet to those who hear him.

Such intimate data accord, if one is prepared to perceive the fact, with formal data. In both respects, poetry gives expression to what exceeds the possibilities of common language. It uses words to express what overturns the order of words. It is the *cry* of what, within us, cannot be reduced; what, within us, *is stronger than us*.

This forces me to recognize the fact that my definition remains vague. Is this due to a lack of precise examples? Perhaps. But to give an example would immediately serve to reveal the inadequacy: my example would be placed in time, and I want to speak about what poetry represents at any period. As a matter of fact, each example would delineate a different meaning, and would suggest that it was not possible to reduce to unity what answers to human forms that are almost alien to each other. For this reason I have had to make do with a difficult-to-grasp definition, and I cannot attempt to make this clear except *after* I have stated that this *cry* varies in accordance with the sorts of emotions dominant in successive civilizations, and in accordance with the possibilities of the contradictory development of poetic language. If you prefer, *not only is the nature of poetry embedded in the subordination of actuality, but poetry is itself actuality.* While poetry may be bellicose, erotic or religious, it is not so without relation to the dominant emotions within a given society. If, in a particular period, the word 'poetic' is defined as something noble – even pompous – this does not mean that poetry must generally be noble or pompous, but that one society fictively desires to maintain the value of emotions which no longer predominate within it. The modalities of poetic language change in accordance with that happening which is the incessant unfolding of the sensibility. On the other hand, the life of the emotions is connected to their poetic expression, and people have feelings that the poverty of a poetic technique can, strictly speaking, limit. On the contrary, the liberty of feelings can liberate verbal techniques; and reciprocally, verbal audacity augments the intensity and liberty of emotion.

(I have discussed these points at some length because the problem today is blurred with polemic. Can poetry escape actuality? Does it need to? The same question can be put in other ways: Should the writer be accountable? Should he be engaged? Generally, the writer is expected to be accountable. But this is not acknowledged to the extent of society asking for accounts! I suspect that literary figures, as they speak of responsibility, must see it in their likeness: as unreal. In truth it is possible that the writer, eager for responsibility, would have no more opportunity of access to the 'castle' than Kafka's land surveyor. The same thing is probably true of actuality: true poetry is born from actuality, it is itself actuality, and consumes the actuality whose flame it is. But the distance between a poet and the actuality remains generally what separates the surveyor from the 'castle'. It is vain to imagine a poetry outside time and able to communicate a human emotion which would have no attachment to class, rivalry, or a change in social relations. Poetic emotion is necessarily that of people in a particular period: it is this emotion alone which the magic of words discloses and transfigures. Poetry turns everything red, finds shrill notes, and communicates a similar awkward strangeness *to the interior of time*. What it expresses is part of the movement of history, and the means by which it expresses it is also a form that this movement takes. But it is not sufficient to say to the poet: this is the actuality you shall express. This might have been so once when one of the misfortunes of this world was tied to the knotted complexity of emotions. We are prey not only to our authentic emotions, but also to those of the past, whose means of expression pursue a sustained restlessness within us. Often we are puppets whose strings are lost in the night. How can we not see in contemporary man a confused chaos of possibilities, a cacophony of worn-out tunes, a suffocation, a ridiculous poverty, which, born from an excess of wealth, is ashamed of itself? This old humanity of heavy industry and indigestible wars which moves forward more rapidly than any before no longer has the feelings to gauge what it is. Its old age recalls the state that follows drunkenness, in which people *are* lived, yet without grasping their possibilities and without living. To shout out *what is*, rather than the mustiness of the past, and, what is more, to escape from the headache to the extent that one shouts it out – to destroy, in the very process of shouting, these habits of shouting which cause one to shout out *what was* and not *what is* – is perhaps no easier than gaining entrance to the 'castle'.

Besides, Kafka possibly identified these difficulties correctly when he described banishment from the castle: thereby, in his own way, he would have been and expressed actuality . . . but he could have done so only by failing, and it is even possible that actuality could be reducible to failure, that Kafka's dejected system would be the only one; but the condition of Kafka's 'success–failure' is doubt. Kafka can 'succeed–fail' only to the extent that he was not certain of failing in advance. And the fact that he had encountered failure signifies nothing even if, as he encountered it, he expressed the actuality. The stakes remain open. Man, it seems, is not definitively separated from what he is: the good fortune of the absentee (of vulgar indifference), and the too lucid misfortune of Kafka, are surely not his final limit.

I will now take a look at Prévert's *Paroles*, the poems of a man who is not part of the literary scene. (When they were collected in a volume, they were already popular. They had sometimes appeared in reviews, but were more often circulated in typed copies. Prévert writes for the cinema, and he prefers films to books because he is attracted by what is immediate, while a book always seems to say: 'I am here and will remain here. I am eternal. It is ME!')

If I want to express what poetry is, I experience a sort of light-headedness when I take up *Paroles*. This is because Jacques Prévert's poetry is poetry precisely as a living denial – and derision – of whatever congeals the mind in the name of poetry itself. . . . For what *is* poetry is also the actuality, in the life of poetry, which is the derision of poetry. 'To exist' in this context means 'to outwit death by means of constant change', 'to become other' and not 'to remain identical with what one is'. But the consent given from one side to a modern conception of poetry is taken from the other: its set purpose is to deny poetry of actuality the name of poetry. This purpose of 'pure poetry' is no less upset in *Paroles*, in which actuality is the theme of poetry, than in the more established 'poetic poetry'. I can thus say that Jacques Prévert's poetry is both the daughter and the lover of actuality. 'It is change. It transforms everything and everything transforms it. Not a portion remains immobile, no place to rest is offered, no looking back, no *it's better like that . . . I await my reward . . .* ' What can be said about this poetry – and perhaps this is also what needs to be said of poetry as a whole – is that it *exists* only on condition that it changes.

Without any doubt there is a defect in a means of expression which is founded in this way on indifference to results (and one seeks it in considering the reason for poetry having this quality of a mirage whereby, as the object of desire, it infinitely slips away): there is little possibility in such circumstances for the work to be worthy of the one who, so to speak, divests himself of it. What I have to say about *Paroles* is without equivocation, but before dealing with some of the pages in which the word is struck, in spite of everything, with inertia, I will say something about the author himself. Not that I consider the work incomprehensible without knowledge of the author, but to my mind Prévert's character is easier to grasp than his writings.

It is curious that in having recourse to the simplest means, in being *effortlessly* within reach of the least manufactured minds (his language is *popular*, his technique is quite straightforward, as much necessarily so as Valéry's language and techniques are *erudite*), Prévert was by no means a stranger to the most cultivated, careful expression. Even if he mocked it, he was well acquainted with it. Between 1925 and 1930 he was to be counted among the surrealists, and if, at that time, he wrote nothing, if he laughed up his sleeve, it still indicates that the concerns of the most subtle and most audacious minds of those times affected him. This is the external aspect, but it means more: there is no one, to my knowledge, who gives such an extraordinary complexion of depth to a pleasant conversation, made up of flashes of wit, black mischievousness, and frenzied verbal play. In the last analysis Prévert's realm is not youth – this would not go far enough – but *childhood*, that light burst of craziness, the gaiety of a childhood which has no respect for 'grown-ups'. This type of bitter awakening, side by side with a wise irony and the 'obstinacy' of the child, has kept him away from any concession to the seriousness of thought and poetry. The child pulls the chair of pretensions to which 'great men' lay claim from under them, making them morose and causing them to perceive in others a vanity which has no meaning other than their own stupidity. But the disconcerting thing about Prévert is that he connects the entire absence of seriousness to the most lively passion. I must also say that his conversation is the most direct and, devoid of hollow confidences, the most ardent I know. In any case, whether he is talking about films, politics, animals or people, I have always heard him talk of just one thing: of what within us is stronger than us and excludes good taste and pretence; and what is most carried away, puerile and mocking, and strangely situates us at the limits of what is and what is not; and, more precisely, of a violent taste for living in a total and indifferent way by someone who does not calculate, who is not afraid, and is always at the mercy of passion (he talked without intellectual baggage, enchanting those who heard him, habitually surrounded by very straightforward, often proletarian, comrades). Nothing is more contrary to the solemn looks which, on several sides, oppose an eternal custom, empty words and blank looks to *puerile* emotion: the tone of indefensible humour, and something frightful and dubious which leads astray, which wrings words and twists laundry . . . . (Moreover, the tone of the poems, their 'at full speed', their simplicity, their verbal extravagance; but the real word is more supple, it exhausts every possibility.) The dialogue of the films gives a more precisely insidious idea of this *way of being*, which is as far from philosophy as the bird from the paper (I am squinting at the moment at my own pages . . .). But a screen character cannot be animated with the same passion as Prévert's character, for whom humour is the *only way of avoiding error*. I mean the error of sentiments, which are nothing if not sentiments of *what is*.

(The person for whom sentiments do not go beyond what *he himself is*, is not free. If he intentionally remains a stranger to the rest of the world, he cannot suppress this residue, and this residue still encloses him. If he denies it, he is the prisoner who denies the prison bars by saying that since it is raining outside, he has decided to stay at home.) Liberty is nothing if it is not fully making use of the present moment (am I free, in that I have *something to do*?). I am free as I live in *immediacy*, for a *now* and not for a *later*. But the moment in which I live in accepted isolation, like the criminal or the depraved, has a flavour of humid shadow and abasement, like a fruit eaten in prison. I live *fully and entirely* in the moment only on one condition: that I no longer hide my plenitude from my fellows.[3] In other words, my integrity will belong to me only if it coincides with the integrity of others. (Not of everyone but of those who, like me, recognize that their integrity depends on that of others, rather than on 'those who put their names in lights . . .' or 'those who do not know what they should say . . .') But the concordance is actuality, and it is within this that sentiments – desires, passions, delights, anger, and other intense states of the sensibility, all of which are means of experiencing the instant – are sentiments of *what is*, of what generally happens to people. Compared with these communicable emotions, the sentiment of *what I alone am* is not merely empty, it also serves to annul. Imagine that I shut myself up in a room to eat a large slice of ham *alone* at a time of famine. No matter what its intensity, the feeling I would experience would be incommunicable (it would be as if it had not taken place). Or what could be communicated about my feeling would be only an unease that would be so much greater in that the other would evaluate the intensity of what is closed to him (due to the refusal to share the ham). The feeling of *what is* would be – if I now try to describe it from the other's point of view – one of unease and the aversion that such an *actuality* generally causes: solitary consumption, in the midst of famine, of a large slice of pork. Of course I could write a song going something like: '*Everyone else is hungry, but not me: I can eat my ham on my own . . .*' But this would be merely to sing the unsingable, communicate what is not communicable, and by making a display of an underhand attitude I would 'bestow sight' not on the pig that was eaten but on the pig who eats. Undoubtedly the great problem for each of us is to pass (as we live in the instant) from the sentiment of *what he is* to the sentiment of *what is*, to separate what is perceptible (desperately, engrossingly) for the man isolated from others (who is locked away) and for the boundless man who is alone free. This is what poetry responds to, awakening us, if possible, to boundless feelings. . . . But it is possible that poetry deceives us. The possibilities of error, seeking the passion which rends and the intense liberty of the present moment, are established through that absence of limits without which the attempt to awaken us to what is perceptible comes to nothing. Of course even the worst poetry still goes beyond the limits I suggested for the pork-eater. The effects of a certain sentimentality are no less related to those that the theme of my song announces. The difference comes from the poet's initiative. . . . But it hardly matters that the feeling evoked touches many people – providing it touches them in such a way that the *limit* of their emotion immediately appears. Emmanuel's poetry has many admirers! . . . It cannot be helped: it is made of the same stuff as my song. Of course the error is possible in two senses, but my opportunity to find the *unlimited* and shake off my *limits* (bearing in mind the sort of pen-pusher I am) is not such that I might hesitate for a long time. In any case, as I said, humour is *the only way to avoid error*, and would not the stake have at least the same value as finding grace for a Christian? From another point of view it is true that the difficulty of humour is attributed to complacency, and most often humour, like poetry, has its limits, or it is an obscene little mistake. But one can no more derive the reason for this lack in humour any more than in poetry.

One of the things Prévert hates most of all is the idea of greatness, and those who talk about it. Nietzsche himself wrote: 'If someone aspires to greatness, he thereby betrays what he is. The best people aspire to be insignificant.' I have often heard Prévert express the same idea. And if one must be grateful to Nietzsche for identifying this, one will also confess that nothing is more human. I say this to indicate the passion, and the degree of passion, tied up in Prévert's humour. It seems to me that in this way he makes an absolutely exact concern of human possibility perceptible: he shares all the humour of the world as well as what one might consider contrary to humour – that is, friendship. Nothing I am aware of in the realm of ideas – which, liquidating the mass of writings, illuminates what is – is so far removed from a pursuit of greatness than these lines from 'Almost':

> . . . the happiness which thinks about nothing . . .
> . . . the misery that thinks about everything . . .

I will now try to indicate more clearly what it is that makes these *Paroles* daughters and lovers of actuality. Some – 'Dinner of Heads' and 'Mutiny', among others – have an overtly Communist and anti-clerical political meaning. . . . 'New Order' is a poem of resistance. 'Vincent's Complaint' tells of Van Gogh's bringing his severed ear to a brothel in the form of a gift. 'This love' is a love poem, and so on. But the pages without object themselves have a meaning: as this is not clearly premeditated, it is doubtless more important.

'Inventory' really has neither a beginning nor an end:

> One stone
> two houses
> three ruins
> four gravediggers
> one garden
> a few flowers
>
> one racoon
>
> a dozen oysters one lemon one loaf of bread
> one ray of sunlight
> one groundswell
> six musicians
> one door complete with doormat
> one gentleman decorated with the Légion d'Honneur
>
> another racoon

one sculptor who sculpts Napoleons
the flower named marigold
two lovers in a large bed
one tax collector one chair three turkey cocks
one cleric one boil
one wasp
one irresolute kidney
one racing stable
one undeserving son two Dominican brothers three grasshoppers one
    tip-up seat
two ladies of the night one amorous uncle
one *mater dolorosa* three sugar daddies two Monsieur Seguin goats
one Louis XV heel
one Louis XVI armchair
one Henry II sideboard two Henry III sideboards three Henry IV
    sideboards
one discarded drawer
one ball of string two safety pins one elderly gentleman
one Victory of Samothrace one accountant two assistant accountants one
    man-of-the-world two surgeons three vegetarians
one cannibal
one colonial expedition one entire horse one half pint of good blood one
    tsetse fly
one lobster American style one garden French style
two potatoes English style
one lorgnette one footman one orphan one iron lung

one day of glory
one week of happiness
one month of Mary
one terrible year
one minute of silence
one second's lack of attention
and . . .

five or six racoons

And so on. Is it excessive to 'see' within these lines 'what is'? Is it not, as
with 'Dinner of Heads' or 'Mutiny' that this immediate world, *impossible*
and stupid, *impossible* and cruel, *impossible* and false? Haunting us to
saturation point . . . such an enraged poetic play of words alone can
'bestow sight' . . . (at least one can 'see' it in that way, 'see' it and not
analyse, 'see' and no longer be able to . . .).

    The same thing is true of 'Procession' which, like 'Inventory', is one
of the most beautiful poems imaginable.[4]

    An old man made of gold with a watch in mourning
    An odd-job queen with a man of England

And workers of the peace with guardians of the sea
A stuffed hussar with a turkey cock of death
A coffee snake with a rattle-mill
A tightrope hunter with a head dancer
A meerschaum marshal with a retiring pipe
A baby in evening dress with a gentleman in nappies
A jail-composer and a music bird
A collector of conscience with a director of fag-ends
A Coligny grinder with an admiral of scissors
A Bengal nun with a tiger of Saint-Vincent-de-Paul
A doctor of porcelain with a repairer of philosophy
An inspector of the Round Table with knights of the Paris Gas Company
A duck in Saint Helena with a Napoleon in orange sauce
A curator of Samothrace with a victory at the cemetery
A tug from a large family with a father of the high seas
A member of the prostate with a swollen French Academy
A parish horse with a grand circus priest
A pious conductor with a bus boy
A little surgeon with a dental devil
And the general of oysters with an opener of Jesuits.

I recall that when 'Procession' first appeared in *Action*, around the beginning of this year, a friend of mine, having put aside his newspaper, recited most of it from memory. That day it was commonplace to ask anyone one met if they had read 'Procession'. Undoubtedly, poems like 'Procession' and 'Inventory' contain an enchantment which inspires the spirit well beyond the simple attraction of wild laughter. Its poetic method is simple: it emerges from surrealist techniques. It is a form of automatism: the poetic element is conferred by means of comparisons and unexpected discoveries that exclude all calculation and fabrication. The poetic element? no doubt . . . But do not images like 'inspector of the Round Table', 'knight of the Gas Company', rather reveal the exact opposite of poetry, serving even to ridicule its dignity? *Actuality* itself (inhuman, vulgar and prosaic humanity) is, as a rule, distanced as far as possible from poetry. The feeling of *what is*, of inhuman humanity . . . is no less proclaimed in a way that serves to intoxicate: the cry goes back to the play in a rapid and almost infinite gush. This has nothing in common with the gaiety of caricature: *the resonance is the effect of poetry*. Born from the actuality of which it is the cry, poetry – in accentuating this cry, and starting with the amazement that created it – gained access to the extreme of possible emotion.

But in truth, it is difficult to appreciate how the disparagement of poetry effects a poetic impact. Minds are, perhaps, used to it, and a few empty formulas, borrowed from the vocabulary of the 'modern spirit', would clinch the matter. Even so, a greater difficulty arises: the presence of actuality. But if one repudiates verbal puns – if one starts, contrariwise, with words to reach consciousness of what the poetic operation represents – the fundamental difficulty remains whether it is such as to allow us to penetrate further into the understanding of what poetry actually is. But for that reason, it is necessary to go back to basics.

It should be recognized that poetry is a cry which bestows *sight* – which reveals what we would not otherwise see: in fact, we must ceaselessly calculate and know – *understand* – with a mind to act. I must demonstrate that the power of poetry has not been given once and for all. What once *bestowed sight* is exactly what later prevents it. It was soon apparent that poetry is also the enemy born of poetry: in being born it turns away from poetry to mingle with the cry the desire for permanence. Between the man (who cries) and actuality (which is), language, whose generality and immaterial character slips smoothly into security, immutability and the Academy, habitually intervenes. In fact, such is the poverty of poetry that in using words to express what happens it tends to stifle the cry of an actual emotion under the disguise of a museum face. Poetry, proclaiming the suspended instant, by the fact that the affecting order of words will survive it, tends to express only a durable meaning: it fixes it in funereal solemnity. . . .[5] But it is not only the immutable character of words which, even before being formulated from its object, distances it from the emotion proclaimed present and fleeting; it separates a sacred language from ordinary language, and noble words from common vocabulary. And in consecrating them to the elevated concern to stir emotion, it slowly uses the emotive value and, without fail, withdraws a power it wanted to be as great as possible.

I have no hesitation in seeking to show that the poetic effect brought about by Prévert's texts takes us back from our time – a period of 'directors of fag-ends' and 'repairers of philosophy' – to that of the stammerings of humanity. (I must say that my claim is not easy to defend, and is so much less acceptable in that, as I think about it, my idea about such stammerings emerges less from a reading of Spencer and Gillen[6] than from dreadfully confused reflections – which even accord, in a sense, with the memory I have retained, generally, from my conversations with Prévert – as confused as could be . . .) We cannot exploit the earth, make tools, raise animals for food – in a word, reduce everything that surrounds us (which affects us in every way) to utilitarian objects (which are not *emotive* but subordinated, and whose meaning is reduced to *it is used for* . . .) without the process disturbing us. Not only is it difficult, but to do it is ceaselessly to destroy an emotional bond that immediately attaches to other powers, which are animals, vegetables, meteorites . . . and other people. I would not claim that our fathers were zoophilous . . . they ate animals without compunction. But to eat something is not necessarily to treat it as an object; to eat is not to deprive what is eaten of palpable value: the food on the table responds to desire when one sits down to eat. It is only the *activity* of man that has made a thing of animals – 'whose meaning is reduced to *it is used for* . . .'. And the loss of palpable value, no matter how far back one goes, seems to have *debased*: it seems that it has always been hard to kill, but harder still to *debase* or to *profane*. What moved the senses was noble – or accursed. Everyday utilitarian activity, which reduced things to the level of use value, was debased. For this reason poetry, chanting out and singing the extremity of emotion in the cry, needed to be distanced from the vulgar world, whose objects could not communicate with desire.[7] Up to the present day poetry has used noble words that were distinct from those that are in ordinary use, and so stained with servility (*waves* for water, *steed* for horse). But the simple withdrawals and separations of classical poetry have little meaning compared with sacrifice. That seems strange in our view, but according to all appearances, men in former times did not submit without unease to the reduction their calculated activity imposed in the palpable world. This activity deprived the world of poetry, or at least of the elements which would become poetry (it changed perceptible values into use values); it seemed necessary to prevent it, if for only one reason: what seems to us poetic today was at the same time experienced as dangerous – that is, as sacred. This is where the necessity for sacrifice comes in; sacrifice returns an element of use value to the world of sensibility. If it was necessary to extract the objects of productive activity from a very menacing world of myths (of mysteries) and festivals (expenditure beyond what is useful), it would at least be necessary solemnly to destroy certain of these objects in order to pacify the injured owner. This is no longer difficult for us to grasp: the world of mystery has lost its darkness; it is only, as I have said, the domain of sensibility – or, if you prefer, of *interest confined to the instant itself*. Like our ancestors, we must take objects away from productive activity to the *interest of the instant itself*. But our ancestors reserved a ritual share of it: sacrifice, in a brief moment of anguish, cast to the wind a richness which – good sense would dictate – should be preserved for the future. This was the reverse of saving (especially of capitalist accumulation).

Clearly, it is strange to situate poetry (and Prévert's poems in particular) in the perspective of a 'clerical' institution. However, I suppose that the obscurity of the debate about poetry derives from cutting the domain of sensibility in two: into art and religion. In any event, both a sacrifice and a poem withhold life from the sphere of activity; both *bestow sight* on what, within the object, has the power to excite desire or horror. The general result of sacrifice is death. It is the ritual death of human beings which fully revealed this suspended and unlimited character of our life which is imposed on sensibility. What we call human nature, which implies a way of feeling, has reached the point where putting a man to death has ceased to be acceptable (and this puts an end to the custom). But it is not only the living victim that the sacrifice illuminates with the excessive gleam of the instant: what the putting to death again reveals to sensibility is the *absence* of the victim. The ritual has the right of fixing 'sensitive concern' at the burning instant of transition: where what exists has already ceased to exist, or what no longer *exists* is, for sensibility, no more than it was. At this price the victim entirely escapes debasement, and becomes divinized. This signifies that he is no longer reducible to human measures, recalling objects to their usage. The *divine*, the *sacred*, which sacrifice bestows to sight, is different from the poetic, and provokes a fearful horror which is connected to the attitude of humiliation. But it is through being undifferentiated, available and without limit (having no particular domain), rather than because of an essential separation, that the poetic is really opposed to the sacred. The poetic use of words, which was first confined to resonant accentuation, gave them, as it set them alight, the power to evoke clearly, and was not set apart in the same way as the ritual destruction of objects: something which had precise, solemn and obligatory ends. But varied as the apparent ends and limited as the primitive techniques may be, poetry is no less directed towards the same aim as sacrifice: it seeks as far as possible to render palpable, and as intensely as possible, the content of the present moment. The *poetic* (capricious, inconsiderate, seething and protean) in a way partakes no less of the *sacred* – immobilizing, cold, and imposing an overwhelming *obligation* that weighs in a great silence. And in the same way, the sacred is poetic. What is strongly suggested to sensibility, and displaced to the process of intelligence, is always to some extent sacred, to some extent poetic.

It is true that it is precisely the demands of poetry that leave it open to the elements, and in the arranging of the rhythm, so to speak, the most empty intentions play a role (there is even a didactic poetry). It is the condition of liberty. The element of death which gives sacrifice such great power can belong to poetry, but it is unrestrained. The theme is given from outside. And as the desire to awaken sensibility calls upon rhythm, the rhythm calls upon the tragic – or epic, or erotic – themes which allot destruction a place. Without this there would be, in the strongest sense, no poetry. Destruction is as necessary to poetry as to sacrifice, but poetry accomplishes it without constraint, since it can, if you like, be used to display knowledge! The meaning of the word *poetic* is no less oppressive: it includes an element of death or concealment that is uncertain only because of the inherently equivocal nature of this component. I mentioned that sacrificial death revealed the *absence* of the victim. Would this *absence* finally become the content of the moment that *sacrifice* or *poetry* 'bestows to sight'? My suggestion immediately has the provocative feel of a paradox, and seems to announce some mournful philosophy. In truth, the thing itself is neither difficult nor depressing. It is easy to recognize that an *object* offered for our consideration – in so far as it is the *distinct object*, associated with the possibilities of producing and using it – is addressed to practical intelligence. If I see a horse in a stable, I see the 'animal that men nurture and harness'. It is to the extent that this distinct character will be destroyed or attenuated that the sight of the animal will affect my sensibility. The horse is taken out of the stable to the abattoir. . . . For the butcher it becomes a quantity of meat worth so much a kilo (which closes sensibility and allows him to perform his task), but my 'animal that men nurture and harness' has now vanished: I sense a presence on the edge of an abyss (whose pit is absence). This *feeling* differs from reasoned sentimentality about death (the death which . . . the death that . . .). To kill the horse is to suppress it as a distinct object: the horse which dies is no longer, as the 'animal that men . . .', something distinct from me. The suppression of this object by its death is the suppression of a barrier between 'the animal' and myself: it becomes the same thing as I am, a presence on the edge of absence. Distinct *subjects* and *objects* no longer exist. In other words, the object – completely different from what I am – transcended me (to *transcend* me means *that it is completely different from me*). The suppression of a transcendent object reveals immanence, a reality which is immanent to me, from which I am not clearly and distinctly separated. The awakening of the sensibility, the passage from the sphere of intelligible (and usable) objects to excessive intensity, is the destruction of the object as such. Or course this is not what is commonly called death (and all the same, in the last analysis sacrifice is a misguided zeal); in one sense, it is contrary to it: in the butcher's eyes a horse is already dead (has become meat, an object). In the world of the instant nothing is dead, absolutely nothing, even if the infinite pressure of death alone has the power to burst in with a single leap. Nothing is dead, nothing can be. No more difference, no calculation to make: the stillness of the lake, the full expanse of the sky in a violent wind, where *happiness thinks about nothing* . . .

This moment of plenitude of the instant, in which the other is no longer 'other than me', in which I am no longer 'other than him', is the *ordeal* of sacrifice, when it *can*, if poetry attains it, be *willed*. But poetry is free, and not only can it be distanced from it but it can attain it overwhelmed, as happens in sacrifice. Tragic poetry, where the theme introduces destruction, is a form of sacrifice in several respects. When Phaedra says, as she dies:

> Already, to my heart, the venom gives
> An alien coldness, so that it scarcely lives;
> Already, to my sight, all clouds and fades –
> The sky, my spouse, the world my life degrades;
> Death dims my eyes, which soiled what they could see,
> Restoring to the light its purity.[8]

it is problematic that such a desirable moment of confusion should be the result inflicted through a fatality. But this does not limit poetry. If I read:

> . . . what god, what reaper of the eternal summer,
> upon leaving had negligently cast
> this golden sickle in the field of stars . . .

the object sold in ironmongers' is carried away by the metaphor, and *lost* in a *divine* infinity. But the black element has vanished. When the element of destruction is no longer externally established, in the theme (when poetry is not simply resonant movement, if the verbal play alone operates upon it a suppression of objects as such), it is no longer a crushing fatality but a deliberate exuberance, a rapid flood tide bearing limits away. It is not the overwhelming sky (annihilating mankind) but, on the contrary, the infinite transparency of mankind playing (recognizing itself) in the infinite transparency of the sky. The invoked God is in fact nothing but man himself, and the absurd confusion of stars with the limited quadrilateral of a field makes man divine through a suppression of his limits only if man himself, almost at the boundaries of his fields, becomes what he calls a god. And I cannot doubt that this surge of poetry 'bestows sight' in the depths of the sky of *what I am* (my presence at the edge of the abyss, which a cry reveals in the instant).

The poverty that begins from that point, given in the same terms (god, gold) of which the poet makes use, means that the poetic, like the sacred, born of a suppression of objects as such, being in essence change, is finally transformed into an object – doubtless removed from vulgar use, but having the durable character of an object. Nothing is more essentially fleeting than the *sacred* or the poetic, both of which contain, at one and the same time, plenitude and the ungraspable brevity of the instant. But *sacred* or *poetic* moments, which die, leave on their disappearance diverse residues. Not only does human memory allow its repetition (custom establishes itself, just as the poem writes itself), but sacred and poetic objects solidify what broke solidity. This is the meaning of entities like gods or God, as well as the meaning of images and 'poetic' conventions. The *sacred* was reborn from the destruction of an object which sacrifice in the first degree makes divine, but a sacrifice in the second degree does not simply destroy the straightforward object: the bull put to death is no longer merely an animal, implicated in man's productive activity; it is *also* the god. Sacrificial destruction kills both the god and the animal, and the death of the object-god is no less required than that of the animal-object. The god-object is not a lesser obstacle to the intense sentiment of the instant than the use-animal. (Wherever religious emotion is desired for itself, it is linked with the death of the divinity.) And just as the sacred is conditioned by the suppression of the sacred-object, in the same way poetry is conditioned by the suppression of poetry. But the possibility of sacrifice is limited: if the regular mechanism assures its rejuvenation, it sticks to the divine substance and remains confined in fear. The sacrifice which kills the god has no result other than the *sacred* which, having gone beyond the moment of confusion, again becomes fixed. . . . When poetry, to which nothing is connected in advance, can destroy without respite, it always makes use of unforeseen means.

Jacques Prévert's poetry is, therefore, poetic, but not in the same way as a work by Boileau, which is so only by virtue of rhyme and cadence (it is true that it observes what the 'moderns' have retained of old conventions: certain typographical arrangements). It is poetry because, in itself, it harshly effects the ruin of poetry. The words in 'Procession' are destroyed by a process of arbitrary association, substituting the confusion of a *doctor of porcelain* for the doctor and the porcelain of everyday life. A *rattle-mill*, a *watch in mourning*, burst forth in the same way as objects defined by their use value. This, with one variant (the rigorous exchange of complements between two couplets of words), is the process which Raymond Roussel's *calfskin soft rails* and *locomotives in ostrich feathers* illustrate (we know that Roussel himself was guided in his work by a rigorous, externally established determination). But a clear faculty to flatten is peculiar to the associations made by Jacques Prévert. Nothing is more abruptly anti-poetic; everything noble is debased: the gentleman wearing his nappies, the meerschaum marshal, the general of oysters. From this perspective, the manic adumbration of 'Inventory' puts the emotive object in the second-hand shop (*Victory of Samothrace* and *day of glory*; *terrible year* and *mater dolorosa*). In addition the rhythm 'clips the wings', radically putting us on the wrong foot of poetic flight. In this way it seems that even the basic element of poetry is directly attained by a destruction of what was given to us as poetry. And this destruction in the second degree is no less than an immediate method liable to 'bestow sight': to the advantage of the confusion resulting from the disparagement of 'Inventory' 'appear' a *stone, flowers, bread, a ray of sunlight*. . . . Besides, what these poems reveal must be made precise. I said they were the expression of an actuality, which is the present world with its questionable values. This world is wretched, and if poems reveal that fact, what they 'bestow to sight' is what one cannot love. In truth, present-day society is vulgar and constructed from man's flight from himself, and it hides behind a set design. But poetry that evokes this society is not confined to describing it; it is also the negation of it. What is 'bestowed to sight' is not, in fact, the hussar of death, nor the parish priest, but the absence of hussar and the absence of priest. The hussar and the priest, representing the present perverted form of life, intercept the light: they are no less of an obstacle to poetry than profane, interested, activity used to be for consciousness of the sacred. If this is clearly understood, poetry is reducible to the '*equality of man in relation to himself*', as Hugo clumsily expressed it, when he used a god to throw the sickle across the stars. But in so far as they reveal the falsehood of man to himself, a '*grand circus priest*', or a '*turkey cock of death*' expresses this 'equality' equally well. So do *stone, flowers, bread* or a *ray of sunlight*.

Notes

1. Published in *Critique*, nos 3–4 (1946).
2. *Donner à voir* is, of course, the title of a collection by Paul Éluard. It is the most accurate – as well as the most simple – definition of poetry: *what bestows sight*. Common prosaic language, on the other hand, does not touch the sensibility, and *bestows knowledge* even as it describes what is perceptible.
3. This is one of the elements involved in the Hegelian notion of 'recognition'. I am referring to A. Kojève's study, 'Hegel, Marx and Christianity', in the same issue of this journal (*Critique*, nos 3–4, p. 339). I would like to take this opportunity to mention that – not only on this point, but generally – my thought flows from the interpretation of Hegelianism that had been explored for several years in a course by Alexandre Kojève at the École des Hautes Études that attracted widespread interest. This interpretation, which reduced the distance between Hegel and Marx (its author is a Marxist, and it could be said, if one accepts his argument, that Hegel is too), also had the interest of an original position, and perhaps a decisive value. The long study one can read below is a substantial résumé of it. The course itself – at least, its outline – will soon appear in an edition published by NRF under the title *Introduction à la philosophie de Hegel*. [Available in English in an abridged edition as *Introduction to the Reading of Hegel*, transl. James H. Nichols, Jnr (1969), New York: Basic Books. – *Translator*]
4. Other poems are no less rich: how can one not mention 'The Thresher', 'The Message', 'The Stupid Wagers' and, most wonderful of all, 'Fishing For Whales'?

5. In the sense of the cry, nothing is more fundamentally anti-poetic, nor more poetic in the funereal sense, than Lamartine's 'The Lake'. The vulgarity of Kafka's stories, on the other hand, liberates a contemporary intensity of actuality.

6. Nevertheless, I would make it clear that the theory of sacrifice, of which I give a glimpse here, is based on elements of the *Intichiuma* in Australia, which has become known through the well-known work of Spencer and Gillen. The *Intichiuma* is an embryonic form of sacrifice among the least advanced so-called 'primitives'. I have considered *Intichiuma* as an elementary organization, less well known than sacrifice, with a view to determining what was general about man's archaic conduct in relation to objects (the study of which cannot be abstracted from the way words are organized).

7. This way of considering the question seems to be opposed to an 'economic interpretation'. But to return to the subject. Once given, this turn away from poetic activity is itself reducible to economic considerations. One day I would like to be able to demonstrate this.

[8. Racine, *Phaedra*, transl. Richard Wilbur (1986), Orlando, FL: Harcourt Brace Jovanovich. – *Translator*]

André Breton:

Ode to Charles Fourier[1]

We are endlessly devoted to this familiar world divided by set square
and rail, where the object and the self are separated from each other,
and in which if I do not want to burn my fingers I must set my face
against the flame that warms me – coldly alien, as the wind is to the wall
which it besieges – and we are so lost in its depths that we need to
diminish what it is that eludes it (as being too trivial or too complicated). This is to no great effect, and this man who seized the world has
managed only to place himself and his home halfway between equally
deceptive and equally incongruous shapes, created by cosmology and
microphysics (a barbarous jumble of images, schemes, indexes and
notions). No less does he subordinate the infinitesimal or immense
universe, by an artifice of thought, to the set-square mentality which
commands reality. The only decision which, in such conditions, would
not be completely ridiculous is to say to what extent scientific research
has deprived this stable world of truth. Not that it has deceived us in
any way, but the clear image we have of it is that, as a whole, it
constitutes only a screen – of a limiting opacity, assembled from a
congealed decomposition of light. To attribute to a tangle of isolated
forms, weighed down with stupor, a greater meaning than necessary
convenience in response to the body's needs is certainly the origin of
that the meanness which, combined with impudence, opposes human
life to the simplicity of the universe.

We emerge from such a sordid delusion by means of poetry. But in
our time, poetry is no longer an expression of pre-established myths, it
is itself the myth (or the 'absence of myth', it doesn't matter which)
which offers us the distracted, and so readily unleashed, movement
that we are. This represents a complete divorce between poetry and
the world of action, to which the strangest myths have remained
connected by positive references. It is not, then, enough for us to
reach, by means of an unsuspected method, a world of passion and

poetic intensity; what we need is, more precisely, to establish a path between the two spheres, for without a counterpart, the negation of the world of production would be only suicide or falsehood.

André Breton has not ceased to seek a solution to this problem which would not simply be a compromise. He has striven, not without obstinacy, to find a path from Marxism to surrealism. It is by no means certain that he has really failed, but he has without a doubt recognized the difficulties involved. For my part, I would not say that the path is impossible. And I do not want to forget that Marx's doctrine has always served as the only effective application of intelligence to practical facts as a whole (this is not true of just any doctrine; no other general doctrine has brought, as it works with the totality of facts, the sort of clear-cut decision that a science brings into a particular domain). But to persist and stubbornly believe in the possibility of a direct path towards Marx could not exclude the desire to find out whether there are other signs in this direction. And it seems to me that we should not be surprised that André Breton now discovers such an sign in Fourier.

In the *Historical Index* of an official Communist Party publication, I note this short entry:

> FOURIER *(Charles) – One of the greatest names of utopian socialism (1772–1837). If his system of social harmony is awash with infantile ideas, it also contains some features of genius in his critique of the capitalist order.*

No one, in fact, would dream of denying the capacity of lucid judgement that the author of the *Theory of the Four Movements* was able to bring to questions of economic reality. Marx recognized him (in the *Communist Manifesto*) as an authentic revolutionary (he is reproached only for having misunderstood the class struggle, which was alone capable of removing a utopian stamp from worthy dreams). But what detained Marx, and what causes economists today – of different schools – to continue to respect Fourier, existed side by side with some propositions that are generally characterized as childish.

Fourier could write, without turning a hair:[2]

> Planets, like plants, copulate with themselves and with other planets. In the same way the earth, through copulation with itself, by fusion of its two characteristic aromas, masculine emanating from the North Pole, feminine from the South Pole, engenders the *cherry*, the sub-pivotal of red fruits, and accompanied by 5 graduations of fruits, as follows:
>
> The earth copulates with MERCURY, its fifth and most important satellite, to engender the STRAWBERRY.
>
> With Pallas, its fourth satellite, the black*currant* or cassis.
>
> With Ceres, its third satellite, the *gooseberry*.

With Juno, its second satellite, the *bunch of berries*.
With Phoebina, its first satellite, NOTHING, *lacunae*.

This sort of thing causes extreme offence to the economist who is dominated by the need for utilitarian knowledge, yet it represents an invasion of poetry into Fourier's work. But does not the fact that a mind so open to poetry nevertheless excelled in the realm of practical reason provide a valuable intimation? Did not what appeared to him in such conditions, and was not contrary to poetry, genuinely respond to the necessities of the path, the bridge, between the two domains? In fact, Fourier's economic theories not only took account of material needs but also gave the passions, which only poetry generally welcomes, a place and a necessity in the ordering of the industrial world. How could Breton, with his interests, not be moved by a project of productive organization in which poetry would not be immediately expelled, as it usually is? And how is it possible to avoid raising the question of whether the crucial possibilities have not been, clumsily, carelessly misunderstood? No one could neglect this problem. It is a question of mankind's harmony with itself, of poetry's harmony with what is useful, and the harmony of the passions with material needs.

André Breton has only given *poetic* expression to the hope the great utopian has sustained in him. But if it is possible to regret that it has not engendered more positive results, how can one not recognize that poetry alone could be their initiation?

Notes

1. Published in *Critique*, no. 18 (November 1947). A review of André Breton, *Ode à Charles Fourier* (1947), Paris: Éditions de la Revue 'Fontaine', translated by Kenneth White as *Ode to Charles Fourier* (1969), London: Cape Goliard.

2. *Traité de l'Association domestique-agricole*, cited by Henri Pastoureau in *Le Surréalisme en 1947*, p. 83.

The Age of Revolt[1]

Even subject to attack as it has been, *The Rebel* emerges as a *major* work. The author of the attack, André Breton, would admit as much. One would have to be blind or of bad faith to deny it.

Albert Camus wanted to grasp what is consistent about the excessive and precipitate impulse which has made of recent centuries a continual process of disconcerting destruction and creation, in which there remains nothing whose aspect has not been radically renewed. This much is certain: the past centuries have little in common with those which preceded them, and in the convulsions that have run through them, the fate of humanity has been brought completely into question. This is why it is so important to try properly to understand what this fever – or rather, this delirium that animates us – signifies; this is why it is finally necessary to shed light into its depths, and on the hidden aspects of a problem generally reduced to outward appearances.

1. The era of revolt

From the outset there is a major reason for us to tackle, with some anguish, the problem of revolt (strictly in the desire to understand). The immense preceding period, on the contrary, was characterized by submission: a succession of submissions and slaveries, whether submitted to unwillingly or accepted willingly. For such a long time the principle of all judgement was reference to authority. Today it is, rather, a contrary movement of revolt that gives our voice a convincing strength. There is no longer anything that arouses respect, friendship or contagion unless it contains an element of refusal. One single word, *conformism*, and the reaction it provokes, sufficiently reveals the change that has occurred. But if we can see that to be a rebel is in conformity with the new principles, we cannot always say why. It is not strange simply that believers themselves react to the accusation of conformism. What has caused such a general rage to occupy the position of revolt in every domain? In any situation, we do not give up until we have reversed the very conditions of action, feelings or thought. It is as if we wanted, through an act of violence, to tear ourselves from the beaten track which connected us, and (the absurdity of this image alone corresponds with this movement) grabbing ourselves by the hair, to pull up and fling ourselves into a world never before seen. It is true that for some people revolt is reduced to more rational aspects. An expression was presented, against which the oppressed had to rise up. But there is no need to challenge this point of view in order to acknowledge it. Since the eighteenth century it is certain that once denied the principle of his humble submission, and losing the divine authority which gives meaning to our limits, man has tended no longer to recognize anything that could *rightly* be opposed to his desire.

It is not simply the condition of economically subjugated man which has occasioned the expression of revolt. It is *in general* that the dominant values of the past have been denied. The spirit of refusal has spread so widely that from Sade to Nietzsche, in one century, there has been no disorder, no subversion, that the human mind has not rigorously carried to completion. Historically, the revolt of the oppressed has no doubt had the greatest impact. But the tidal waves of language – if language really is, as one must believe, a key to mankind – are not unworthy of interest. These are unprecedented, and coincide with historical changes which are equally so. We must also pay the closest attention if Albert Camus is now bold enough to consider the unity and consistency of this movement.

2. A discourse on fundamental revolt

It is true that surrealism has doubtless been the first to try to reveal this consistency. But surrealism did not go beyond strong affirmations. In proportion to the possibilities and the needs of intelligence, this might seem insignificant. At the same time, surrealism tended to define a moral position which responded to this double movement of revolt. In a way it vaguely sketched out what today Albert Camus tries to make precise. Both for Albert Camus and for surrealism it is a question of finding a fundamental movement in which man fully assumes his destiny. If one wants to understand a profound book, one must relate it to the state of mind from which it evolved and to which it responds. I am saying not that Albert Camus is a surrealist, but that surrealism was the most visionary (and sometimes the most felicitous) expression of this elementary state of mind.

It may therefore be legitimate to begin this discussion of *The Rebel* from the perspective of André Breton's attack on it.

First I must mention the paradox that is immediately apparent (using completely excessive language, Breton would say it is 'unacceptable in every respect'). Anyone who attentively reads the allegations made by the author of *Nadja*[2] in a calm and impartial way, and with the texts to which they refer to hand, notices a disarming disproportion between the complaint made and the consequences drawn from it. This is all the more surprising in that the two men enjoyed a close friendship before the breach: 'For a long time,' we read, 'I have had *complete* [my emphasis] confidence in Albert Camus. At the Pleyel meeting in December 1948, you may remember, I was moved to offer him personal homage, saying that following the Liberation I considered that his was the clearest and most honourable voice . . . ' But here we are in the world of all or nothing: since then Camus has spoken of Lautréamont whom, apparently, he had read without feeling the drawn-out thrill that passes through Breton (as it does through me) at each reading. So it is a matter of a sacred element which Albert Camus does not recognize as such. It is not really what Camus actually said about Lautréamont that is at issue. It is that his tone is inappropriate to the mystery which the *Poésies* does not surrender. I do not think that the incriminating passage takes sufficient account of the excessive, frantic and provocative character of this 'conformist' text: can one imagine a conformist character that the *Poésies* could possibly satisfy? Nevertheless, Camus's dialectic, based upon the opposition of the *Poésies* to the *Chants de Maldoror*, reveals (without fully exploring it) a movement of Lautréamont's mind which goes to the heart of revolt. 'Poetic revolt' − which calls for excess, 'theoretical spite', and all types of disordered states − is dismissed as banal. It seems to me that the experience of poetry (to the extent that the excess of revolt carries it to the extreme degree of negation) should confirm the identity on this point, in *Maldoror* and the *Poésies*, of a complete disordering and scrupulous observance (both ridiculous and ambiguous, it is true) of the rule. No doubt Albert Camus has, with regard to Lautréamont, drawn no other consequence from this identity than the explanation of the thread connecting surrealism to Stalinist Communism (this contention is not untenable, but is it necessary to connect it to the elusive slippage of *Les Poésies*?), but the impulse of the entire book has the same import: the mind which has unrestrainedly roused revolt experiences the absurdity (and non-viability) of its

attitude, but discovers there an unexpected truth: the general existence of a good which is *worth all the problems of revolt*, 'something . . .
which demands that we take care'. 'The rebel, in the etymological
sense, makes a volte-face', and if he speaks – more simply, if his
conduct is human rather than animal – it is necessary for him to state
and conceive what it is that justifies his attitude, and merits the risk of
confronting death. But the very movement of revolt signifies that the
rebel shares this inviolable and sovereign element (which can neither
be subordinated nor submitted to without denying itself and withering
away) with whoever rebels with him. In the movement of initial revolt,
the mind, in the process of expressing its position, becomes conscious
and, as it speaks, realizes the benefit which is available to all and
requires people to rise up against the blows inflicted upon them.
Camus says it: 'In our everyday trials revolt plays the same role as the
"cogito" in the order of thought: it represents the first evidence. But
this evidence draws the individual from his solitude. It is a common
ground upon which everyone founds their first principles. I rebel
therefore we exist.'[3] So revolt as it attacks morality – to the extent that
morality becomes the base of the established order – is no less, from
the first moment, engaged on a moral course. Rather more: its impulse
alone releases a value that goes beyond vulgar interest: it is a benefit
more precious than the advantage, or the favourable condition, of life;
which even exceeds life (and is distinct from it), since we are ready to
sacrifice life in order to preserve it.

It is difficult to avoid making an association between this view, which
is in a way inspired, and the surrealist state of mind. The difference lies
in the stormy and hesitant mode of expression, sometimes even laden
with a barely intelligible upheaval, to which surrealist expression is
intentionally bound.

Cold analysis succeeds the delirium of fever. While it lacks its blind
vehemence, it emerges in this way from Breton's apparent awkward-
ness as he tries to found *his* morality, despite his intolerance of the past.
It also emerges from the separate domain in which Breton wanted to
establish a world which would *properly* belong to him. Can we forget the
starkly brutal incomprehension with which Dostoyevsky's work was
treated in the *Manifesto of Surrealism* – a great deal more thoughtless
than Camus's treatment of *Poésies*? Breton has always had the habit of
replacing a rigorous development of thought with an audacity and an
(often subtle) displacement of the question at issue: what he says with
an unrestrained power touches the sensibility or the passions. This
barefaced lack of control has been instrumental in giving him both a
wide public and a paucity of meaning and fragility of support. But it
has authority principally over the incomplete character of the world in

which he wants to enclose man's existence. Particularly troubling is his refusal to accept a more appropriate method. He does not want to acknowledge that judgements founded on strength of feeling have little possibility of convincing anyone or, rather haphazardly, possess a persuasive power of the vaguest kind. In the final analysis, the present world lacks rigour, simple lucidity and, in particular, breadth of vision: each person is enclosed within a restricted world on which he gazes with an unchanging perspective. If André Breton did not feel such discomfort as soon as the results of the dazzling – but too rare, too difficult to create – plays of perspectives he has regulated around him are disturbed, if he did not completely lack imagination once outside his marvellous domain, he would have recognized the treasures that Camus's book brought him. He would have considered even a profound divergence in the way of judging *Poésies* to be of little consequence. But he has no imagination, not even a simple curiosity, when it comes to ordinary things. When he unreservedly admired Lenin it probably never occurred to him that Lenin, *without any doubt whatsoever,* would merely have shrugged his shoulders at the frenzy of *Maldoror.* (Perhaps even now Breton would contest such incontestable evidence . . .) Today Albert Camus's thought retains the greatest regard for Lautréamont, even though undoubtedly with great discretion. Here we are a long way from the most penetrating but often blinding vision of fever. In reading Lautréamont, Camus has felt only a lukewarm admiration. He replies to Breton's first attack: 'From a literary perspective . . . I must say that I consider *War and Peace* to be a far more important book than *Les chants de Maldoror.*'[4] But Breton does not want to see that dizzy and multiplied divergence is inherent to the human condition, and that it is necessary to realize this clearly if one wants to retain hope of not simply talking to deaf ears. In his attitude he has the rather strange fault of implying that apart from a small number of people who resemble him (or those who lend themselves to this confusion), the world contains only ignoble human trickery. This is the only way he can implicitly explain why people are so rarely like him. This is also the only meaning – and it is no less implicit – when he speaks (in relation to the offending passage in Camus) of false witness.[5] False witness! Quite simply, that means: he does not see what I see.

Anyone else would say to himself without further ado: There is no way I can subscribe to this summary judgement, but if the author is mistaken and risks misleading others; if I am sure, in the present case, that he is wrong, I must nevertheless try to understand why someone I believe to be honest – someone, moreover, in whom I have placed 'all confidence' – can speak in this way. Unless he has other reasons, which he does not mention, Breton ought to have been all the more prudent and recalled the apologies that accompanied the most recent edition of his *Manifestos*, the second of which contained personal attacks that have since become regrettable. If Breton had known how to dominate the moment of passion, which caused him to consider insensitivity to the work of Lautréamont as proof of moral vulgarity, he would also have recognized that in Camus, by a concurrence of intentions and initial reactions, the surrealist experience encountered the means to render clear and indisputable the profound necessity to which it had responded. The unity of poetic revolt and the historical process, whose manifestation surrealism once proposed as its elementary task, is revealed in the fact that an unconditional revolt is the basis of the dazzling revelation of well-being and its grip over man, the consequent basis of a movement of revolution which postulates the sovereignty of justice.

3. In the realm of misunderstanding

At this point I am obliged to make my own position clear. It is a little paradoxical that I should be the one to reveal what these 'adversaries' have in common, and that a final coincidence of their views (of which an absurd polemic underlines, in fact, the depth and the objectivity) gives the dominant truth of an era its firmest foundation. In point of fact, this curious 'accord' developed against a position I had taken, the aspects of which I have sometimes represented in this journal, and of which I will here set out the principle, adapted to the terms of the present development: the opposition between *well-being* (identical to the *sacred*) and *justice* (which derives from the benefit identical to what is profitable).

Thus, by revealing the mistake through which the opposing parties have struggled (in a disagreement to which only Breton gave its venomous quality), it is my error in particular that I would confess. And as far as my admission and its reasons accordingly allow me to clarify the significance of Albert Camus's position, I would add to the parallels between the surrealist experience and *The Rebel* the experience which, in my opinion, is common to both of them as well as to myself.

Before considering this, let me make a simple fact plain. In the whole of this incident there is a purely accidental opposition. I feel rather annoyed with what appears to be no more than an error made by André Breton. But to this extent I am his adversary only on the surface. On more than one occasion, following some old difficulties over twenty years ago, I have expressed my agreement with the surrealist position, at least in the sense in which I understand it. In an open letter to the editor I have even publicly refused to publish in *Les Temps Modernes* because of the impertinent way Sartre spoke about the surrealists in this review.[6] This is of no consequence: I mention it merely to underline the fact that, in the general train of thought, I am more often in agreement with Breton than with Camus.

It is more important to insist on the high regard and interest that *The Rebel* reveals for the character of the person who today attacks it. The long passage that deals with surrealism[7] cannot pass for an agreement on the part of Camus. It is a concise critique which, in my opinion, stands as an outline. Perhaps the author lacked the information of those who experienced the daily ebb and flow of the movement. But would one reproach someone with a lack of understanding and love when he writes: 'a great call to absent life armed with a total refusal of the present world'? Camus continues:

> As Breton so marvellously put it: 'Incapable of accepting the fate destined for me, affected in my highest consciousness by this denial of justice, I am careful not to adapt my existence to the ridiculous conditions of life in this earthly existence.' According to Breton, the mind cannot be found fixed either in life or beyond it. Surrealism is determined to respond without respite to this disquiet. It is 'the cry of the mind turning back against itself and determined desperately to break these chains open'. It cries against death and the 'ridiculous duration' of a precarious situation. Thus surrealism places itself within the ranks of the impatient. It lives in a particular state of wounded fury as well as in the rigour and proud intransigence which assume a morality.[8]

Later he adds:

> in the meanness of his time – and this should not be forgotten – he has been the only person who has spoken profoundly about love. Love is morality in a state of trance serving as a homeland for this exile. Certainly a dimension is still lacking here. Being neither a political party nor a religion, surrealism is perhaps nothing but an impossible wisdom. But it is the proof that there is no comfortable wisdom: 'We demand and will be content with nothing less than the hereafter in our days,' as Breton admirably wrote. The splendid night in which he took pleasure while reason, called to action, unleashed its armies on the world, in fact perhaps announces those dawns which have not yet broken, and the advent of René Char, the poet of our renaissance.[9]

Thus the sentence in which Breton, without having the patience to read the whole book, accuses the man who – because he understood it – so precisely interpreted the impulse of his revolt of rallying 'to the side of the worst conservatism and the worst conformism',[10] will stand as a stupefying example of inexcusable misunderstanding.

4. The dilemma of revolt

History itself is perhaps – in any case, it certainly seems to be – an interminable misunderstanding. Nevertheless, the aim of discourse is to resolve the difficulty men have in understanding each other: a restricted view, considered in its relation to language as a whole, to the exhaustive and coherent thought to which all isolated thought aspires, has no meaning except in the moment in which it contradicts itself. (This is why a thought full of vitality does not rest until it catches itself out.) It is first necessary to confront the misunderstandings, which attract and bring not only a promise of resolution, but also this agonizing power that causes night to fall, giving us an obscure sense of the death by which it is engulfed.

I have such a strong desire to portray what is and what I must live with precision, and the exact portrayal of things seems to me so closely linked with the possibility of it being communicated in the clear agreement of minds, that the mere thought of those who could understand each other being separated by these violent disagreements makes the pursuit of reflection and language seem first odious and then ridiculous to me. The meaning (and the fate) of revolt is at stake. We can wisely (as happens in the synod, or as a congress now does) seek an agreement based on a preliminary *submission* to the assembly's decisions. But we then risk absurdly demonstrating that synods and congresses are right, at least to the extent that they spare us the discordances of revolt. Often it seems that on the side of rebels there is only caprice and the sovereignty of unstable humour, and contradictions multiplied without restraint. In fact, this is enough to submit revolt indefinitely to the spirit of submission! This necessity is inscribed in the destiny of mankind: the spirit of submission has the efficacy so lacking in insubordination. Revolt leaves the rebel faced with a dilemma which depresses him: if it is pure and headstrong he will reject the exercise of all power, will push powerlessness to the point of nourishing himself with the complacency of incontinent language. If he compromises with a quest for power, then his revolt becomes allied with the spirit of subordination. This is where the opposition between literature and politics comes in: one is rebellion with an open heart; the other is realistic.

How, on the one hand, do we sever the impulse of revolt from the contrary inclination to force others to our will? On the other hand, how do we avoid the dangers of verbal incitement, of an impotent multiplicity of opinions in which language can no longer measure up to the reality of action, gets carried away, becomes frustrated and finally exhausts itself? This is not simply a problem for Albert Camus; it is the problem for all people today who experience the poverty of their time; in short, it is the most urgent contemporary problem to be confronted.

5. The only response to the dilemma of revolt is restraint

It is to Albert Camus's credit that he is the first person to pose the problem in its entirety (as it is André Breton's good – or bad – fortune to have, despite himself, clarified its uncomfortable aspects). We can reject the efficient solution offered by tyrannical revolt: of a transition (revolutionary at the moment of completion – in the sense in which astronomers understand the term – a perfect movement of 'revolution') from the revolt of the best to the submission of all. (For tyrants, in tyrannical revolt, are themselves subject to the tyranny they exercise over others.) Still, we must ask whether a revolt that refuses tyranny can achieve anything other than ferment and discordant verbalism. It is not certain, and if it is true that Albert Camus offers a solution that goes beyond blind rage, it remains to be proved that it gives us the power to proceed to action without turning to murder and tyranny. Only the future can authentically decide this, but we can question here and now whether this solution escapes the difficulties we have already noted (and which surrealism is so far from resolving, having only ever given such brutal instructions about it that it belonged on the side of the exasperated demand and the scream uttered to no avail).[11]

Camus does not hide his aversion to excess: he proclaims it. His philosophy is expressly based on the principle of the golden mean. He is not afraid of confronting head-on this juvenile state of mind, which condemns what is not *cut and dried*, and promises to compromise itself as completely as possible. Camus is not against purity; he is against method and the desire for the absolute.

According to him:[12]

> restraint . . . teaches us that an element of realism is necessary to any morality. Completely pure virtue is murderous; equally, an element of our morality is necessary to all realism: cynicism too is murderous. For this reason humanitarian verbiage has no more basis than cynical provocation. Finally, humankind is not entirely to blame, for it did not start history; but it is not completely innocent either, since it continues it. Those who go

beyond this and affirm humanity's complete innocence end up in the mania of definitive culpability. Revolt, on the contrary, sets us on the path of calculated culpability. Its one hope – but an invincible one – culminates in innocent murderers.

6. The first impulse of revolt is beyond measure

No praise is too great for a language which is as far from naive phraseology as it is from artful realism. But it is easy to respond like Breton, and put one's money on the prestige of an incorrigible refusal to listen . . . . 'a revolt into which "restraint" has been introduced? Emptied of its passional content, what remains of revolt?'[13] As if he did not have, before his very eyes, the remnants of a revolt that had been reduced to verbal violence for thirty years.

We are again in the realm of misunderstanding, in which Breton wants to confound the initial impulse with the consequences he desires. There is no doubt that Breton has formulated the most precise images of the first – passional – impulse of revolt: even today, it is what is most laden with excess that serves to clarify what is most essential. But on this point one could generally agree that if the necessities of revolt finally lead us to the need for restraint, in the first instance revolt exists in its excessive movement. But having started out in excess, we also need to understand the necessity of coming through it to restraint.

Perhaps there is no truth that needs to be surpassed (more rapidly, but also more easily) than the one which Breton defined in this celebrated passage:

> The simplest surrealist act consists in descending to the street with revolver in hand and shooting at random, as fast as one can, into the crowd. Whoever has not, at least once in their lives, had such a desire to make an end of the trivial system of debasement and cretinization in place has his own place marked out in the crowd, belly in line with the barrel . . .

I certainly accept that it is not possible to live in this dead-end, but I cannot agree with some of the reactions to this passage. Breton is right to insist on this much. It is clear that 'it always goes without saying that in [his] mind the author of such an action acts in the realization that he will immediately be lynched'.[14] He adds:

> It is a question – metaphysically speaking – of a fully conscious outrage against humanity, which is of such a nature to strike out against both 'self' and 'other' and which, no matter how little one might reflect on the fact, is

not without affinities with Jules Lequier's final outrage against 'God'. I admit that I have passed, and in a quite fleeting way, through nihilist despair. My consolation would be that I have had illustrious predecessors:-

> To war, to vengeance and to terror,
> My mind! Let us turn in the snapping jaws: Ah! Pass by,
> Republic of the World! We have had enough
> Of Emperors, regiments, colonials, peoples.

I wanted to quote the whole of this passage. It has the virtue of grasping revolt in the moment when its excess is unleashed: the dazzling and mortal vertigo in which man tears himself from the submission imposed upon him. In this I am not too far away from Albert Camus' description of Rimbaud as (in his life, if not in his work[15]): 'the poet, the greatest poet, of revolt' – Rimbaud, who could give 'revolt the most strangely appropriate language it has ever received'.[16] I don't linger on the distance today between Breton and a statement which is already twenty years old. Nor on Albert Camus's insistence on placing 'metaphysical revolt' on the clearly distinct paths of crime (in particular of Nazi violence). The passage about 'revolvers' has nothing to do with political bestiality: without a doubt, it even brings into play the bewildering wonders of suicide. Moreover, this elementary form of revolt has more than a verbal existence: it is the *amok* of Malaysia, whose practice (which is *traditional*) was not so rare. Tired of enduring the weight of the world, a man would suddenly see red: he would race into the street and stab those he encountered by chance with a kris until he succumbed in his turn to the blows of the frightened crowd. It is odd that in at least one area of the world such an intense gesture responds to custom, to the extent that it seems to become less criminal madness than a sacred act. We search in vain for a more complete revolt. Nothing has more profoundly corresponded, no matter what its purely physical foundations, in such a complete way to the spirit of this metaphysical revolt which, Albert Camus tells us, is 'the impulse by which a man raises himself against the human condition and creation in its entirety'.[17] It is 'metaphysical because it contests the aims of both man and creation'.

For the *amok* there is no longer any misunderstanding; nor is there for his victims.

But what about those who saw him thirsty for death, who survive and perhaps took part in killing him?

The European crowd, perhaps more heavily subjugated, would succumb to spite; but I can depict a prouder and more open audience which would not be deaf to this sovereign protest, even if it has had to protect itself from it. It would know without any *misunderstanding* that the *amok* was determined, in a flash of lightning, to deny what limited him, rather than accept a limited existence: for this reason it would bow down before the *amok*, whose death has the significance of a genuine sovereignty.

My way of considering the issue is paradoxical, and seems very different from that of Camus, for whom the rebel is defined by the desire to see the value of revolt recognized in himself. But before that, must we not consider the revolt which blinds – and desires to remain blind – in death?

7. Revolt, sovereignty, and the criminal and rebellious character of royalty

In the first part of this article I stated my intention to show not only the essential accord between Breton and Camus, but also the concordance of their common position with my own.

It is a question of establishing a value founded on revolt, and *using* it to give a basis to traditional law, which condemns falsehood and demands from us loyalty towards others. Of course justice itself is implied in the morality defined by this value. Words like revolt, loyalty and justice are not without ambivalence, and I would like to show that the fundamental requirement of such a morality is sovereignty. Thus, the morality of revolt – which, as we shall see, lays the foundation for justice – would, nevertheless, not be based on it: its foundation is the will to exist in a sovereign way.

This does not clearly emerge – at least not straight away – from Camus's book. Moreover, I must recognize that the proposition in itself is not so clear. I will now endeavour not only to prove it but to give it an everyday meaning.

When Camus talks about the motivation of revolt, this is ambiguous. At first this motivation seems to be injustice and the suffering that results from it. Albert Camus seems by no means a stranger to pity, but we still need to know *what* this suffering is that is the object of pity. He rightly says: 'Revolt is born of the exhibition of irrationality in the face of unjust and incomprehensible conditions.'[18] But equally, he can state: 'Revolt is the refusal, within man, to be treated as a thing.' 'Treated as a thing' signifies, in Kant's vocabulary, as a means, not as an end. This refusal positively expresses itself by a demand that within man revolt is the will to be sovereign (to belong to oneself and no one else).

Albert Camus is not the only person to see the great tide of challenge which has been rising for two centuries as being inspired by a demand for sovereignty. Marx established the alienation of the proletariat as the principle of the class struggle. But often this fundamental element is veiled. As a rule, sovereignty and the autonomy of existence are abstract formulas. More material satisfactions are generally considered more important. If it is a question of freedom, this is because of the familiar images this great word immediately evokes, like prison and repression. It is not that sovereignty inevitably has to be abstract, but to the extent that a common representation is connected to it, it is not popular. Above all else, sovereignty is realized in the fact of divinity, or of kings. The 'sovereignty of the people' remains an unreal statement; it means the *sovereignty* of *labouring* people *submitting* to work, and sovereignty is defined by the fact that it refuses submission and is, above all, the fact of existing in the world with no end other than to exist! This is in contradiction not with the work to come or already achieved, but with *current* work – or the *essence* of work, assumed in its *laborious* quality, in the qualification of *worker*. We must be precise about this: the worker can be sovereign if he desires to be so, but only to the extent to which he lays down his tools.

Let us move on.

Camus himself has left things obscure – so much so, it is true, that they become portentous and irresolute. It seems to me – and I feel very strongly about this – that his pity is addressed above all to those who want to become sovereigns and are shattered by what remains irreducible within them. I even believe that the word *pity* itself betrays the strength – that is, the sovereignty – of such an impulse, which is a matter of solidarity (although Camus finds this word too vague, and would prefer to use 'complicity', which raises the curtain on tragedy). In its essence sovereignty is guilty; it could even be said that in a way it is equivalent to guilt. Camus knows this very well, reminding us of Saint-Just's words: 'No one can rule innocently.'[19] This remains ambiguous if one understands the question of ruling in the vulgar sense of governing. But sovereignty resides in crime just as its divine and majestic humours do, being, like revolt, beyond all laws. 'Saint-Just postulates . . . that it is axiomatic that all kings are rebels . . .'[20] Is not sovereignty the fact that one would prefer to die, or at least to place one's life on the line, rather than submit to the weight that overwhelms man? At its most extreme limit, this weight is not simply servitude or suffering, but death. Like Albert Camus, we ourselves can rebel against death, but who cannot recognize that there is in revolt *first of all* a particular will towards excess, and that one cannot *extract* restraint from sovereignty? This was even the affliction of sovereignty at an extreme of wanting to protect the sovereign existence of the king from death, even if it implies more than the vain counterpart of this glaring truth: 'Every king', says Camus, 'is guilty by the very fact that he wants to be a king. And is he not thereby consecrated to death?'[21] In the same way the modern rebel exists in crime: he kills, but in his turn he accepts that his crime consecrates him to death: he 'accepts dying and paying for a life with a life'.[22] In human terms there is a curse on all sovereignty, as on all revolt. Anyone who does not submit must pay, for he is guilty. These archaic terms cannot be the final word: mankind's innocence has never really been definitively lost. But sovereign life, as it responds to the desire to be an end in itself without any expectations – without, as a means to other ends, being subordinated – needs to take guilt and retribution on to itself.

8. Retribution for the king's guilt

Guilt is excess, but retribution is the return to *restraint*. It is true that retribution is not always the fact of sovereignty, but it is so clearly connected with it that if one thinks about the most ancient times or primitive forms, the myths and rituals in which it took shape reveal the counterpart of the sovereign's excessive powers. By means of his prerogatives, a single individual is able to incarnate mankind's intractable nature, at least liberated from the obligations which overwhelm the mass of people. The people may have demanded this elevation as an aspect of the common law, and to this extent such a person would even cease to be human – would in a way, without such elevation, succumb under the weight of a distress and submission which would be limitless, but the counterpart is that a fatal curse falls upon someone who has received divine prerogatives. Sometimes this curse is averted: royalty may be associated with a mythical infirmity.[23] Or religion requires the king to abase himself to the level of the most wretched of his subjects before a celestial power which utterly overwhelms people. In other instances a simulacrum of sacrifice, or the sacrifice of a substitute victim, serves to release him. But often the king must pay for his divine privileges by being ritually put to death; and so, strictly speaking, royalty itself becomes a terrible burden.

Moreover, sovereignty is most often confounded with military power, which in accordance with the terms used by Hegel in the dialectic of master – *Herr* – and slave – *Knecht* – belongs to the master – in other words, to the person who pays *with his life* for the privileges of mastery (the *Genuss*, the exuberance, and the fact of raising the whole weight of material life for himself). (For Hegel, the master and the slave choose their fate: the slave prefers submission to death, the master death to submission; but the master, lacking the experience a man acquires in servitude (essentially the experience of work), cannot reach the state of a complete person, something which is attained only by the slave in revolt. One would have to say that the sovereignty of the master (or the king) is an inconsequential sovereignty: retribution is paid despite it and by whoever contradictorily *uses* his *sovereignty* as a thing which he possesses.)

9. Revolt and restraint

Normally, the only thing apparent in the life of the great and of kings is crime (in the most vulgar sense of the word): at the very least, abuse of power and exploitation of the weak to the advantage of vested interests. The nobility and royalty use violence to confiscate the fruits of others' work for their own profit. To this extent it is easy to see no more than misappropriation, and to fail to recognize the initial meaning of the impulse, which lies in a refusal to accept man's common condition as a limit.

There is in historical sovereignty something quite different from this refusal – a slumber, rather; the exploitation of property acquired by the violence of refusal. In the exercise of royalty there is even something contrary to this refusal that is clearly emphasized if we consider the situation, found in India, of the king put forward as a victim at the celebration of a festival, for a potential *amok*. The *amok* who killed the king succeeded him (almost in the same way as the king of the woods of Nemi, whose murder in ritual combat is Frazer's point of departure in *The Golden Bough*). Or he was immediately slaughtered. In this significant theme the animal state is rediscovered, for sovereignty was the act of someone who refused human law, which overwhelms man and *bends* him to its will. Whoever reigns following the *amok* is opposed to a new *amok* being performed, but his objection is only half-hearted: if it comes to it he will offer himself to death, since he accepts the principle of retribution. But the sovereign can entirely betray the truth of his power, and no longer retain anything of his *sovereign* origins and his original complicity with violence. From that moment he passes over to the other side. He reduces the power and privileges open to him simply to a means; he rejects custom, and *governs* rather than reigns. He can even govern simply to advance his own personal interests. In so doing he renounces *sovereignty* (except the name) and nothing about him transcends, in any sense of the word, an organization of interests (a subordination of very moment to a calculated protection of interests). He becomes a mere caricature of a sovereign. His presence is now no more than an asset: it tells us to look for an authentic sovereignty at the opposite extreme to the despised institution.

These detours have taken us a long way from Albert Camus's argument. Nevertheless, this has served to prepare the way for the indirect succession to which the 'rebel' can lay claim.

'The rebel' attains his merit from his revolt, from his refusal to bear the weight which overwhelms and subdues people. He sees how much attention is devoted to the irreducible part of himself, which can undoubtedly be broken, but which *in a profound sense* maintains so much violence within him that he cannot even envisage subjection and compromise. He can do nothing except succumb or betray himself. His awareness of such a simulacrum of sovereignty before which history has placed him immediately diverts him away from *animal* solutions and he is contemptuous of the blind path, and of those gaudy privileges, substitutes for holiness, of those *willing to pledge allegiance*. From the outset he is on the side of those who refuse established sovereignty, and his revolt – contrary to that of sovereigns of the past – is *conscious* of itself, both within him and in others. This part of him which is never reducible to the law, which derives from the immensity of being within him, which is an end in itself and cannot be treated as a means – he knows he can spare it by working, by allowing another – reducible – part of himself to submit to the law. He cannot be taken in by appearances which would show, on the one hand, slaves submitting to work and, on the other, proud wild beasts cheating as they sink to the calculation of the revenues arising from the work of others. He knows that this indomitable part of himself exists within *all* other people, even if they have denied it. The old system of the world in which this was not (or was no longer) perceptible, where falsehood reigned, is exactly what he refuses, and is the very object of his revolt. He is not really opposed – not, at least, in a *profound* sense – to that part of the sacred which, in the old falsehood, leaked out; and his protest is made *profoundly* against the common condition, against the ineluctable necessity for the partial subjugation of man's life to work.

But this protest, tied to those movements of excess which stir human life, no longer takes place in *excess*. The 'rebel' knows he can do a certain amount of work, on condition that he does not make his *whole* life a cog in the system subordinated to the requirements of work. And it is also the effect of *restraint* within him no longer to aspire to that power he struggles against.

He now knows that by taking the place of those he has fought against, he inherits above all their excess, and destroys within himself everything that matters most to him: the 'complicity of men with other men'. At a stroke all the benefits of his revolt are nullified. He destroys within himself (and those he henceforth governs) the energy that sustained him. And there no longer remains within him, or among those who are (willingly or unwillingly) his followers, anything other than *excess* transformed into terror and tyranny.

10. Revolt, poetry, action

This brings me back, through my own analysis, to the essential impulse of Albert Camus's thought. I do not feel that the comparison I have introduced between this impulse and my own starting point *does anything* to distort it, and even makes it explicit. But I would like to make one point clear: my own thought seemed to me to be left hanging for want of reaching the conclusion drawn at the end of this generally admirable book, whose profound sense I hope I have conveyed.

It is true that the point of departure of these comparisons, which seem to me to establish a coincidence, could still be considered debatable. One could doubt that Camus's revolt could be confounded with an urge towards sovereignty.

It seems natural to me to go on to the author's marked interest, in opposition to all political theoreticians, for the moral positions established within poetry and, going beyond poetry, within literature as a whole. The poetry (and the literature) of our time has only one meaning: an obsession with a sovereign surge of our life. This is very much why they are so frequently connected with revolt. (Nevertheless, the literature and poetry Camus talks about generally have nothing to do with the efforts, however moving or not they may be, of 'engaged' writers.) What is at issue is the negation of the limits of the real world, of those limits which so often besmirch a sovereignty whose exact meaning is given in poetry, a sovereignty which *is* poetry.

This reveals, of course, how much the theme of this movement in its entirety is in constant accord with surrealist research, in which – it goes without saying – its *excess* goes beyond literature to place at stake the sovereignty of the instant (which alone is its end), as opposed to the writings which remain simply as its visible traces. But to the same degree, *restraint* has not been lacking in André Breton's revolt, which anticipated Camus in this will for justice (putting an end to the surfeit – and the trickeries – of the initial excess). In the same way, surrealism, at first seduced by the vehemence and stratagems of realist politics, soon distanced itself when it recognized how *excessive* these elements were.

Nevertheless, the surrealists remain isolated by their distance from clear thinking, which is the key to Camus's attitude. Breton is capable of profound insight and audacious propositions, but he disdains analysis and seems to feel no need to establish a comprehensive view. If he finally settles for the quietism of the captain of a sinking ship (something which does sometimes seem worthy of admiration), it is a quietism that remains *unaware* of the leaks which would awaken him to the sentiment of death.

Undoubtedly there are minds for whom such *moral* questions have no force. And it is true, as I have said, that there is no certainty that such a starting point will lead to a conclusion. Camus relies upon restraint for the solution, and quickly passes over the subject. Nevertheless, he shows optimism, and perhaps he is right to do so. Would the essential thing be no longer to be taken in by the indulgences which have led to such inextricable situations? It especially seems to me that the time has come to recognize that the *rebel* cannot hope to succeed those he fights against without compromising the inherent value of revolt. Why is it, in the government or management of things, as everything indicates, always a question (here I am not talking about sovereignty) of a will to oppress rather than to maintain, apart from management, a force of revolt which would limit its powers? This could be the meaning of the trade-union action which Camus himself supports in his crucial book. No one could claim in advance that a will towards restraint could not, in going beyond empty provocation, 'separate the movement of revolt from the contrary inclination to force the other to bend to one's own will'.

Notes

1. Review of Albert Camus, *L'Homme révolté* (1951), Paris: Gallimard. Published in *Critique*, no. 55 (1951).

2. 'Dialogue between André Breton and Aimé Patri on Albert Camus's *The Rebel*', *Arts*, 16 November 1951.

3. *L'Homme révolté*, p. 36. This passage, and more generally the analysis I am taking into account, is found in the chapter entitled 'The Rebel'.

4. 'A letter from Albert Camus in response to André Breton', in *Arts*, 19 October 1951. This first letter was justified by 'Sucre jaune' (*Arts*, 12 October), in which Breton attacked Camus after publication of an article in *Cahiers du Sud* taken from the pages in *The Rebel* devoted to Lautréamont.

5. 'Dialogue' (*Arts*, 16 November), p.1. This is the complete sentence: 'I do [not] believe in the final virtue of a thought whose trajectory relies on arbitrary interpretations and does not recoil, if necessary, before false witness.'

6. The pages of *Les Temps Modernes* to which I am alluding are reproduced in *Situations II* (Gallimard, 1945), pp. 214–29, in which the author adds some notes, one of which reads: 'Does [Breton] fully realize the intrigues of which he is the object? To clarify the facts, I would reveal to him that M. Bataille, before publicly informing Merleau-Ponty that he was going to withdraw his article, had informed him about his intentions in a private conversation. This champion of surrealism then declared, "I have a lot of things against Breton, but we need to stand together against Communism." "That's

reason enough."' I would mention that it was Merleau-Ponty who one day brought the existence of this note to my attention, and that he added: 'I don't remember very well what I said to Sartre, but it could not have been exactly what you said to me, and I am sure that Sartre has not reproduced exactly what I said to him.' This is only to be expected, but what is more surprising is that someone should reproduce a conversation which he had not himself personally heard. . . . I do not remember what I said to Merleau-Ponty, but I did remember precisely the phrase, which is easy enough to remember without distortion; this made me realize that Sartre could attribute to me a comment so completely different from what I really think. Perhaps my thought differs from what I actually said, but I know very well that it has not changed: I think the text Sartre quotes contains truths which distort the truth, and that this summary execution reinforced the Communist position in the realm of literature, with which I do not agree and with which I do not believe Sartre himself agrees. At that time I was far from alone in thinking that Sartre's attitude was tiresome: it was not a question of an intrigue on my part, but of a little external agitation to which I would not give way so easily today. Sartre is the only one who is involved in intrigues, attributing to me a remark which would attract the hostility of both Breton and the Communists towards me! But the fact is that this is not a matter of any great interest to me. Since Sartre's passage has come to my attention while I was trying to trace a reference, I believe it is good, in spite of everything, that now three years have elapsed, this is my chance finally to put an end to the matter.

7. *L'Homme révolté*, pp. 119–20.

8. ibid., p. 127.

9. ibid.

10. 'Sucre jaune' [reprinted in *La Clé des champs* (1967), Paris: Jean-Jacques Pauvert, pp. 300–4. – *Translator*]

11. Yet the demand is not without incoherence or laxity: a few people remember the Matta affair, in which Matta was excluded owing to a suicide which followed (without clearly being an effect of it) the separation of a husband and wife. This touches, in an undeniable way, the 'worst conformism' at the antipodes of revolt.

12. *L'Homme révolté*, p. 366.

13. 'Dialogue between André Breton and Aimé Patri . . . ', p.3.

14. ibid.

15. [In fact Bataille reverses what Camus says, which is: ' . . . Rimbaud was the poet of revolt only in his work. His life, far from the myth it has sustained, illustrates only . . . an assent to the worst possible nihilism.' – *Translator*]

16. *L'Homme révolté*, p. 115.

17. ibid., p. 40.

18. ibid., p. 21.

19. ibid., p. 50.

20. ibid., p.150.

21. ibid.

22. ibid., p. 216.

23. The work of Georges Dumézil shows the significance, in the imagination of antiquity and the Middle Ages, of the idea of the Mehaigné king, the infirm king.

André Masson[1]

The potential of the human mind is apparent to anyone who writes like a *rodeo* horse: no one could expect anything more than to be perched on the back of such a crazy mount for just one moment. A little later – if not straight away – this knight will 'bite the dust'.

It is useless to make recriminations; to say, as though the truth were finally speaking (since in fact it is now *I* who speak!): 'the problem was poorly posed'. Had my intelligence been of the highest (which would be to say *the most anxious*, for without anguish . . . but at the same moment *the most contented*, for anguish . . .), I would still live bogged down in that mud in which problems are poorly posed. And here I am making decisions, and I am not disheartened. (In the end it doesn't matter: like others, I will take my turn, and will soon enough be lying 'scattered' over the arena . . .)

I am not without my own obstinacy: I want to travel further and suffer more. I undertake nothing that I do not take to the impossible, and everything seems to me to be conditioned in such a way that we know only its ridiculous aspects as long as we have not seen that on one point it touches on an aspect of 'what is' which can be neither seized nor not seized; neither known nor not known; *and which confines us*.

If I talk about a painter people are amazed when, before even saying anything about him, I place everything in question. This state of mind reigns uncontested in its immense scorn for anyone who is a *painter* – but not only a painter, of course: for a *writer*, a *minister* or a *juggler* . . . , the complete personnel of a large house. I do not believe it is wrong to be scornful of functions and services, and consequently of those who are charged with them. To put oneself in service is to be servile. In a world where everyone has their own service to perform, there reigns – necessarily – a great contempt for *all*. (Perhaps I am exaggerating; the world is deceptive, but this is what it adds up to.)

The first on the scene when it comes to contemptuous contempt-ibles, a *critic*, declares: 'We do not want *thought painting*.' This opinion is defensible, but in listening to it one accepts for painting – and for the painter – limits that are analogous to those of service. The question this involves is important: should the work of art be a response to a demand, in the same way as other functions and services are? If not, then should it function as a calling into question of what is 'given': human conventions and existence itself?

Others have tackled the problem of the artist and the work of art vigorously. They rightly speak about commitment and totality. Every-thing is linked, and every work is committed: we need to realize that, even if it causes us to perish. But if we talk about commitment, it can be understood in two ways. To be committed could mean to serve a defined activity such as a revolution, a war, a political reform, an effect of agricultural or industrial production. But I could perhaps also be committed to a totality – in other words, to the very thing to which warlike, political or industrial action refers and subordinates itself . . .

Therefore, I will start – I must start – with a rather inscrutable distinction. On the whole, this is a little unfortunate: my intention is to discuss the art of André Masson, who rightly rejects such distinctions. Even now I am obliged to say that every work by André Masson *is* a totality; this character of totality dominates it, is its strength, its seduction and its power to distance. In one respect this does not accord very well with my analysis: totality's nature is to assert itself without words, even to scorn the desire for analysis. It *is* like the striking fist – in other words a blow – while for myself, I speak . . .

But at this point, must I remain silent or simply say: 'It is totality, and as such it is vain to try to add to it'? On the contrary, I believe I must define a general difficulty: I can do one of two things – either I (in communion or not with others, or the others) exist in a total way for whatever action is necessary (in an economic or military sense . . .) or I remain a means (economic, military, etc. . . .) which is used by totality. But in the first case I must affirm myself with silence, not with explanations. For by seeking to explain, *I would serve* what I speak about, instead of being it. In this way Masson affirms without serving, and remains silent. By speaking, I can only serve his affirmation.

Even so, is it certain that I serve it?

I betray it to the extent that I serve (and who will wash these *intellectual bloodstains* off me?).

I express an internal debate that others from the outside would hear with an ear infinitely open to the void of discourse. As if. . . . Neverthe-less, this debate had meaning only experienced in the dead of night, in

the same way as the faithful were once overwhelmed by their representation of God. In truth this desire to 'exist in a total way' (in which
thought and being itself are no longer subordinated to some subser-
vient occupation) is, nourished by solitude, the development and
denuding of the drama which was sketched out in Christian meditation (Nietzsche was the first to have experienced and defined this
settling of accounts: since God is dead, I cannot detach my thought out
of the depths into which it had been plunged by what anguish and the
unfathomable opened up, taking a final degree of violence to its logical
conclusion; it will be necessary for me to be God myself: overwhelmed
by vastness, since in the end it is only the void, I must cease to be less
than what vastness seemed to be because, God being dead, I must
replace him).[2]

After Christianity, we are faced with two possible paths. 'God is
dead' has two possible meanings for us. For some, God is considered
purely as a master principle, represented on earth by authorities
empowered to act on his behalf and to whose orders men must submit
in their daily lives. For them, his death simply has an emancipatory
meaning: they are now free to *serve* man rather than God. The others
are not opposed to the first, but slowly begin to feel – and to live –
through the void that death has left. For them this void is the
revelation of man's potential, which cannot henceforth be anything
other than *totality*, and can no longer be action in the service of others.
(That these others would no longer be God, but men, does not get rid
of the problem!) To serve men is not mankind's whole potential; each
person must also be *the reason why* others serve and, if necessary, die for
him, and *the reason why* cannot be reduced to the exchange of proper
behaviour (I die in order for you to live because, had it been necessary,
you would have died so I might live). No! Now I ask *the reason why* we
both live.

I think it is now time to apply my problems to the history of art.

Nothing is more common than for a painter to accept the reduction
of his being to painting.

Living in a world in which to paint is one possible function, he
chooses it as his limit. His ambition is confined to producing fine
paintings, and he narrowly devotes his life to finding the best possible
means of personal expression. From this moment he defines this *means*
as an end, for he must deny his servility. It is easy, since foolishness,
falsehood – and plasticity – have few limits: art lovers, merchants and
critics form a closed world in which all activity appears to be subordinated to mastering the mode of graphic representation. What is
expressed no longer matters; it is the *means* of expression that alone
constitutes the *grail* of this futile chivalrous order.

Nevertheless, it is not as futile as it seems at first.

This domain of means at least offers a loophole. All traditional means are asserted as a law which one can possibly breach, and this painter, attached as he is to his scorn for what painting is not, finally comes out of it by means of a negation of the limit he wanted to uphold. At this moment his passion ceases to be painting, and becomes liberty . . .

And for a while the apparent servility which confines us to a single function becomes a ruse, by which the decision to become free refuses an empty liberty and gives itself a precise object.

But only for a while.

The infringement of given laws depends on the power that maintains those laws. And as the infringement tends to divest them of all power, so it tends to become empty in its turn.

Thus the question of the thing expressed is raised again.

The simple use of a liberated (if you prefer, revolutionary) mode can express this 'thing' which is the opposition of oppressed to oppressor, which is desire for liberty in action. It must be said that it does not matter to non-initiates (but fundamentally, nothing ever matters, except for initiates . . .). In any case, it is a possibility with no future.

Like any human enterprise of putting these means into practice, painting is confronted with this settling of accounts, and must become a means – that is, something other than what it essentially is.

And finally, art is encouraged to commit itself. However, if it remains a refuge of 'art for art's sake', painting can no longer simply express art itself.

Surrealist art (both its writing and its painting) has as its end the expression of *thought*. But the thought surrealism defines rightly seems *freed* from the world. In surrealist art a halt is made, without the slightest doubt. Emerging from the emptiness of art for art's sake, it can neither serve action nor form a totality. It expresses only a part of the human sphere. This is true to such an extent that from the origin of surrealism we can distinguish two rather separate moments: that of empty liberty (innocence, automatism), which is expressed in *works* that finally become monotonous and themselves powerless; and that of total affirmation of the meaning of this empty liberty by the *being* who experiences it. Over and above this, the work requires an externally affirmed intellectual judgement if surrealist activity is to be given the value of totality. And as in general one sees the interest of surrealist painters (and writers) lingering on their works, this results in a world which is neither servile nor complete, but which in long run is nothing at all.

André Masson's art is somewhat – but firmly – distanced from pure surrealism, in that the thought it expresses is no longer, as in automatic writing, *disengaged* from the world, but becomes integrated with it and invades it. This thought has a quality of totality in that it is limited neither by discursive thought nor by the automatism of dream. There is a resultant danger which surrealism wanted to prevent (by means of the separation I have spoken about). But it could not dispense with discourse and had to maintain, by a positive intellectual judgement, the meaning of what, by definition, slips away in all directions. What André Breton did not see (or did not say) is that as a rule one cannot escape this impasse. Added to what exceeds it, the affirmation made by the intelligence suppresses its essence, which is to exist outside intelligence. This is why it seemed legitimate to suggest (as Jean Wahl did) that surrealism did not exist before it was defined, but that is not completely true: Rimbaud or Blake, to whom Wahl refers, like Masson today, did not dissociate poetic vision from the intelligence.

A moment ago I said that this difficulty is born of the desire 'to exist in a total way', and no longer to be 'in service'. It has meaning only experienced in 'the dead of night'. This is something that cannot exactly be resolved. All we can do is accept that it carries us to breaking point. It is useless to hope to banish the intelligence (with the latter ejected, there would remain only the void, powerlessness and madness – or pure aestheticism). From that moment, we can only remain in the impossible.

Notes

1. Published in *Labyrinthe*, no. 19 (1 May 1946).
2. This does not mean 'to be God' but to be myself as fully as possible, both for myself and, in respect of equality and ordinary communication, for another; to be this unlimited grandeur that the idea of God suggested (it suggested it badly, since it subjugated as well as suggested). Is this not the same end that Breton indicated when he spoke of determining the 'point of the mind at which life and death, real and imaginary, past and future, communicable and incommunicable, high and low, cease to be perceived contradictorily'?

Surrealism and God[1]

In a sense the word *surrealism* is an absence of a word. The word *silence* also reveals language's power to deny even as it affirms, since a perfect negation of language, a perfect silence, is inconsistent with the use of the word. In the same way the *absence* of a word is a delusion, it is nothing but a series of words.

In itself and independent of a given historical meaning, *surrealism*, it is true, does not mean 'language beyond words' but, rather, 'language beyond things' (it stands above the real which, according to etymology and logic, is the order of *things*). But it comes to the same thing. *Things are what they are only because of the meanings words give them.* This book would not be the thing it is without the word *book*: it would be whatever it is for a dog. Besides, it is essential to realize that we could not live without these things which are words, just as we could not live without these words which are things. But words and things enclose us, stifle us; and it is very difficult for us to escape from them, to find ourselves beyond words and things. The surrealists asked (even before describing themselves as such): why do you write? A man who writes (in the sense understood by the word *writer*) is a man who does not want to be the thing man is for the employer; and the same goes for someone who reads him.

The surrealist definition of literature also has the virtue of revealing the point at which literature (or surrealism) becomes problematic. Literature begins with good intentions, but is caught in the trap of words, which finally alter the intention. As he passes from the passion which moves him to written expression, the writer encounters words that he believes submit to his passion but which, rather, reduce it to their enslaved movement. Words link together, and if we are to follow their thread, we need to recognize that every element serves the meaning in some way. In so far as he turns away from both action and science, the writer is someone who does not give reasons, and remains profoundly silent. But how? If I remain obstinately dumb, the world in which I write would speak for me! It would reduce me to the dimensions of its small talk. I would be submitted to the common activity, just as a break for rest is believed to be the necessary complement of work.

Lautréamont said that the 'intellectual bloodstain', which is the mania for giving explanations, could not be washed away. And in fact it cannot. I succumb to the use of words like *to be, effect, succumb, use*. In being assembled together, these words, through the very process that links them, announce my servitude. And it is not enough to recognize it for it to cease to exist. In fact, even the writer who is most against discourse (i.e. 'the order of things' and the servile language which expresses it) cannot be content to turn his back. He is constrained to express himself on the level of discourse; he is constrained to have an intellectual position. But this is something painful for him, and he does it unwillingly, grinding his teeth and giving way to impatience. The knowledge that he should remain quiet commits him to vaticinate.

Few things I have read have been more disagreeable than the 'surrealist documents' collected together and published by Maurice Nadeau. Of course I read all of them as they appeared, but collecting them together frightens me. I can transform my unease only by means of a comical word: I can call them *edifying*.

These texts, in their incessant repetition, are edifying in that they reveal the disregarded *taboo* (the interdiction) which is different from the one they intended to defy. What they say, in fact, cannot be *said*: here I do not mean to condemn the surrealists, but to point out a profound difficulty. There is nothing here with which I am in disagreement. I think that every free man, in his non-servility, has a fundamental affinity with what they express. How can one not hate this society, and its poets, if they insist on taking themselves and me for things? The established order imposed on us is the constant negation of all that is irreducible and proud. Anyone who is not a rebel cannot be a *friend*, since he is the *enemy* of man. But it ought to have been possible to dispense with its *expression*, and to express it is already to recognize the established order (to recognize it at least to the extent of discussing it). The *negation of things that surrealism is* has itself become a *thing*. The glue of words makes an entity, a durable being, condemnatory and necessary, of what *is* not (in the sense in which Sartre talks about the 'moment that is not'). In the same way the instant cannot be durable; but it genuinely is the wound, it is the shame of language that words expose: it would be necessary, in order to speak, that the word *being* should designate what the moment *is*, something which is impossible (surrealism, then, does not exist, since it cannot be named). But what, then, should the surrealists do? Keep silent! Instead they had to devote themselves to writing these texts and tracts that tear at the heart, which call so portentously for the silence that should have been safeguarded at all costs, but *simply could not be*.

This is not in any sense a critique, but an apology for surrealism. I do not believe that anyone has esteemed it more highly. *Conflict* justifies, it reports what, with good reason, seems susceptible to criticism, the shaky and dated elements, the tedious aspects of the works. And conflict is necessary for anyone who seeks to grasp what the texts mean: if you stop at their surface meaning, at the words, you forget that even the person who wrote them was forbidden in advance to employ them. This is even why they clash: they wanted to clash, they implied intolerance and slipped into chaos. This unpleasant tone? This exaggeration? This tendency to turn grey into black? How could one imagine they could be avoided if one recognizes the impossibility of using words to reach the dazzling truth which founds them, which is the truth of the proud and insubordinate man (the truth that is poetry)?

These elements are perhaps necessary if one wants to understand exactly the meaning of a final pamphlet to be added to those repudiated[2] by Nadeau. This pamphlet (*À la niche . . .*) begins: 'While rationalism's closed face suggests that the enemy has definitely lost all trace of courage, a recrudescence of activity is manifest on the complementary face of religion.'[3] This military realism is astonishing, yet the sentence introduces an inevitable protest. The surrealists (there are fifty signatures) protest against the inextricable misunderstanding raised by a controversial argument among Christians. For the latter, 'to deny God is still to affirm him . . . to combat him is still to support him, to detest him is still to long for him'. The idea of God (I do not write *god* with a small g, since this generally refers to entities in which the Church Fathers saw the Devil) is in truth either the most inconsistent or for some the most enduring, according to the necessity of the moment: one way of entering into a sacred silence, and keeping a right of sovereign definition and legislation for language, actually led to this confusion. The numerous Christians who praise surrealism finally seem naive, but they have been led astray by the demands of theological discourse, which condemns their pliancy as much as Breton's position does. Between surrealists and Christians there is certainly the deepest abyss, which is definitively indicated by the last sentence of the pamphlet, which speaks of 'an irreducible aversion to all abased being'.

Notes

1. Review of Maurice Nadeau, *Histoire du surréalisme II. Documents surréalistes* (1948), Paris: Seuil; and 'À la niche les glapisseurs de Dieu!' (1948), Paris: Éditions Surréalistes. Published in *Critique*, no. 28 (1948).

[2. This word is presumably a printing error in the original, and should in fact read 'republishes'. – *Translator*]

[3. Bataille slightly misquotes this sentence. In my translation, I have followed the original wording of the surrealists' document, – *Translator*]

Happiness, Eroticism and

Literature[1]

Sexual pleasure is offered to man by life as an incomparable blessing. The moment of the sexual act is one of resolution and gushing forth – it presents the perfect image of happiness.

These value judgements, even though they have a major role in the scheme of things, are considered null and void if it is a question of going to the heart of the matter. Without any doubt at all there are solid reasons for this, the first being that if these judgements were true it would, in spite of everything, be necessary to contest them, for if we were to admit them our lives would no longer be possible. No one founds their conduct on the antinomy between moments of bliss and a humanly organized life. In truth, eroticism is dangerous precisely because of its value. As we recognize it, we take the risk of destroying both ourselves and our works.

But simply to confront this difficulty is not to get to the heart of the matter. Finally, someone asks, in all its profundity, the question of what sexual pleasure means. This is not an insignificant question: it is almost impossible not to start by considering how the 'lost good', to which the best part of man's endeavour is devoted, could really differ from sexual pleasure? In other words, is not value, set in contrast to the world of things, defined decisively by the extreme point of sexual pleasure?

What is most evident in all this is that since sexual pleasure is by its very nature happiness, and desired as such, value is detached from it because it nevertheless has the sense of unhappiness. The pleasure of the body is unclean and baneful, and man in a normal state – let's be precise: man engaged in ordinary activity – condemns it, or accepts that it should be condemned. Only the rake does not pretend to disdain the activity whose seduction exhausts him. In truth this activity consumes our reserves of energy so dangerously that we contemplate it with anguish. It enraptures and frightens us: it frightens us because it enraptures us and it enraptures us all the more profoundly because it frightens us. But the dread which transfigures its value demands that, provisionally, we evade this value, and that our humanity actually depends on the extent to which we deny it: for man the sexual act is animality, it is divine only when it is fallen, and its fall is its condition – so much so that our conduct is always treacherous: either we betray our truth of the night during the day, or we hypocritically aspire simply to denounce the conventions of the day.

*

These violent contrary movements within us, which confine humanity – language and life – within the conditions of falsehood, are found *in literature*, to which they give the disguised face of truth. If the glacial expression of clear language is deceptive, if literature fascinates, it is because the desire, proud or exhausting, for laughter and love relentlessly maintains us in its grip. But in literature we come up against the same obstacle as in love. Literature has meaning only as happiness, but this quest for happiness that causes us to write or read seems in truth to have the contrary meaning of unhappiness. If we consider tragedy, it brings terror rather than pleasure; and if we consider the joy of comedy, it is a joy that is equivocal, for we laugh at a fall from grace, if not at a misfortune. The art of the novel requires vicissitudes which produce anguish, and it is commonplace to say that the depiction of happiness is boring.

But literature's vocation for unhappiness seems so necessary to most people that if the writer evokes pleasure he does so with dark overtones suggesting something distressing. Miller himself succumbs to this concession, to which Sartre has undoubtedly given the most mournful tone. Often the depiction of auspicious sexual pleasure seems distant from real sexual pleasure, since happiness lacks a sort of malicious and sovereign vigour which is in the nature of unhappiness. The expressions which announce bliss give the feeling of poetic insipidity (if not venal pornography). Some recent literature, which no longer consents to suppress moments of resolution, offer in this respect a desolate landscape. In truth, a recently published anthology gives a feeling of defeat. It is true that men of letters have tried: they pressed ahead with the appearance of audacity, but this audacity is itself a confession of their discomfort. And it is not chance that has demanded this miserable choice and hasty introduction, this feeble display of failure or shameful pleasures. If the body triumphs, language, which expresses such triumphs, has the power only to acknowledge a movement of retreat.

Literature translates this movement towards happiness that has been deflected towards unhappiness in several ways. But it does not really abort into the form of tragedies or anguished tales: there the unhappiness serves as a stimulant, a failure which reveals the power to confront it. While recent literature, as it portrays sexual pleasures, tends more strangely to betray happiness and to misunderstand the poetic sense of unhappiness.

Perhaps there is something insincere about this, but it seems to me that modern writers often docilely obey rhetorical rules they are unable to formulate. Perhaps I am mistaken, but the sexual passages in *The Age of Reason* never strike me as 'true'; I saw in them the effect of this unrecognized rhetoric limiting literature and imposing on it a sort of tribute to unhappiness – which balances a desire for the happiness it really is. The absence of incisive movements of anguish and the general reduction of 'privileged moments', the predominance of everyday life, undoubtedly demanded these joys which deny joy without having affirmed it; it is a pleasure which anticipates its own failure.

If we want to grasp clearly this dance passing from life to death, from heaven to hell, it is necessary first to recall its material data. As a rule we are separated from happiness, whether conceived in the positive sense of pleasure or in the negative sense of rest, because before we can be happy we must find the means to be so. The thought of happiness thereby urges us to work to attain it. But the moment we work, far from bringing ourselves nearer, as we would have liked, to the moment in which we would grasp happiness, we introduce a distance between ourselves and happiness. The moment we work we set ourselves in search of happiness (which is not a thing) in the same way as we seek the immediate results of work, whether houses, clothes or food. We even tend to identify it with such results, particularly if we are talking politically.

This stands out more clearly if we specify that happiness is considered by us to be something to be acquired, even though its demand is to pass to the contrary sphere of expenditure. From the most abundant expenditure, which is sexual pleasure (accompanied by luxuriousness and ostentation) to the lightest form, which is rest (a negative expenditure: the resting man does not consume very much, but he consumes without producing), we cannot be happy unless we enter the domain of anguish. If one excludes pathological conditions, the only means man has of escaping anguish is through work. My anguish begins from the moment I feel I have, rightly or wrongly, expended more than I have acquired in a given period. (In terms of resources, there is no distinction between physical energy and material goods, but to them must be added the problematic sense of the power of work.) Of course, sexual pleasure suspends anguish, but at the same time it makes it more intense: in everyday circumstances, the more I spend in the warmth of pleasure and sensuality, the more I weaken my situation. No doubt we retain the power to strike a sensible balance between acquisition and expenditure, and often sensual satisfaction, by liberating morbid inhibitions, restores this balance in us (and compensates for the loss experienced by the sense of the power of accumulated work). But this risk, determined by anguish's propensity for delusion (which either adds to or curtails the sum total of immediate anguish according to the action of the disturbed imagination), generally means only that the loss of energy does not magnify anguish, and that work, or the acquisition of goods, does not diminish it – so much so that happiness, considered unequivocally, must resolutely be said to serve to increase the sense of anguish.

It goes without saying that this way of considering the question is not commonly accepted. Happiness is *always* confounded with the resources which make it possible. This means that the word 'happiness' is used for both acquisition and expenditure, and our representations vary in accordance with our frame of mind. If we are in a mood for celebration, raising our glasses and living in a state of warmth and attraction, happiness is equated with what amuses us, but in the calm of study we want no more than the coherent efficacy of ideas, and happiness is reduced to the resources without which we could not be content. To this extent the drinker is wiser than the studious (or political) man: he takes into account only the warmth which issues from the consumption of resources. And reasoning does not see that to place happiness within the sphere of acquisition is to substitute for warmth a way of life which excludes it. For such a warmth announces the return of anguish. Drunkenness is followed by unpleasant awakenings. The happiness that excludes drunkenness is reduced to life untroubled by anguish. The happiness of reason resolutely becomes the negation of happiness, since the happiness of drunkenness is the beginning of unhappiness.

This dialectic is millenarian. And it is difficult to see how to escape the reasonable and well-established idea of happiness. The reasonable man puts forward a compromise: he refuses to give fleeting pleasures the name of happiness. As a result the word is given a reduced meaning sanctioned by its use. In consequence, the discussion generally becomes problematic through the refusal to admit that such terms might have a double meaning. Happiness does not refer merely to what has a lasting value, but also to what is momentary (if we say: 'I am as happy as could be'). And no one can prevent the word from being

freely used in both cases. I merely want to show that the meaning of
duration is necessarily tied to the denial of the meaning of the instant
(and vice versa). The person who perceives happiness in what lasts
cannot take the moment into consideration: for him value is connected
to the acquisition of resources, and their expenditure is of interest only
in so far as they are favourable to the continuance of happiness.
Reciprocally, duration is no longer important in the value of the
instant. Reason casts the instant into the hell of anguish. Doubtless the
importance of the instant can even completely disappear if one opts
for duration. But if this is so, it is *in spite* of the conscious intention. In
these circumstances what endures of the instant is not its strong value,
and is never its affirmation. Positive happiness or expenditure is
limited to insignificant modalities, and they can never be recognized
for what they are.

As a result, what has most meaning for man, what attracts him most
strongly, are the extreme moments of life which, because of their
extravagant nature, are defined in terms of a non-meaning. It is an
enticement, a moment which should not happen; it is the stubborn
animality of man that his *humanity* is devoted to the world of things and
reason. Thus the most intimate truth falls into an odious and inaccessible obscurity.

But for all that, it is still not suppressed. It is only drawn into the
night. The rational refusal of anguish and the submission to work
could only cause consumption to lose its final value. Duration merely
suggests wretched compromise: its feeble attraction is all the more
limited in that anguish itself is attractive. But our desire to hold on to it
consigns our most intimate moments to something monstrous, something disgraceful. This does not mean that such moments have lost
their underlying value – rather, that the fundamental value is no
longer humanly accessible on the same plane, since it has gained an
aspect of monstrous shame, and we have lost consciousness of it. In this
way anguish, having been exiled along with happiness, is no longer
simply anguish. It has become intimately united with happiness and
has, in a way, become more distressing in so far as it no longer
responds to a simple hazard like fear: the hazard which anguish resists
results from a possibility of extreme happiness. But not only is our fear
redoubled by the fact that danger attracts us; equally, the resistance of
anguish increases the intensity of our happiness if we finally surrender
to its attraction. It follows, therefore, that the quest for a grail, in which
man laments his lost happiness, is linked with the pursuit of anguish, to
the extent that profound pleasure can be experienced only in anguish.

*

All this is strange – the more completely so, perhaps, for the person who expresses it and is no longer required, like the reader, to make the effort to understand it.

Besides, I could continue only with difficulty if I did not now have some way of going from oppressive reasoning to poetic expression. Pleasure, in fact, cannot be defined as a logical category. On the very point upon which it is in question, the powerlessness of language is ridiculous. In other respects poetry liberates a truth different from that to which it seems connected: it is then simply poetry. Pleasure is not poetry. Poetry is merely the power I lack, and how not to dwell on it (if, being of rare quality, it actually does exist) in the expression of happiness. Literature is usually so miserable, it is led astray by so many detours from the simplicity of joy, that I am really moved when I read among Rimbaud's poems (no matter how uncertain the step) these lines in which felicitous animality is rediscovered:

> HE: Just the two of us together,
>   Okay? We could go
> Through the fresh and pleasant weather
>   In the cool glow
>
> Of the blue morning, washed in
>   The wine of day
> When all the lovestruck forest
>   Quivers, bleeds
>
> From each branch; clear drops tremble,
>   Bright buds blow,
> Everything opens up and vibrates,
>   All things grow.
>
> You rush about, and alfalfa
>   Stains your white gown,
> As the shadows beneath your eyelids
>   Fade in the clear dawn.
>
> Madly in love with the country,
>   You sprinkle about
> Like sparkling champagne bubbles
>   Your crazy laugh.
>
> Laughing at me, and I'd be brutal
>   And I'd grab your hair
> Like this – how beautiful,
>   Oh! – In the air
>
> Your strawberry-raspberry taste
>   Your flowery flesh!
> Laughing at the wind that kissed
>   You like a thief . . .[2]

Perhaps this is nothing. In this edition this poem follows on from the last verse of 'Venus Anadyomene':

> She bends and shows the ulcer in her anus.

The final rejoinder responds to the *rhetoric of unhappiness:*

> SHE: And be late for work?

This is still the moment when literature becomes weary and cannot really rediscover its initial pure blaze, and all I have done is to pose the problem anew without shedding light on it.

*

Malcolm de Chazal has, perhaps alone in our time, given a resolute expression to the happiness of sensuality.

A few articles[3] have brought the Mauritian author of *Sens-plastique* to notice. It would be difficult to describe Chazal's work except by using the passages in which he expresses himself. It is true that he once sketches, as a sort of key to his thought,[4] a kind of 'philosophy of sexual pleasure'. Again, it would be vain not to quote it at more length: 'Any genuine introspection into the realm of the senses', he writes in the preface of *Sens-plastique*,[5]

> is vain and incomplete if the two greatest sensory phenomena of existence, birth and death, do not, in the process, deliver up some of their secrets. Yet how can we enter into the 'depths' of birth, how can we 'discover' death, except by becoming too dead to describe it? Nevertheless these two essential phenomena of life can be 'explained', through an experience available to all, in the sexual act, which is a death–birth in one which has generally been intellectualized through pornography or desperate sentimentality. Since the act of love lies at the universal crossroads of the senses, the mind, the heart and the soul, it constitutes a place-condition in which death and birth encounter one another halfway, and where complete man 'intersects' with himself. For this specific reason the act of love is the greatest source of knowledge and the most wide-ranging field of study of the innermost workings of human existence.

This affirmation is valuable not simply because of its clear content, but by a swift movement in which thought composes itself as it decomposes. An incessant acceleration and a dislocated liberty of movement cause Malcolm de Chazal's thought to take the form of a prism in which the reflected objects multiply the aspects that are set in motion with the speed of an arrow. This world of motion is as different from common reflection as the abrupt and dazzling flight of an insect is from a mammal's bearing. The exactitude of his thought is not of the same order as that of the sciences: this thought proceeds by intuition, and the revelation given is of a poetic order. But the facets of its light are centred on a vision that generally establishes a sense of the transparency, penetrability and immanence of all things, and of the beings between them.

This process has much in common with that of William Blake[6] and his liberty is structured in the same way as Blake married heaven and hell in the universe. Malcolm de Chazal writes: 'We reject in the Devil all the elements of God we do not understand. Equally, the Devil is surrounded with far more mystery than God himself.'[7] Chazal talks about God and the angels in the same way as Blake does: he places them in a world in which they are separated from nothing, where they lose themselves, where they appear no longer to be anything other than man demanding his most elevated and limitless vista. 'God', he writes, 'is the only neutral point of ideas, as the "dead calm" is the pivot of the cyclone. As men we are always to the left or right of an idea. If we were right in the centre of any of our ideas we would lose consciousness of ourselves, and would become reabsorbed into God.'[8]

This is not the place to decide the precise meaning of this standpoint, but it would be misjudgement not to say that it refers back to a sort of frozen manner of frenzy which, in a way, is frenzy in its pure state. This merciless reflection – better than other slipping or strangled ones – offers an account of it: 'If we had a tail, what declarations of love would not, at each moment, come flowing from this member that today is non-existent! . . . '[9]

This mad-insect play of thought, thrown into the night of sexual pleasure, passes through it with immense lightning flashes in which we recognize nothing of what was once defined (but could perhaps finally be what we do *know*).

I will present them in the order in which they are to be found in the book (who would dream of presenting them in a different light?):

> *The act of love is the letter which will not be answered. It is the bottle cast into the sea drifting towards eternity. It is the only sensation that does not bring a shock in return. In the same way that water can never return to its source, it is the one pleasure that cannot be recaptured. (p. 41)*

> *Dalliance in love is the heart and senses playing at blind man's buff, perpetually approaching each other without ever touching. If they did touch the pleasure would be*

*so great that the body, at this moment, would melt like a candle approaching a furnace.
(p. 49)*

*Like beauty in retreat progressively divesting her forms as desire mounts, the sensation
of internal nakedness rises within us with increasing intensity and, to the extent that the
flame augments love, man experiences the sensation of complete nakedness only at the
ultimate peak of sexual pleasure. (p. 65)*

*In sexual pleasure we become partially disembodied in what is a miniature resurrec-
tion. Perhaps death is a spasm extending into the beyond, just as a baby's first cry
blends with the lover's on reaching orgasm. (p. 98)*

*Sexual pleasure is a game of leapfrog in which, no matter how far one jumps, one is
constrained each time to land on the support one sought to transcend. Freed of this
'support', one would leap into the beyond. Death is the 'support cleared', the supreme
leap of life. (p. 10)*

The act of love is death in microcosm, birth in its amplitude and life brimfull. (p. 112)

*It is the sensation of birth that the soul experiences, the sensation of death that the body
feels, the frightful pull which comes to us with all the anguish of death. Sexual pleasure
is nothing other than a core of birth inside a death's shell; all its 'dizziness' lies in that
precise moment when the 'shell' falls from the almond, like a ripe fruit falling from the
tree. (p. 114)*

*Sexual pleasure places the body in short-circuit. In sexual pleasure one feels the toes in
the head, one's own mouth a little bit all over the body, knees in the place of the
shoulders and shoulders in the thighs, since in the meantime the arms have entirely
migrated to the torso: one would seek the kidneys in vain: like a ship without a helm they
navigate a little throughout the body. (p. 138)*

*Sexual pleasure transforms the spinal cord into a lone finger, as if to caress the brain
from within. (p. 138)*

*Death is a perilous leap by the feet and birth is a perilous leap by the head. Sexual
pleasure is a leap of the loins, like those leaps into the air of the dancer which,
conjoining perilous leaps of head and feet as one, proceeds from the stammering of the
balancing pole between the hands of the tightrope walker. Sexual pleasure is a
hesitation between Heaven and Earth, in the same way that the thunderstruck stare of
the dying man seems fastened to space. (p. 139)*

*Sexual pleasure has no 'neutral', for it is thrown into gear by life. Birth is sexual
pleasure in sudden gear and death is sensuality in 'neutral'. (p. 146)*

*Sounds and light are associated. If colour has a tone, it also has a timbre. If the tone of
colour is uniform with its texture, the timbre varies according to the region of the body
the fabric clothes. The forms of the body give colours their timbre. Flute-like in the
folds of the armpits, drum-like on the hindquarters, clarinet-like on the forearm,
saxophone at the top of the thighs, castanet on the knees that the dress slaps, oboe
around the region of the neck; the colour on the bust is a xylophone on which two
hammers of felt and cotton wool tap and tap again on the breasts. (p. 146)*

As happens in the silence of night when the walls cry out, there is in the complete silence of sexual pleasure a crackling through our entire frame that causes our bones to howl in the same way as a man in agony 'undergoing' the sound of the collapse of his disintegrating frame, or as a baby in the process of birth senses its bones crack in its first sensation of the motion of flight of its body into life, or like a newly launched yacht creaking through its whole hull as its sails take the first gusts of the winds in the open sea. (p. 160)

As a pursued fish feels itself, due to fear, 'become water', so in the mutual pursuit that is sexual pleasure — fear of joy, joy of fear — bodies liquefy in the waters of the soul, and we become all soul, and our body becomes tiny. (p. 270)

I do not know if it is worthwhile emphasizing the fact that such sentences reach the summit of verbal possibilities: the mystics have perhaps never discovered, in the descriptions of their ecstasy, such an intoxicating subtlety, reaching a tangible point with incisive precision, the point at which the sensibility is overturned. The object of such flashing play of light is no longer indirectly referred to: its vision is no longer sought – or eluded – through a depressing accommodation to anguish, or through recourse to a foul or ridiculous disgrace. Burning space in the image of light, thought ignores both detours and halts. Not that anguish has vanished, but it has been consumed in the flash of light, and all that remains of it is a halo of night, giving to light its intense brilliance.

Moreover, the link between Malcolm de Chazal's 'vision' and anguish must be clarified. He writes: 'Sexual pleasure is the greyhound race of desire, in which the pursuer always falls short of the line, unable to reach its prey.'[10] But later he describes sexual pleasure as 'time assassinated for a moment and rendered indivisible with touch'[11] – as if the greyhound had touched its prey. The contradiction, given here in the truth of the object, expresses it more accurately than logical fidelity. But the second form that the expression of this thought takes is not the whole story, and Malcolm de Chazal repeats: 'If the notion of time was completely abolished in sexual pleasure, the soul would pass away.'[12] Sexual pleasure is possible, in general, only on the condition of suppressing all difference: not only must the hiatus of time existing between desire and the response to it be annulled (the greyhound must seize its prey), but the lovers must overcome this difference which separates them to the end: 'Complete sexual pleasure,' says Malcolm de Chazal, 'enables us to taste through the other's palate. How far we are from this ideal and this sublime goal! . . . '[13] But although it would have excluded 'perfection', the thought is so precise as to present, when it speaks of the difference between beings, the same vagueness as when it speaks about the difference of time.

Discretion itself is in keeping with the fact that sexual pleasure communicates a 'feeling of fusion with the other', but the slippage from one to the other cannot be achieved if we continue to live.[14] Death alone would abolish the difference, and since death is inaccessible, we are powerless to 'discover' it except 'when we are too dead to describe it'. Instead of the perfect unravelling of the drama, of the death of the actors, what remains by default is the movement towards the point of unravelling. It is Malcolm de Chazal's feat to have 'seen' sexual pleasure in a movement[15] in which the essence of the movement *stands out* (as eyes struck with horror *stand out*), since it insists on the feeling – which accelerates and precipitates it – of the impossibility of rest. Literature habitually lingers only on descriptions of rest: it weighs it down and engulfs it in anguish. It states what it is that makes the movement necessary, but the movement is lacking, and only impossible states remain. These *states* are not accepted in the movement; the hiatus between desire and the object, and the difference between beings and death, are never acceptable. The movement, on the contrary, is the refusal of it. But serious literature, refusing impossible *states*, does not refuse them as the movement does. Undoubtedly, it always sees the possibility of movement, but the desire to describe it drives it away, or what it seizes is only a movement reduced to a *state*, which it refuses in its turn. It is, in truth, only the play of consciousness hoaxed by the effects that evade it. It endlessly describes situations and enumerates all forms of loss (Sade has shown the immensity of this domain); it can then affirm as a fact the movement of sexual pleasure connected to this loss, but if it wants to seize the movement itself, it cannot follow it. To do that one would need to stop it: and depression results if it is stopped; it is no longer the movement that is described, but the state which results from its pause.

This is not a termination. Malcolm de Chazal proves that with incomparable mastery. But we readily notice here that the evasion of consciousness is sustained by all this anguish which the movement surpasses in counterpart as it lures away its vertiginous development. As a rule, the moment of sexual pleasure remains outside the field of representations of consciousness. This is not to say that consciousness is unaware of it, but that it has not left tangible traces of it; that it is still what is foreign, unknown, dwelling in darkness, without rights or power, and is denied in those moments when consciousness affirms itself. Thus the explosion of sexual pleasure within consciousness remains at a standstill. And one cannot talk about it, one can draw it into the clear field of consciousness only on condition that one reverses thought's usual direction.

But I am now led to say the strangest thing: others have already reversed the usual direction of thought. We know these explosions of words against a field of darkness, these precipitations of a phrase in pursuit of a movement that is too quick for it. The language of mystics differs little from that of Malcolm de Chazal, and the comparison is all the stronger in that the great contemplatives have always borrowed part of their vocabulary from the erotic. The sentiments the divinity inspired in them seemed to them comparable to the feelings the lover inspires in the beloved. Besides, it has never escaped them that the spiritual rapture of ecstasy does not entirely differ from that of the senses in the sexual act. I am not seeking to denigrate religious experience (I have little time for those doctors who claim, in their inexperience, to be able to equate mystical phenomena with mental disorders that can be observed in clinics). But I cannot fail to recognize that mystical theology has, from the beginning, evoked these balancing motions of being and non-being – that the 'I die of not dying' of Saint Teresa has a stress recalling Chazal's sentences; that in consequence the extremely delicate thought of mystics has *paid attention* to this movement that habitually escapes consciousness and gives it verbal expression.

Thus the question of the unity of man's affective life is posed. Although we choose different routes, perhaps we may be seeking the same object. Malcolm de Chazal does not turn away – or at least, does not resolutely turn away – from what we might call the classical spiritual tradition, and he insists upon the relation between sexual pleasure and a strictly religious life. 'Sexual pleasure', he says 'is pagan at the start and becomes sacred towards the end. The climax comes from the other world.'[16] He wonders if 'sexual pleasure would not by chance be the first step to the spiritual beyond.'[17] He is more precise: 'Sexual pleasure is a plunge, "arms held tight around the body". We do not know what happens to the right nor to the left in this black room of infinity. If our soul could hold out its arms at that precise moment, we would touch the shell of the spiritual world.' In truth, he is not very far from expressing the ultimate content of his research.

'Everything is sensuality,' he says; and this sensuality, 'which sets the tone', would not be reduced to the purity of intense sensation. Such would be 'the absolute of the new' which is 'complete nudity'. 'Up to a point it is possible', he says, 'to define Handsome, Ugly, True, False, Good, Evil and other universals of language – but not Nudity. To describe Nudity in its essence would be to describe God . . . '[18] It is possible that this quest leads to an undifferentiated point, and that as the sensualist reaches his object, Nudity, he also reaches the common object – the irreducible object – of the spiritual world, and of the senses. Here we must not dread being distanced from the essence and specificity of the carnal world.

There are two possibilities of thought in the face of the object that is nudity – which, indeed, is the specific object of sensuality (it determines it, sustains it, and carries it to the extreme). Malcolm de Chazal has shown that it is possible on the one hand to release it from its motivation. From that point, it appears as irreducible, as a 'sheer drop', and unfathomable. Doubtless it is most important that one tries to *explain* the effect of nudity, but one cannot avoid the feeling of getting further away from this object – and from its effect – while if we consider it as a 'sheer drop', the object is synthetically offered to consciousness by the truth of its effect. But just as I can consider the object in two ways, I can equally strive to explain its effect in two ways. There are two sorts of explanation which, proceeding in the same way, still have opposing meanings. I can explain. My explanation would be founded on the possibility – vaguely given, perhaps, but as a rule given – of taking the explanation to its logical conclusion in which everything would be explained, without limits, and all darkness would be transformed into light. I am still not really separating myself from this method if I recognize that in the end I am powerless to reach it, for in this case my regret continues to imply the possibility that escapes me. But I can explain in order to gain access to the inexplicable – both to the object I want to find, and to the object I seek – which attracts me in consequence of a considered choice. Let us be clear about this: it is now no longer a question of something inexplicable whose explanation is still lacking (when I do not know how the bee returns to the hive). But it is the *irreducibility* of what, in any case, could not be explained. Thus I am able, in that nudity which gives me a sensual feeling of total novelty, to tell myself that I have finally reached the irreducible: at this moment I can still wonder if I have really reached a pure irreducibility which genuinely cannot be reduced. I then strive to reduce it, with a contrary intention to that of the sciences, for the good reason that I cannot reach an authentic *irreducibility* before having done everything to reduce it.

In this way my approach would finally rejoin the more direct approach of Chazal. But in the process, without having loosened the ultimate aim, I will have elucidated the essence and specificity of the sexual.

This leads us back to the analysis of properly erotic literature.

*

Literature runs aground (it cannot restore a rich sound) if it strives towards the depiction of happiness. Its aim is, rather, the pleasure which will result from reading; but pleasure, despite appearances, cannot be directly attained: a novel must bring into play difficulties or downfalls, which induce anguish or laughter, otherwise it will not make interesting reading, and will give no pleasure. The strangest thing about this is that the expression of sexual pleasure itself does not escape this law. Erotic literature can undoubtedly dwell on the description of the most blissful states, but its impulse generally involves the suggestion of greater attractions. But clearly it cannot be confined to the portrayal of feminine beauty; it always calls forth the intervention of an *irregularity*, whether it be distressing or ridiculous.

Nudity embodies the principle of this irregularity, but whether it can be ridiculous or distressing depends on circumstances, as well as on the character of the person who is naked. Or course, it is still possible to say that nudity is natural, and that to laugh or to be distressed by it is against nature. But to assume that 'naturism' is right only displaces the question. If human nudity is considered natural, and placed on the same level as animal nudity, we have nullified its sexual meaning in our civilized world. But even extracted from nudity, the sexual element no less retains from it the power of anguish or laughter that nudity has for unnatural man, who is in fact normal man.

The difficulty in determining the nature of the *sexual* is that if we consider it as an object, the object considered never has anything which, of itself, offers a content in which one could recognize why the very particular necessities of sexual activity exist. In fact the sexual object, which determines sexual conduct, is variable. And finally, it seems that any object whatsoever is inclined towards having, in a given context, the power to evoke sexual conduct. Finally, it is the latter which is fundamental. Being nothing in itself, nudity has the anguished or absurd meaning which we stated was only the index of sexual conduct, or at least recalls the latent presence of a sexual world. If literature takes upon itself the explicit depiction of sexual activity, it thereby chooses objects and décor that have the power to determine the reader's sexual conduct, or at least the frame of this conduct. But it is clear as we read it that these objects must, in some way, become distressing or absurd for us, and that this quite strangely maintains the 'language of immediate interest' as far as loss and misfortune are concerned.

But if we try to go to the root of the explanation of the *sexual*, allowing ourselves to be brought back from the object to conduct, it finally seems that the 'conduct' transmits the simplicity of happiness to us. Sexual activity, at least while it is taking place, could even be considered happiness itself. But in fact things are not so simple: we still need to understand why objects which cause anxiety or amusement are precisely those which serve as an index in the sexual world.

In fact if we consider things in their simplest aspect, we see first of all only a clear determination. Sexual conduct and everyday behaviour are mutually exclusive. There are two incompatible modes: one in which erotic acts occur, the other in which the different acts of social life occur. There are probably paths leading from the second to the first, but they never do so easily.[19] This reminds us of the seasonal behaviour of certain animals, such as reindeer, which live in couples during the mating season, and in packs for the rest of the year. But this general observation has little meaning. In this view, the sexual world and the social world, no matter how incompatible they might be, can still appear in a sort of equality – which is to say that, all in all, the difference between them could be analogous to the opposition between south and north, plant and animal, or female and male. This is not without interest, for if nuances alone contrast sexual behaviour to what excludes it, we immediately cease to understand. What seems strangest is that by wanting to come closer to the specificity of eroticism, it is possible to move further away from what it is, which is not only different but contrary to what excludes it. For between an erotic act and any other act (buying a gift, having dinner, making conversation) there is an gulf, an opposition which must be described as terrible, even if it is slight. It is the opposition of death to life and absence to presence: without any doubt, sexuality is a desperate negation of what it is not.

This, which emerges unambiguously, could not be considered clearly except in a detailed analysis of the content of erotic literature.

This analysis should obviously be global. To consider only the work of Sade seems at first glance dubious. But it is perhaps too theoretical a consideration. It very often seems that Sade confined himself within the form of an obsession which is a long way from general behaviour, but this is not certain. In spite of everything, the erotic world he describes possibly serves to magnify the most commonplace responses, and it would be vain to believe it alien to such responses.

*

There is a crucial difference between the universe Sade depicts and the world we experience. As a rule, sexual activity unites beings, while Sade defines it – *in his work*, if not in his life – as the negation of partners.

Maurice Blanchot insists on this aspect as a basic principle. (His study devoted to Sade differs from other similar studies in that it *reveals*

Sade's thought, and allows it to emerge from a profound night that was probably obscure for Sade himself: if Sade had a philosophy, it would be futile to look for it anywhere but in Maurice Blanchot's study. Reciprocally, it is possible that Blanchot's thought is completed by being measured against Sade's, since the achievement of both is to have demanded what thought generally refuses: the hypocritical *community* and the complicity of minds – an accord which, in truth, is completely the contrary of the *unicism* of Sade!) In fact this negation of partners is, rather, the essential element of the system. Eroticism partly contradicts itself if it turns the movement of death (which, as a rule, is what it is) to communion. Sexual union – and this is analogous with the rest of life – is profoundly only a compromise, a half-measure, which is of value only between life and death. It is separated from this communion which limits it only so that sexuality can freely manifest the exigency at its base. If no one had the strength – at least in writing – to deny absolutely the bond which attaches him to his fellows, we would not have Sade's work. Sade's actual life allows an element of boastfulness in negation to appear, but this boasting itself was necessary for the elaboration of a thought whose expediency does not accept servile principles, does not accept principles in which utility, mutual assistance and kindness are more meaningful than seduction. It is not difficult for us to understand the impossibility of pushing what seduces us to its logical conclusion, if we take into account the difficulties which could result for other people of surrendering entirely to our desires. On the contrary, in no longer taking account of others, these desires, even if their affirmation is only 'literary', are offered to us without misrepresentation.

'[Sade's] morality', says Maurice Blanchot, 'is founded as a first principle on absolute solitude.' He

> says so over and over: nature causes us to be born alone, and there is no relation between one man and another. The only rule of conduct is to prefer everything that favourably affects me and take no account of any resulting evil I might cause others. The distress of others, no matter how great, always counts for less than my pleasure. It is of no consequence if I must buy the feeblest enjoyment through an extraordinary catalogue of serious crimes since pleasure is my delight and is within me, while the consequences of crime do not affect me because they are external to me.

*

In so far as the bond between destruction and sexual pleasure is considered, Maurice Blanchot's analysis adds nothing to Sade's fundamental affirmation: in this, Sade, who in other respects is inconsistent, expresses without respite the paradox of crime being the foundation of sensuality as a certified truth. This aspect of Sade's work is presented in such a way that one can add nothing to it: on this point Sade's thought is at its most explicit, and his consciousness is at its clearest. He had the certitude of having made a decisive discovery in the sphere of knowledge. But one notices how restricted the cohesion of the system is. If the isolation of the sensual individual is not, as a rule, established as the most perfect isolation, the intimate relation between criminal destruction and sensual pleasure slips away, or at least can express itself only feebly. To gain access to this truth necessitated being placed in the illusory perspective of isolation. Nothing is more moving to read than the absurdity of the continual negation of the value one being has for another: this negation continually gives this thought the value of a counter-truth, and draws it towards the most commonplace contradictions. Life does not confirm it, or confirms it only in part. Not that isolation in this life has never come into play (it is even possible that it has the final say), but it did not come into play alone. It is difficult to reduce what we know of Sade's character to a sham, something which distinguishes him profoundly from the odious heroes he depicts (I could mention his love for his sister-in-law, his political career, his disgust at the sight, from his prison window, of the guillotine in action; and, finally irrefutable, his concern with writing and the 'tears of blood' he shed on the loss of a manuscript). But the falsehood of isolation is the truth condition of a relation between love and crime, and one cannot even imagine Sade's work without the resolution with which he denied the value man has for man. In other words, the true nature of sexual attraction can be revealed only literally in the bringing into play of impossible characters and scenes. Otherwise it would remain veiled, and the pure sexual act could not have been recognized in the mists of tenderness, for finally love is usually communicated; its very name has connected it to the existence of others. It is as if a man, in order to be sovereign and no longer a thing, by being forced to make things of everyone else, releases sovereignty from its condition, and his failure is thereby of the deepest kind, and echoes back to the community of equals.

The very excess with which Sade affirms his truth is not of a kind that makes it easy to admit. But he compels consideration. Maurice Blanchot has sought to illuminate Sade's thought, but I can now add some precision. From Sade's representations it is possible to perceive that affection cannot change the fundamental role played by death. Affection, as it uses the destruction brought about by this play, cannot make of it its contrary. In the most general way, sexual behaviour is opposed to everyday behaviour as expenditure is to saving. If we behave in accordance with reason, we acquire all sorts of goods, we work to augment our resources or our learning, and strive in various ways to acquire more. As a rule, such conduct determines our sense of ourselves in social life. But at the moment of sexual fever we behave in a completely different way: we expend our energy without restraint, and squander a considerable amount of our vitality violently and with no profit to ourselves. Sexual pleasure has so much in common with destruction that we have named the moment of its paroxysm the 'little death'. In consequence, the objects suggesting sexual activity to us are always connected to some disorder. Thus nudity is the collapse, even the betrayal, of the aspect of ourselves given to us through our clothes. But in this respect much is required to satisfy us. In general, passionate destruction and reckless betrayal alone have the power to cause us to enter into the world of sex. To nudity is added the peculiarity of half-naked bodies which artfully give the suggestion of being áll the more *naked*. Suffering and sadistically inflicted death defer the moment of collapse; by no means do they run counter to it. In the same way prostitution, erotic vocabulary, the inevitable connection between sexuality and excretion, contribute to make the world of the senses a world of loss and destruction. It appears that our only true happiness is to spend vainly, and we always want to be sure of the uselessness of our expenditure; we want to feel as far away as possible from the responsible world in which augmentation of resources is the rule. But we could go further, since we would like to oppose it, and commonly in eroticism there is an impulse towards aggressive hatred, an impulse towards betrayal. This is why distress is connected to it, and why, in counterpart, if the hatred is powerless, and the betrayal involuntary, the erotic element becomes ridiculous.

*

In this respect, Sade's system is simply the most consistent and extravagant form of sexual activity. Moral isolation suggests the lifting of restraints, and also alone reveals the most profound meaning of expenditure. Anyone who admits the value of others is necessarily limited, and is obscured by this respect for others which prevents him from experiencing what, within him, is the only aspiration which is not subordinated to the desire to accumulate material or moral resources. Nothing is more commonplace than a momentary incursion into the world of sexual truths, sustained for the rest of the time by a funda-mental refutation of these same truths. Solidarity prevents man from occupying the place denoted by the word 'sovereignty'. Man's respect for his fellows introduces a cycle of servitude, of subordinated moments in which we immediately violate this respect, since we deprive man in general of his sovereign moments (of what he possesses that is most precious).

'The nucleus of the sadeian world', on the contrary, is, according to Maurice Blanchot, 'the demand for sovereignty affirmed through an immense negation'. Here the essential good which man generally serves is revealed (and withholds the strength to reach the place where his sovereignty would be accomplished). The essence of the sexual world is not simply the expenditure of energy, but negation taken to the extreme – or, if you prefer, the expenditure of energy is itself necessarily this negation. Sade calls this supreme moment 'apathy'. 'Apathy', says Maurice Blanchot,

> is the spirit of negation applied to the man who has chosen to be sovereign. It is, in some way, the cause and principle of energy. Sade's argument appears to be something like this: today the individual embodies a certain quantity of strength. Most of the time he wastes his strength by transferring it to benefit those simulacra called others, God or the absolute; by such a dispersion, he wrongly exhausts his possibilities by squandering them; but even more, he founds his behaviour on impotence, for if he expends his energy on others it is because he feels that he may need their support himself. This is a fatal failure, because he thereby enfeebles himself in a useless expenditure, and he wastes his strength because he believes he is weak. But the true man knows that he is alone, and accepts the fact; he denies everything within himself, the heritage of seventeen centuries of cowardice, which relates to others rather than to himself; feelings like pity, gratitude and love. He destroys such feelings, and as he destroys them he regains all the strength he would have needed to devote to such debilitating urges, and – even more important – he extracts from this work of destruction the beginning of a true energy. It must be clearly understood that in fact apathy does not consist merely in destroying 'parasitic' affections; equally, it is opposed to the spontaneity of any passion. The depraved man who immediately plunges into his vice is simply a freak who will lose himself. Even the great profligates, perfectly endowed with the talent required to be monsters, are destined for disaster if they are content to follow their inclinations. Sade insists that if passion is to become energy it must be compressed, and mediated through an essential moment of insensibility; only then will its potential be realized. Early in her career, Juliette is ceaselessly criticized by Clairwill because she commits crime only through enthusiasm; she lights the torch of crime only from the torch of passions, and places profligacy and the effervescence of pleasure above everything. Dangerous indulgences. Crime is more important than profligacy; 'cold-blooded' crime is greater than crime carried out in the fervour of passion, but crime 'committed in the hardening of the sensitive part', crime that is dark and secret, matters more than anything else, because it is ·

the act of a soul which, having destroyed everything within itself, has accumulated an immense strength, which will be identified completely with the acts of total destruction being planned. All those great libertines, who live only for pleasure, owe their greatness to the fact that they have annihilated all capacity for pleasure within themselves. This is why they carry out such frightful abominations, otherwise the mediocrity of ordinary sensuality would be enough for them. But they have made themselves insensitive: they intend to use their insensitivity (which they have crushed and denied within themselves) to experience pleasure to the full and they have become 'ferocious'. Cruelty is merely the negation of the self, carried so far that it is transformed into a destructive explosion. Insensibility causes a quivering through the whole being, says Sade: 'the soul ascends to a type of apathy which is soon metamorphosed into pleasures a thousand times more divine than those that their weakness procures for them.'[20]

This passage had to be quoted in its entirety, since it illuminates the central issue. Negation cannot be separated from these paths in which the sensual is not made palpable but in which its mental mechanism is taken apart for inspection. And in the same way sensuality, separated from this negation, remains furtive, contemptible and powerless to take its supreme place in the light of consciousness. 'I would like', says Clairwill, Juliette's companion in debauchery, 'to contrive a crime which would have a perpetual effect, so that even when I no longer act, there would not have been a single moment of my life in which, even while I slept, I did not cause some disorder, and this disorder could expand to the point where it would result in wholesale corruption or a disturbance so absolute that its effects would still continue beyond my own life.' Who would finally dare not to recognize within himself a taste for sensual pleasures that would find its extreme continuation only at this point? Who would finally dare to refuse sensuality, in its abasement, a value which the interests of reason cannot rival? Who would dare to refuse to see in sensuality, from the point of view of an eternal instant, the ravishment without which the divine (distressing, cruel, and the negation of man) could not have been conceived?

This excessive negation has two aspects. First, it divinely denies the separated being, the precarious individual in the face of the immensity of the universe. It denies him, perhaps, on behalf of a no less precarious other, but one who, by the fact of his universal negation, if he affirms himself to the extreme degree of affirmation, nevertheless does so only as a denial – so much so that from the beginning, being logically the soul of extinction, he contains nothing which does not reveal itself in advance with similar effects to those he himself bears from all quarters. Undoubtedly, this latter affinity with cruel destruction is not commonly manifested by Sade's heroes. Nevertheless, one

of his most perfect characters, Amélie, expresses it as completely as
one could desire:

> She lives in Sweden, one day she goes to find Borchamps . . . The latter, in
> the hope of a monstrous execution, has just delivered up all the members of
> a plot against the sovereign (a plot he had himself hatched up) and this
> betrayal has excited the young woman. 'I love your ferocity,' she tells him.
> 'Swear to me that one day I will also be your victim; since I was fifteen my
> only thought has been to perish as the victim of the cruel passions of
> libertinage. I don't want to die tomorrow, I dare say; my extravagance does
> not go so far as that; but this is the only way I want to die: to make my death
> the occasion of a crime is an idea that causes my head to spin.' A strange
> head, which receives a worthy response: 'I love your head to the point of
> madness and I believe we can do great things together.'– 'It has rotted,
> putrefied, I acknowledge the fact!' Thus 'for the integral man, the complete
> man, no evil is possible.' If he harms others, what pleasure! If others harm
> him, what joy! Virtue gives him pleasure because it is weak and he can crush
> it and, likewise, vice, since he takes gratification in the disorder which
> results from it, even if it be at his own expense. If he lives, not a single
> incident of his life cannot be experienced with happiness. If he dies, he
> finds in his death a still greater happiness and, in the awareness of his
> destruction, the crowning of a life that only the need for destruction
> justifies. Thus in the universe the negator is present as an extreme negation
> of everything, and this negation also permits him no shelter for himself. For
> as long as it lasts the strength of denial probably confers a privilege, but the
> negative action that it exerts with such a superhuman energy is the only
> protection against the intensity of an immense negation.

*

Who does not perceive here that in any case the contemplated effects
exceed the human sphere: this sort of conclusion has only ever been
conceived under a mythical form, which situates it, if not outside the
world, at least in the domain of dream. The same thing is true in Sade's
work, but – this is the second aspect of this negation – what is denied
here does not serve to uphold some transcendent affirmation. It is with
a rare violence that Sade opposes the idea of God. In truth, the only
profound difference between his system and that of theologians is that
the negation of isolated beings (which no theology, except in appearance, accomplishes less cruelly) holds nothing existent in reserve above
it to offer consolation, not even an immanence of the world. This
negation stands at the summit, and that is all. It is clearly very much
held in suspension, very disconcerting, and this is equally so for the
person who recognizes that this unique potential cannot be attained.
(Sade's representations are in fact so perfect that in their way they

leave the ground, and whoever seizes them – in as much as they can be seized – knows at once, from the outset, that they are alien[21] to his personal potential.) Finally, this ultimate and inaccessible movement, the very idea of which leaves us breathless, substitutes an impossible human instant for the image of God, but this necessity no less compels recognition, and in a more logical way than that of God once did. For the idea of God was a resting-place, a time of pause in the vertiginous movement in which we are swept along. Sade's negation, on the other hand, signifies man's power to accelerate rather than stop this movement. It is no longer a question of knowing. To know to what vault the idea of God provided the key was to offer oneself the possibility of sleep, while Sade's negation leaves the spirit faced with a truth which is neither of nature nor of the universe, nor of anything, but the absolute negation of nature and the universe, as if there were in nature – and in the universe – an ultimate possibility, at the extreme a possible trans-cendence, in the dissatisfaction of being, in the obsession with a passage from being to non-being. Perhaps this is not necessarily transcendence: being emerges from itself only on condition of no longer being, but desires as a possibility, an impossible transcendence. At this point of the explanation, understanding evaporates all of a sudden, the irreducible is here, such that a poetic – or negative – expression has had the immediate power to reveal its presence in *sensuality*.

Notes

1. Review of Malcolm de Chazal, *Sens-plastique*, 2nd edn (1948), Paris: Gallimard [part of this book has been translated by Irving Weiss and published by SUN books: New York (1979) – *Translator*]; Maurice Blanchot, *Lautréamont et Sade* (1949), Paris: Minuit; *Anthologie de l'érotisme: De Pierre Louÿs à J.P. Sartre* (1949), Paris: Nord-Sud. Published in *Critique*, nos 35/36 (April/May 1949).

[2. In Arthur Rimbaud, *Complete Works* (1976), trans. Paul Schmidt, New York: Harper & Row. – *Translator*]

3. See *Critique*, no. 20, p. 3. One should add the pages André Breton has devoted to him in *La lampe dans l'horloge* (Robert Marin, 1948 pp. 41–51) [reproduced in *La Clé des champs* (1967), Jean-Jacques Pauvert, pp. 149–55. – *Translator*]

4. André Breton has very justly stated about this:

The very key to such a work – a key that Malcolm de Chazal has, moreover, clearly wanted to leave in the door – resides in *sexual pleasure*, in the least metaphorical sense of the term, envisaged as a supreme line of resolution of the physical and the mental. It is astounding that it has been necessary to wait until the middle of the twentieth century for sexual pleasure, in its capacity as a phenomenon which maintains an unequivocal place in the conditioning of the whole of life, to find the means of speaking of itself and nothing else without worrying about the masks with which hypocrisy covers it any more than about the licentious trimmings of defiance under which it succeeded so well in concealing itself. (*La lampe dans l'horloge*, pp. 46–7)

5. This preface is not reproduced in the second edition of *Sens-plastique*, to which this study refers. It is included in the first edition (Port-Louis, Mauritius, 1947).

6. 'The eyes of fire, the nostrils of air, the mouth of water, the heart of earth,' wrote Blake. It would be easy to give more examples.

7. *Sens-plastique*, p. 39.

8. ibid., p. 220.

9. ibid., p. 266.

10. ibid., p. 3.

11. ibid., p. 137. In the same sense: 'Sexual pleasure is an involution towards Infinity. It is death in reverse, birth taken against the grain where time and space are abolished' (p. 108).

12. ibid., p. 136.

13. ibid., p. 160.

14. 'Sexual pleasure is a double bind between two carnal cities, in which each body collides with the walls of the other, and which would be forced in vain. If one climbed over a wall, one would fall into the beyond' (ibid., p. 48).

15. At one point he insists on this character: 'Sexual pleasure', he says, 'is the powerful sensation we can have of speed' (ibid., p. 32).

16. ibid., p. 124.

17. ibid., p. 108.

18. ibid., p. 125.

19. I need not mention that this must be connected to detailed analysis, founded on a common experience but leaving a considerable margin for ambiguous facts.

20. *Lautréamont et Sade*, pp. 256-8.

21. Maurice Blanchot has formulated the relation of Sade's thought to that of the totality of men very precisely:

> We do not say that this thought is viable. But it shows us that between the normal man who encloses the Sadeian man in a blind alley and the Sadeian who makes of this blind alley an escape route, it is the latter who knows most about the truth and logic of his situation and has the deepest insight into it, to the point of being able to help the normal man to understand himself as he helps him to modify the terms of all comprehension. (ibid., pp. 262-3)

Index